Managing Successful Projects
with **PRINCE2**

Office of Government Commerce

London: TSO

Published by TSO (The Stationery Office) and available from:

Online
www.tsoshop.co.uk

Mail, Telephone, Fax & E-mail
TSO
PO Box 29, Norwich NR3 1GN
Telephone orders/General enquiries: 0870 6005522
Fax orders: 0870 6005533
E-mail: book.orders@tso.co.uk
Textphone: 0870 240 3701

TSO Shops
123 Kingsway, London WC2B 6PQ
020 7242 6393 Fax 020 7242 6394
68–69 Bull Street, Birmingham B4 6AD
0121 236 9696 Fax 0121 236 9699
9–21 Princess Street, Manchester M60 8AS
0161 834 7201 Fax 0161 833 0634
16 Arthur Street, Belfast BT1 4GD
028 9023 8451 Fax 028 9023 5401
18–19 High Street, Cardiff CF10 1PT
029 2039 5548 Fax 029 2038 4347
71 Lothian Road, Edinburgh EH3 9AZ
0870 606 5566 Fax 0870 606 5588

TSO Accredited Agents
(see Yellow Pages)

and through good booksellers

First edition Crown Copyright 1996
Second edition Crown Copyright 1998
Third edition Crown Copyright 2002
Fourth edition Crown Copyright 2005
Third impression 2006
ISBN 0 11 330946 5

Printed in the United Kingdom for The Stationery Office.

ACKNOWLEDGEMENTS

The original design and development of PRINCE2 was carried out by a consortium of Duhig Berry, WS Atkins and Penzer Allen, under contract to the former CCTA (Central Computer and Telecommunications Agency). Parity Consulting is acknowledged for assisting the consortium in the design and development of the PRINCE2 model. In particular, OGC would like to express special thanks to all members, over 150 individuals and organisations, of the PRINCE2 User Review Panel, and the large number of other contributors, who gave their time freely to input ideas and comments during the quality reviews.

OGC has continued to develop and improve the definition and presentation of PRINCE2 within this reference manual. OGC would like to thank the following individuals and organisations for their contributions and ongoing support to PRINCE2 throughout all the phases of its development:

Mike Allen	Department of Education and Employment
Dick Bennett	Duhig Berry
Colin Bentley	Hampshire Training Consultants
Alan Berry	Duhig Berry
Ken Bradley	SPOCE
Graham Connellan	Independent Consultant
Brian Coombes	The Projects Group
Jeremy Cox	Parity Consulting
Alan Ferguson	AFA
Rob Herson	Parity Consulting
Mike Kirk	Promit
Tony Levene	Quality Projects
Tim Lulham	DHL Systems
Patrick Mayfield	Pearce Mayfield Associates
Nick Morgan	Xansa (formerly Duhig Berry)
Ian Santry	Civil Service College
Alison Thurlbeck	Methodica
Ben van der Wijngaart	Tanner James Management Consultants
Mark van Onna	Pink

Barry Wall   Vega Consultancy Division

Peter Weaver   PWA

OGC would also like to thank the following individuals and organisations for their contributions and support throughout this revision of PRINCE2.

Project Board

Project Executive   Anne-Marie Byrne, OGC

Senior User   Eddie Borup, The Best Practice User Group

Senior Suppliers   Richard Pharro, APM Group Ltd and Janine Eves, TSO

Project Manager

Janine Eves, TSO

Project Team

Colin Bentley, Emma Jones, David Atkinson, Alan Ferguson

Project Assurance

The Best Practice User Group, led by Chris Churchouse

FOREWORD

Today most organisations are experiencing unprecedented levels of change. Change has become a way of life for organisations that need to achieve greater efficiency and better value for money, and to be more effective or competitive in order to thrive. Managing the inherent risk associated with change and innovation is essential to successful project delivery.

Projects bring together resources, skills, technology and ideas to achieve business objectives and deliver business benefits. Good project management helps to ensure that risks are identified and managed appropriately, and objectives and benefits are achieved within budget, within time and to the required quality.

PRINCE2 is recognised as a world-class international product and is the standard method for project management, not least because it embodies many years of good practice in project management and provides a flexible and adaptable approach to suit all projects. It is a project management method designed to provide a framework covering the wide variety of disciplines and activities required within a project. The focus throughout PRINCE2 is on the Business Case, which describes the rationale and business justification for the project. The Business Case drives all the project management processes, from initial project set-up through to successful finish.

Many organisations are employing the skills and services of external suppliers, working alongside in-house resources, to enhance their ability to deliver successful projects. PRINCE2 provides a mechanism to harness these resources and enable the team to integrate and work together effectively on a project.

The success of PRINCE2 in the public and private sector makes it easy for me to commend the PRINCE2 approach to you. I am confident that PRINCE2 will help you to deliver better projects and achieve success.

Peter Fanning
Deputy Chief Executive Officer
Office of Government Commerce

CONTENTS

Acknowledgements	iii

Foreword	v

1	**Introduction**	**1**
1.1	Why use a project management method?	1
1.2	Benefits of using PRINCE2	2
1.3	Support for PRINCE2	4
1.4	Structure of the manual	4
1.5	Using the manual	5
1.6	PRINCE2 terminology	6

2	**An introduction to PRINCE2**	**7**
2.1	What is a project?	7
2.2	The scope of PRINCE2	8
2.3	PRINCE2 in context	9
2.4	Overview of PRINCE2	11
2.5	The processes	12
2.6	The components	17
2.7	The techniques	18
2.8	Process and component links	19

3	**Introduction to processes**	**21**
3.1	Management levels	21
3.2	Structure of each process description	22
3.3	Diagram and text notation	23

4	Starting up a Project (SU)	25
4.1	Fundamental principles	25
4.2	Context	26
4.3	Process description	26
4.4	Appointing an Executive and a Project Manager (SU1)	28
4.5	Designing a Project Management Team (SU2)	31
4.6	Appointing a Project Management Team (SU3)	34
4.7	Preparing a Project Brief (SU4)	37
4.8	Defining Project Approach (SU5)	40
4.9	Planning an Initiation Stage (SU6)	43

5	Initiating a Project (IP)	47
5.1	Fundamental principles	47
5.2	Context	47
5.3	Process description	48
5.4	Planning Quality (IP1)	50
5.5	Planning a Project (IP2)	53
5.6	Refining the Business Case and Risks (IP3)	56
5.7	Setting up Project Controls (IP4)	60
5.8	Setting up Project Files (IP5)	63
5.9	Assembling a Project Initiation Document (IP6)	65

6	Directing a Project (DP)	69
6.1	Fundamental principles	69
6.2	Context	69
6.3	Process description	70
6.4	Authorising Initiation (DP1)	74
6.5	Authorising a Project (DP2)	76
6.6	Authorising a Stage or Exception Plan (DP3)	81
6.7	Giving Ad Hoc Direction (DP4)	85
6.8	Confirming Project Closure (DP5)	89

7	Controlling a Stage (CS)	95
7.1	Fundamental principles	95
7.2	Context	96
7.3	Process description	97
7.4	Authorising Work Package (CS1)	98
7.5	Assessing Progress (CS2)	102
7.6	Capturing Project Issues (CS3)	105
7.7	Examining Project Issues (CS4)	107
7.8	Reviewing Stage Status (CS5)	110
7.9	Reporting Highlights (CS6)	114
7.10	Taking Corrective Action (CS7)	117
7.11	Escalating Project Issues (CS8)	119
7.12	Receiving Completed Work Package (CS9)	124

8	Managing Product Delivery (MP)	127
8.1	Fundamental principles	127
8.2	Context	127
8.3	Process description	128
8.4	Accepting a Work Package (MP1)	129
8.5	Executing a Work Package (MP2)	132
8.6	Delivering a Work Package (MP3)	134

9	Managing Stage Boundaries (SB)	137
9.1	Fundamental principles	137
9.2	Context	137
9.3	Process description	138
9.4	Planning a Stage (SB1)	139
9.5	Updating a Project Plan (SB2)	142
9.6	Updating a Project Business Case (SB3)	144
9.7	Updating the Risk Log (SB4)	146
9.8	Reporting Stage End (SB5)	147
9.9	Producing an Exception Plan (SB6)	150

10	Closing a Project (CP)	153
10.1	Fundamental principles	153
10.2	Context	154
10.3	Process description	154
10.4	Decommissioning a Project (CP1)	156
10.5	Identifying Follow-on Actions (CP2)	160
10.6	Evaluating a Project (CP3)	162

11	Planning (PL)	167
11.1	Fundamental principles	167
11.2	Context	168
11.3	Process description	169
11.4	Designing a Plan (PL1)	171
11.5	Defining and Analysing Products (PL2)	174
11.6	Identifying Activities and Dependencies (PL3)	176
11.7	Estimating (PL4)	180
11.8	Scheduling (PL5)	183
11.9	Analysing Risks (PL6)	188
11.10	Completing a Plan (PL7)	190

12	Introduction to the PRINCE2 components	195

13	Business Case	197
13.1	What is a Business Case?	197
13.2	What should a Business Case contain?	198
13.3	Developing a Business Case	199
13.4	Development path of the Business Case	200

14	Organisation	203
14.1	Overview	203
14.2	The PRINCE2 project management team	208
14.3	Project Support	217

15	Plans	219
15.1	Benefits of planning	219
15.2	What is a plan?	220
15.3	What are the elements of a plan?	220
15.4	The PRINCE2 approach	222
15.5	Levels of plan	223

16	Controls	227
16.1	Purpose of control	227
16.2	Controls overview	228
16.3	Project start-up	230
16.4	Controlled progress	233
16.5	Controlled close	244
16.6	Stages	246

17	Management of risk	251
17.1	What is risk management?	251
17.2	Risk principles	252
17.3	The risk management cycle	254
17.4	Risk profile	258
17.5	Budgeting for risk management	259
17.6	Mapping the management of risk to the PRINCE2 processes	259
17.7	Interdependencies	263
17.8	Further risk management considerations	263

18	Quality in a project environment	265
18.1	Purpose	265
18.2	What is quality?	265
18.3	Quality management	265
18.4	The quality path	266
18.5	Making project quality work	273

19	Configuration management	275
19.1	Purpose	275
19.2	Definition	275
19.3	Baseline	277
19.4	Managing the configuration	277
19.5	Configuration management method	280
19.6	Configuration management and change control	282
19.7	Configuration management and a Project Support Office	283

20	Change control	285
20.1	Purpose	285
20.2	Project Issue management	285
20.3	Authority levels	287
20.4	Integrity of change	288
20.5	Management of change and configuration management	289

21	Introduction to techniques	291

22	Product-based planning	293
22.1	The four products of product-based planning	293
22.2	The benefits of product-based planning	293
22.3	Producing a Product Description of the final product	294
22.4	Producing a Product Breakdown Structure	294
22.5	Writing a Product Description	300
22.6	Producing a Product Flow Diagram	302
22.7	Product-based planning example	303
22.8	Further examples	307
22.9	Guidance on creating a product-based plan	311

23	Change control technique	315
23.1	Change control steps	315

1
INTRODUCTION

PRINCE (**PR**ojects **IN** **C**ontrolled **E**nvironments) is a structured method for effective project management. The method was first established in 1989 by CCTA (the Central Computer and Telecommunications Agency). PRINCE was developed from PROMPTII, a project management method created by Simpact Systems Ltd in 1975. PROMPTII was adopted by CCTA in 1979 as the standard to be used for all government information system projects. PRINCE superseded PROMPTII in 1989 within government projects.

CCTA (now the Office of Government Commerce) continued to develop the method, and PRINCE2 was launched in 1996 in response to user requirements for improved guidance on project management on all projects, not just information systems. PRINCE2 is based on the experiences of scores of projects, project managers and project teams, who have contributed, some from their mistakes or omissions, others from their successes.

PRINCE2 is a *de facto* standard used extensively by the UK government and is widely recognised and used in the private sector, both in the UK and internationally.

1.1 Why use a project management method?

Project failures are all too common – some make the headlines, but the vast majority are quickly forgotten. The reasons for failure are many and varied. Some common causes are:

- Insufficient attention to checking that a valid Business Case exists for the project
- Insufficient attention to quality at the outset and during development
- Insufficient definition of the required outcomes, leading to confusion over what the project is expected to achieve
- Lack of communication with stakeholders and interested parties, leading to products being delivered that are not what the customer wanted
- Inadequate definition and lack of acceptance of project management roles and responsibilities, leading to lack of direction and poor decision making
- Poor estimation of duration and costs, leading to projects taking more time and costing more money than expected
- Inadequate planning and co-ordination of resources, leading to poor scheduling
- Insufficient measurables and lack of control over progress, so that projects do not reveal their exact status until too late
- Lack of quality control, resulting in the delivery of products that are unacceptable or unusable.

Without a project management method, those who commission a project, those who manage it and those who work on it will have different ideas about how things should be organised and when the different aspects of the project will be completed. Those involved will not be clear about how much responsibility, authority and accountability they have and, as a result, there will often be confusion surrounding the project. Without a project management method, projects are rarely completed on time and within acceptable cost – and this is especially true of large projects.

A good project management method will guide the project through a controlled, well-managed, visible set of activities to achieve the desired results. PRINCE2 adopts the principles of good project management to avoid the problems just identified and so helps to achieve successful projects. These principles are:

● A project is a finite process with a definite start and end

● Projects always need to be managed in order to be successful

● For genuine commitment to the project, all parties must be clear about why the project is needed, what it is intended to achieve, how the outcome is to be achieved and what their responsibilities are in that achievement.

1.2 Benefits of using PRINCE2

Organisations are becoming increasingly aware of the opportunities for adopting a project approach to the way that they address business change. They are aware of the benefits that a single, common, structured method for project management can bring:

● A method that is repeatable

● A method that is teachable

● Building on experience

● Ensuring that everyone knows what to expect, where, how and when

● Early warning of problems

● Being proactive, not reactive, but also able to accommodate sudden, unexpected events.

Projects may exist in their own right, may have relationships with other projects or may be part of a larger programme of work. PRINCE2 is applicable in all these situations. PRINCE2 provides the organisation with:

● Controlled management of change, in terms of investment and return on investment

● Active involvement of users and stakeholders throughout the project to ensure that the product(s) will meet the business, functional, environmental, service and management requirements

● An approach which distinguishes the management of the project from the development of the product(s), so that the management approach is the same whether the project is to build a ship or to implement new working practices.

PRINCE2 provides benefits to the managers and directors of a project and to an organisation through the controllable use of resources and the ability to manage risk more effectively.

PRINCE2 embodies established and proven best practice in project management. It is widely recognised and understood, providing a common language for all participants in a project.

PRINCE2 encourages formal recognition of responsibilities within a project and focuses on what a project is to deliver, why, when and for whom.

PRINCE2 provides projects with:

- A controlled and organised start, middle and end
- Regular reviews of progress against plan and against the Business Case
- Flexible decision points
- Automatic management control of any deviations from the plan
- The involvement of management and stakeholders at the right time during the project
- Good communication channels between the project management team and the rest of the organisation
- Agreement on the required quality at the outset and continuous monitoring against those requirements.

Project Managers using PRINCE2 are able to:

- Establish terms of reference as a prerequisite to the start of a project
- Use a defined structure for delegation, authority and communication
- Divide the project into manageable stages for more accurate planning
- Ensure that resource commitment from management is part of any approval to proceed
- Provide regular but brief management reports
- Keep meetings with management and stakeholders to a minimum but at the vital points in the project.

Those who will be directly involved with using the products or outcomes of a project are able to:

- Participate in all the decision making on a project
- If desired, be fully involved in day-to-day progress
- Participate in quality checks throughout the project
- Ensure that their requirements are being adequately satisfied.

For senior management of the project, PRINCE2 uses the 'management by exception' concept, i.e. management agree a plan, and then let the Project Manager get on with it unless something is forecast to go wrong. Senior managers are kept fully informed of the project status without having to attend frequent, time-consuming meetings.

1.3 Support for PRINCE2

There are many service providers offering training, consultancy, tools and services for PRINCE2, thus ensuring a competitive supply of services to support organisations in their implementation and use of the method.

There is an international accreditation programme for trainers and consultants, ensuring a high quality and consistent level of service to organisations. There are professional qualifications in PRINCE2 that assess an individual's knowledge of the method and ability to apply it to project scenarios. In addition, there is an active user group dedicated to the support, promotion and strengthening of the method.

1.4 Structure of the manual

There are five major parts to this manual, as shown in Figure 1.1.

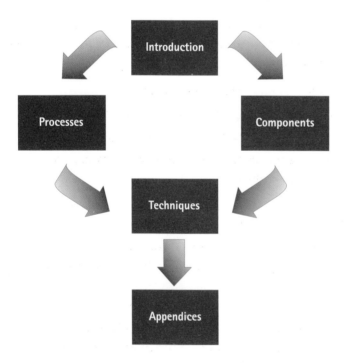

Figure 1.1 Structure of the manual

Introduction presents the basic principles governing project management and how PRINCE2 addresses them; it also shows how PRINCE2 fits with the related topic of programme management.

Processes describes the PRINCE2 process model, explaining what has to be done to manage a project by bringing together and applying the principles in a successful manner.

Components explains and describes the major elements of project management, such as organisation and control, and how PRINCE2 incorporates them. These components represent the 'raw materials' of good project management, including quality management and the management of risk.

Techniques explains some techniques of project management that are specific to PRINCE2.

Appendices offer Product Description outlines for PRINCE2 management products, role descriptions, a series of 'healthcheck' questions for organisations to ask themselves when using PRINCE2, risk categories and a suggested filing scheme for management documents.

In addition, there is a full glossary of terms.

1.5 Using the manual

This manual is aimed at people who will be playing a part in a PRINCE2 project or those who wish to understand how PRINCE2 contributes to the project management process; this would include senior managers responsible for the overall direction of a project, Project Managers, project auditors, quality assurance personnel and members of the project team. In addition, line managers of project personnel may find it useful to gain an appreciation of their staff's involvement in a project by reviewing *An introduction to PRINCE2*, Chapter 2.

This manual has been designed to provide a complete reference to the PRINCE2 method. As such, the entire manual provides essential reading for all Project Managers. However, the following is offered as a focus for specific groups:

- Project Managers coming to PRINCE2 for the first time should:
  - read and understand *An introduction to PRINCE2*, Chapter 2 to appreciate the overall approach that PRINCE2 takes to creating and managing a project
  - use the process descriptions in the *Processes* section as the basis for planning a project and deciding on resource requirements
  - read and understand the *Components* section to familiarise themselves with the interaction between the components and the processes

- Project Managers already familiar with PRINCE2 should read and understand the process model described in the *Processes* section to appreciate the changes of emphasis and process-driven approach

- Senior managers who will be involved in a project at Project Board level should gain an appreciation of PRINCE2 and their roles within a project by studying *Introduction*, Chapters 1 and 2; *Business Case*, Chapter 13; *Organisation*, Chapter 14 and the description of the process *Directing a Project*, Chapter 6

- Programme managers with PRINCE2 projects in their programme should gain a clear understanding of the approach that PRINCE2 takes to creating and managing a project.

1.6 PRINCE2 terminology

The following terms are the most important to understand with regard to PRINCE2 and are all included in the Glossary. Readers should familiarise themselves with them to prevent any possible confusion when using PRINCE2.

Business Case is used to define the information that justifies the setting up, continuation or termination of the project. It answers the question: 'Why should this project be done?' It is updated at key points throughout the project.

Customer is used to represent the person or group who has commissioned the work and will be benefiting from the end results.

Product is used to describe everything that the project has to create or change, however physical or otherwise this may be. Results of projects can vary enormously from physical items, such as buildings and machinery, to intangible things such as culture change and public perception.

Programme is a collection of projects that together achieve a beneficial change for an organisation.

Supplier is used to mean the group that is providing specialist resources and skills to the project or is providing goods and services to create the project outcome required by the customer and user(s).

User is defined as the person or group who will use or operate the final product. In some situations, the customer and user may be the same group of people.

2

AN INTRODUCTION TO PRINCE2

2.1 What is a project?

PRINCE2 defines a project as:

A management environment that is created for the purpose of delivering one or more business products according to a specified Business Case.

Another definition of a project might be:

A temporary organisation that is needed to produce a unique and predefined outcome or result at a prespecified time using predetermined resources.

PRINCE2 additionally supposes that those responsible for the project may not have experience of working together to produce a similar set of outcomes or results for the same customer in the past; that co-ordination between those working on the project will need to be well organised; and that the responsibilities shared among those undertaking the work, those managing it and those sponsoring it will need to be clearly defined.

A PRINCE2 project, therefore, has the following characteristics:

- A finite and defined life cycle
- Defined and measurable business products
- A corresponding set of activities to achieve the business products
- A defined amount of resources
- An organisation structure, with defined responsibilities, to manage the project.

Each project falls within a specific business context. A project may be stand-alone, it may be one in a sequence of related projects or it may form part of a programme or corporate strategy.

A project, by its nature, is a temporary structure, created to achieve a specified business benefit or objective. When the work has been completed, the project is disbanded.

A project has a life cycle, which is the path and sequence through the various activities to produce the final product. The term 'life span' is used to describe the life of a product. The two should not be confused. Figure 2.1 shows how a *product life span* might start from the initial idea or conception, through to the operation of the product, finishing with the eventual scrapping of the product when it comes to the end of its usefulness. The *project life cycle* covers the tasks of specifying and designing the product, through to its testing and handover into operational use. PRINCE2 covers the project life cycle plus some pre-project preparation.

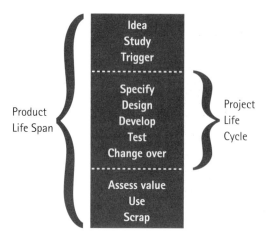

Figure 2.1 Product life span and project life cycle

2.2 The scope of PRINCE2

Figure 2.2 shows where PRINCE2 fits into a business and project environment. PRINCE2 is not intended to cover all subjects relevant to project management. The project management techniques and tools needed will vary according to the project type and the corporate environment. There are also certain aspects of project management that are well covered by existing and proven methods and are therefore excluded from PRINCE2. Examples of these aspects are:

- People management techniques such as motivation, delegation and team leadership

- Generic planning techniques such as Gantt charts and critical path analysis

- The creation and management of corporate quality management and quality assurance mechanisms

- Budgetary control and earned value analysis techniques.

PRINCE2 covers the management of the project and the management of the resources involved in carrying out the activities of the project. It does not cover the specialist techniques involved in the creation of the products. This is the job of other methods, although PRINCE2 must interface with them to enable information on such areas as estimating to be provided for project management.

Although PRINCE2 is centred on the project, it begins before the project does by preparing the ground so that the project starts in an organised and controlled manner.

Another often critical project area is purchasing. PRINCE2 assumes that the project is run within the context of a contract. The contracting process is not included within the method itself. Contracting and purchasing are themselves specialist activities (like software engineering) and can therefore be managed using the PRINCE2 method. If purchasing or contracting is to be undertaken during the early stages of the project, changes may be needed to the Project Board and other parts of the project management team once these stages have been completed. For example, it may be appropriate to have a senior representative of the purchasing department as a member of the Project Board (in the role of Senior Supplier) until suppliers are appointed.

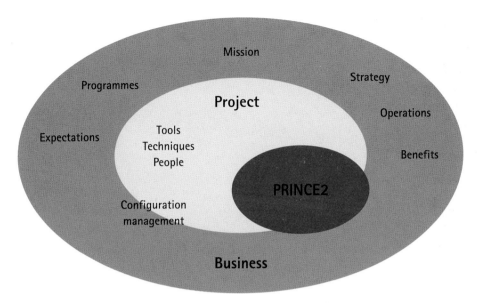

Figure 2.2 The PRINCE2 relationship with projects and business

Contract and purchasing issues will also increase the importance of a complete and accurate Project Initiation Document (PID), which will need to be kept in line with the text of the contract(s). Where PRINCE2 describes project roles, the conversion of these into formal job definitions for a particular project will also require careful attention, for example, Project Assurance, the approval of Product Descriptions and the allocation of risk 'ownership'.

2.3   PRINCE2 in context

PRINCE2 may be used on any type of project in any environment. It contains a complete set of concepts and project management processes that are the minimum requirements for a properly run and managed project. However, the way in which PRINCE2 is applied to each project will vary considerably, and tailoring the method to suit the circumstances of a particular project is critical to its successful use.

PRINCE2 projects are always focused on delivering specified products to meet a specified Business Case. PRINCE2 enables the project to capture and retain a definition of the business benefits that are the driving force behind the project itself. The benefits are stated in the project's Business Case. Benefits can take many different forms:

●   Financial, in the form of additional profit or avoided costs

●   Strategic, by providing a platform to move towards one of the organisation's strategic aims

●   Legislative, by fulfilling some absolute requirement laid down by head office or a government body.

Throughout a PRINCE2 project, the Business Case is reviewed and progress is measured against any revised expectations of achieving defined benefits. During any project there are often opportunities to discover new benefits, which may enhance the project's product or indeed impact on another project. However, any deviations from the original Business Case must be controlled through the Project Board.

Within any project there are stakeholders with an interest in the project and its product, including:

- Customers, who have commissioned the work and will be benefiting from the end results

- User(s), who will use or operate the final product. The customer and user may be the same group of people

- Suppliers, who are providing specialist resources and/or skills to the project or are providing goods and services

- Sub-contractors, who provide products or services to the supplier.

The customer/supplier environment assumes that there will be a customer who will specify the desired product, make use of the final products and (in most cases) pay for the project, and a (prime) supplier who will provide resources and skills to create that product. PRINCE2 is written from the standpoint that these two parties come from separately managed areas and typically from commercially separate organisations. Where, as may often be the case, both customer and supplier have a common management, this will influence the composition of the project management team.

Whatever the team composition, the customer should always participate (throughout the project) in the creation and verification of products.

A project, by its nature, is set up to introduce change and the future is always less predictable than with routine work. During the project, the specification of products will inevitably undergo change. These changes need to be controlled because they can easily destroy the project's chance of success. Controlling changes is linked to version control, a topic that is covered within PRINCE2 under configuration management. Configuration management is an essential part of project control as it is focused on controlling the products being delivered, knowing where they are at any point in time, what their status is, who is working on them and which is the latest version.

In addition, projects can be large and complex, dealing with novel or unusual factors. Risk is therefore a major factor to consider during project management and PRINCE2 incorporates the management of risk into its processes.

Whatever the nature or size of a project, PRINCE2 defines an initiation stage that covers the planning and definition of the project. The initiation stage enables a management review before making any commitment to later stages and their associated resources and costs.

There will be many higher-level details surrounding the project. These will need to be dealt with by other methods and approaches, such as programme management. PRINCE2 is aimed at the middle ground between these higher-level, more strategic details and the specialist techniques required to create the technical products.

Few projects can be completed entirely in isolation from other work. PRINCE2 projects may exist as part of a programme, contributing to the realisation of benefits of a larger organisational change. In a programme context, the outputs from one project may be used as inputs by another project. There may be other dependencies between projects, such as shared resources. PRINCE2 places strong emphasis on the products that the project is required to deliver and so provides a firm basis for defining the boundaries.

Feasibility studies

In some situations, a feasibility study might be required to investigate the situation and determine options for the way ahead. Using PRINCE2, the optimum approach would be to handle the study as a separate and distinct project.

Figure 2.3 shows the (relatively) simple life cycle for a feasibility study project. It has one Project Plan, one Business Case, one set of risks and one final product – the recommendation. The possible options may each vary enormously in their costs and timescales. Each option would have a different Project Plan, Business Case and set of risks, but at the end of the feasibility study project there is one recommendation. A PRINCE2 project is based on getting a clear definition of the final product, a Project Plan and a budget by the end of initiation. If the feasibility study were part of the PRINCE2 project, coming before the development of the recommended solution, then it would not be possible to get a clear definition of the final product before the end of initiation since this definition would depend on the option chosen during the feasibility study. The appropriate option should be chosen in a separate feasibility study project, allowing the second project to proceed with a straightforward set of project information.

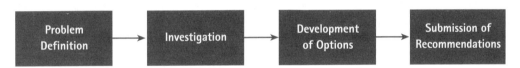

Figure 2.3 Life cycle of a feasibility study project

2.4 Overview of PRINCE2

PRINCE2 is a structured project management method based on the experience of scores of project managers, who have contributed, some from their mistakes or omissions, others from their success.

PRINCE2 has a process-based approach to project management. The processes define the management activities to be carried out during the project. In addition, PRINCE2 describes a number of components that are applied within the appropriate activities. Figure 2.4 shows the components positioned around the central process model.

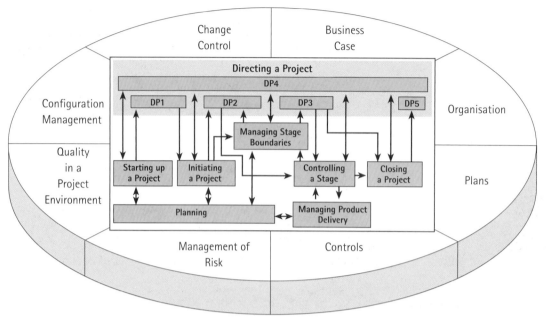

Figure 2.4 PRINCE2 processes and components

2.5 The processes

The PRINCE2 process model, shown in Figure 2.5, consists of eight distinctive management processes, covering the activities from setting the project off on the right track, through controlling and managing the project's progress, to the completion of the project. The common *Planning* (PL) process is used by four of the other processes.

Any project run under PRINCE2 will need to address each of these processes in some form. However, the key to successful use of the process model is in tailoring it to the needs of the individual project. Each process should be approached with the question: 'How extensively should this process be applied to this project?'

The objectives of *Closing a Project* are, therefore, to:

- Check the extent to which the objectives or aims set out in the Project Initiation Document have been met

- Assess to what extent all expected products have been handed over and accepted by the customer

- Confirm that maintenance and operation arrangements are in place (where appropriate) including any relevant training

- Make any recommendations for future work (Follow-on Action Recommendations)

- Capture lessons resulting from the project and complete the Lessons Learned Report

- Prepare an End Project Report

- Archive the project files

- Produce a Post-Project Review Plan

- Prepare a recommendation to the Project Board to notify the host organisation of the intention to disband the project organisation and release the resources (end project recommendation).

2.5.8 Planning (PL)

Planning is a repeatable process and plays an important role in other processes, the main ones being:

- *Planning an Initiation Stage* (SU6)

- *Planning a Project* (IP2)

- *Planning a Stage* (SB1)

- *Updating a Project Plan* (SB2)

- *Accepting a Work Package* (MP1)

- *Producing an Exception Plan* (SB6).

Apart from a plan, the process produces:

- A Product Checklist, which is a table of the products to be produced by the work planned, with space for planned and actual dates for delivery of draft, quality-checked and approved products

- The Risk Log, updated with any risk situation changes made as a result of the planning activity.

2.6   The components

Each component is described in further detail in the *Components* section of this manual, showing how the particular subject affects project management and providing guidance on when and how to address the issues.

Business Case	The existence of a viable Business Case is the main control condition of a PRINCE2 project. The Business Case is verified by the Project Board before a project begins and at every major decision point throughout the project. The project should be stopped if the viability of the Business Case disappears for any reason.
Organisation	PRINCE2 provides a structure of a project management team and a definition of the responsibilities and relationships of all roles involved in the project. According to the size and complexity of a project, these roles can be combined or shared.
Plans	PRINCE2 offers a series of plan levels that can be tailored to the size and needs of a project and an approach to planning based on products rather than activities.
Controls	PRINCE2 provides a set of controls which facilitate the provision of key decision-making information, allowing an organisation to pre-empt problems and make decisions on problem resolution. For senior management PRINCE2 controls are based on the concept of management by exception, i.e. we agree a plan, then let the manager get on with it unless something is forecast to go wrong.
	In order to promote sound management control, a project is split into stages as an approach to defining the review and commitment points of a project. (Using stages also helps to reduce the amount of work that the Project Manager needs to plan in detail at any one time.)
Management of risk	Risk is a major factor to be considered during the life of a project. PRINCE2 defines the key moments when risks should be reviewed, outlines an approach to the analysis and management of risk, and tracks these through all the processes.
Quality in a project environment	PRINCE2 recognises the importance of quality and incorporates a quality approach to the management and technical processes. It begins by establishing the customer's quality expectations and follows these up by laying down standards and quality inspection methods to be used and by checking that these are being used.
Configuration management	Tracking the components of a final product and their versions for release is called configuration management. There are many methods of configuration management available. PRINCE2 defines the essential facilities and information requirements for a configuration management method and how it should link with other PRINCE2 components and techniques.
Change control	PRINCE2 emphasises the need for change control, and this is enforced with a change control technique plus identification of the processes that capture, analyse and progress the change control.

2.7   The techniques

PRINCE2 offers very few techniques, preferring to leave the choice of technique to the users of the method and according to the circumstances of the project. But in support of the method the manual does contain details of three techniques: product-based planning, change control and quality review.

PRINCE2 provides a product-based start to the planning activity. It also provides a planning framework that can be applied to any type of project. This involves:

* Establishing what products are needed

* Defining the form and content of each product

* Determining the sequence in which each product should be produced.

Part of the product-based planning technique enables the project to define the standard of quality to which each product must conform.

Every project needs a technique for the control of changes. For organisations that do not already have a suitable technique, PRINCE2 describes a change control technique.

PRINCE2 also describes a specific technique, quality review, which is particularly suitable for the quality testing of document-based products, although its principles can be applied to any form of quality testing and review.

2.8 Process and component links

It is often difficult for newcomers to PRINCE2 to understand the main relationships and links between the processes, components and techniques. In which processes are the components used? Where is this technique used? Figure 2.6 gives a picture of these links.

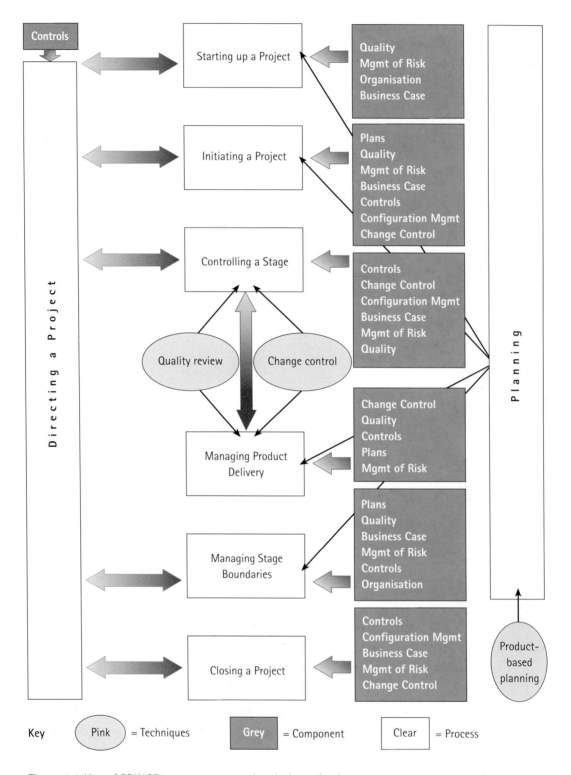

Figure 2.6 Use of PRINCE2 components and techniques in the processes

3
INTRODUCTION TO PROCESSES

3.1 Management levels

Project management is seldom straightforward enough to be a simple, linear process. In a PRINCE2 context, there are four management levels to take into account (see Figure 3.1).

Figure 3.1 The four management levels

These management levels are reflected in the PRINCE2 process model.

- At the highest level is corporate or programme management. While not part of project management as such, this higher management level is important, as it will often set the business context for one or more projects

- Within the project itself the highest level is *Directing a Project* (the Project Board work). This level is for key decision making and direction setting

- At the next level, *Controlling a Stage*, a great deal of management effort is expended in day-to-day planning and control. This is largely handled by the Project Manager

- The lowest management level, *Managing Product Delivery*, is handled by Team Managers.

There are two major ways in which these levels interact:

- The higher-level processes exercise control over the lower levels. For example, *Controlling a Stage* provides the Work Packages that define the work for *Managing Product Delivery*

- The output of the lower-level processes provides the inputs that allow the higher-level processes to function effectively. For example, *Controlling a Stage* provides essential planning and control information to enable the effective conduct of activities in *Directing a Project*.

3.2   Structure of each process description

Each process within PRINCE2 is described using the following structure and format.

3.2.1 Fundamental principles

Under this heading the following questions are addressed:

- Why have this process?
- What is it aiming to achieve in project management terms?
- Why is this process fundamental to good project management and hence a minimum requirement of PRINCE2?

3.2.2 Context

This section puts each process in context with the other processes and with activities going on outside the scope of PRINCE2. A context diagram supports each context description. The context diagram shows the major information flows into and out of the process.

3.2.3 Process description

This section describes the process by explaining the objectives and how the process fulfils the fundamental principles. The steps involved in carrying out the process are described.

No attempt has been made to lay out the steps in a strict sequence, since such a hard and fast sequence seldom exists. However, they have been listed in as logical a sequence as possible.

3.2.4 Scalability

Any project run under PRINCE2 will need to address each of the processes in some form. However, the key to successful use of PRINCE2 is its tailoring. Each process must be approached with the question: 'How extensively should this process be applied to this project?' For each of the main PRINCE2 processes, there is a section describing the factors to consider when tailoring the process to fit the needs of the project.

3.2.5 Responsibilities

This section specifies who should be accountable for the successful conduct of the process and responsible for its management. These are only stated for the sub-processes, as it is at that level that responsibilities can be decided.

3.2.6 Information needs

This section contains a table of the important information required for the sub-process to function and achieve its objectives. Some entries will be products, such as plans and reports; others are in the nature of decisions.

3.2.7 Key criteria

This section highlights the main issues that will dictate the ultimate success or failure of the sub-process.

3.2.8 Hints and tips

Projects by their nature are very varied. The environments within which they operate also vary tremendously. The PRINCE2 processes lay out the anticipated requirements for the vast majority of projects in most environments. The *Hints and tips* sections provide some guidance on the application of PRINCE2 in certain circumstances and indicate how PRINCE2 might be applied in practice. They are not expected to be a definitive guide. It is strongly advised that this section be fleshed out using best practice and normal approaches for each project environment that adopts PRINCE2.

3.3   Diagram and text notation

The following symbols are used in the various types of diagram used in the *Processes* chapters.

This is a repository for all management products that are created and may be used in many other processes.

This symbol indicates the archiving of project documentation.

This represents people or bodies outside the PRINCE2 identified roles, such as corporate or programme management.

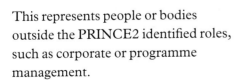

Capitalisation

All PRINCE2 products are denoted by the use of upper case letters for their initials, for example, 'Business Case'. Other products which may be useful in practice but are not considered as an integral part of the method are shown with lower case letters for their initials, for example, 'project closure recommendation'.

4
STARTING UP A PROJECT (SU)

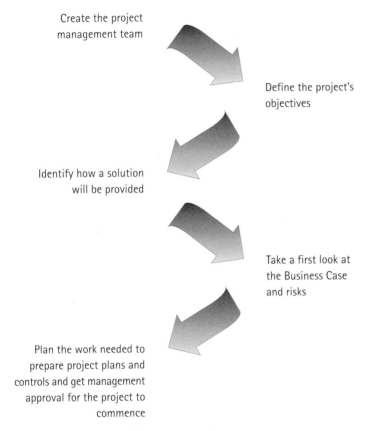

Create the project management team

Define the project's objectives

Identify how a solution will be provided

Take a first look at the Business Case and risks

Plan the work needed to prepare project plans and controls and get management approval for the project to commence

Figure 4.1 Overview of Starting up a Project

4.1 Fundamental principles

- There must be a basic business requirement that triggers the project. Indeed, before any work is commenced or resources are committed, there is a requirement to be able to answer the basic question: 'Do we have a viable and worthwhile project?' This question must be answered honestly to ensure that resources are not committed and wasted

- Nothing can be done in the project until responsibilities are defined and key roles have been filled. Someone has to 'kick-start' the project into being and make the first decisions

- Certain base information is needed to make rational decisions about the commissioning of the project

- An initiation Stage Plan must be submitted for approval before the initiation stage can be entered.

4.2 Context

This is the first process within PRINCE2. The project begins once this process has been conducted and the Project Board has approved commencement of project initiation. In terms of processes, it leads to *Authorising Initiation* (DP1).

Projects can be identified in a variety of ways and thus have a wide variation in the information available to the project management team at the time of start-up. The trigger for the project is the Project Mandate. This is normally provided by corporate or programme management. It is accepted that the Project Mandate may be anything from a verbal request to a complete Project Brief.

The process expects the existence of information explaining the reason for the project and the outcome expected. This set of information has been given the title Project Mandate to avoid confusion with more rigorously defined sets of information created within PRINCE2. The process *Starting up a Project* (SU) should be of short duration relative to the size of the remainder of the project.

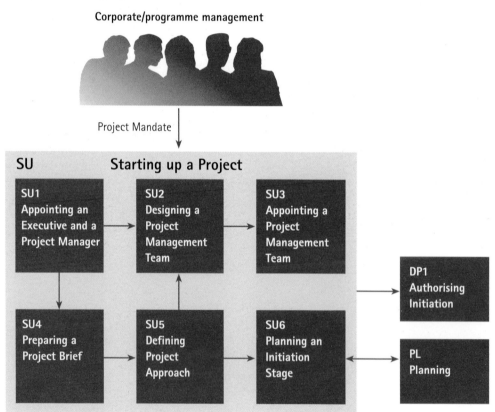

Figure 4.2 Starting up a Project

4.3 Process description

The work of the process is built around the production of seven elements:

• Designing and appointing the project management team

• Ensuring that the information required for the Project Brief is available

- Establishing the Project Approach

- Establishing the customer's quality expectations

- Creating an outline Business Case

- Setting up a Risk Log

- Creating the initiation Stage Plan.

The objective of the process is to enable a controlled start to the project by ensuring that:

- All the necessary project management authorities exist for undertaking the project

- Sufficient information is available to formalise the terms of reference for the project

- Individuals are appointed who will undertake the work required in project initiation and/or will take significant project management roles in the project

- The work required for project initiation is planned

- The organisation that will host the project team is informed of the existence and implications of the new project.

The process begins by receiving from some external source the definition of a problem or opportunity that the project has to satisfy. 'Project Mandate' is a term used for whatever information comes in to trigger the project, be it a feasibility study or details on the back of an envelope. The closer the quality of information in the Project Mandate can get to the ideal described in the Product Description outline for the Project Mandate (see Appendix A), the easier the start-up process will be.

An additional input that will help with the creation of both the initiation Stage Plan and Project Plan is the Project Approach, explaining the way in which it is intended that the end products of the project be produced.

If the project is part of a programme, the programme should provide the Project Brief and Project Approach and appoint some, if not all, members of the Project Board, thus eliminating much of the work required in this process.

Whilst the process model shows two parallel sets of processes to do with assembling a project management team (SU2 and SU3) and agreeing terms of reference and Project Approach (SU4 and SU5), in practice there will be considerable interplay between these two elements of work. This will depend on how much is known about the nature of the project, and how much has already been agreed about the structure and content of the project management team.

The target work location is informed of the impending project and requests are made for any appropriate logistical support required to carry out project initiation.

4.3.1 Scalability

There are a variety of approaches to this process, which fall into three categories:

- It is a stand-alone project and all the steps of this process will apply. If this is the case, there is little problem in deciding which steps to carry out

- This project is part of a programme. The programme has passed down documentation that is either a complete Project Brief or even a Project Initiation Document. The Project Board may already be defined; the Project Approach and the Risk Log are controlled at programme level. In other words, all the work of *Starting up a Project* (SU) and most of the initiation work has been done. In such a case, the work of this process is simply to check whether any more work needs to be done on the start-up products and that all the information provided is still correct and current

- The third possibility is that the project is very small. In such cases the process can usually be handled in an informal manner, possibly only taking a matter of minutes. A Project Manager should avoid the temptation to bypass it altogether.

Hints and tips

It will not always be appropriate, or indeed possible, to appoint the entire project management team prior to the start of initiation. But at least the Executive and the Project Manager should be appointed, so that the input to initiation can be prepared and decisions can be made.

Lessons Learned Reports from similar previous projects should be referenced to inform the set-up and conduct of this project.

If the Project Approach is not defined within the Project Mandate, or it cannot easily be identified, then consideration should be given to redirecting this work as a feasibility study to define the appropriate Project Approach. Once completed, the feasibility study will provide an excellent Project Mandate for the main project.

4.4 Appointing an Executive and a Project Manager (SU1)

4.4.1 Fundamental principles

To get anything done in the project, you need a decision maker and someone to undertake the planning.

4.4.2 Context

Before initiation of the project can begin, there must be a plan for that initiation work. The appointment of the Executive and Project Manager is a prerequisite for this work.

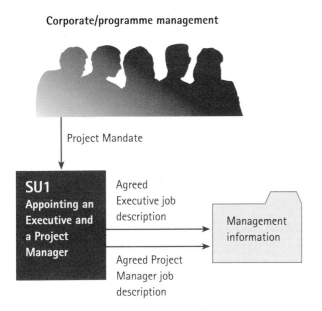

Figure 4.3 Appointing an Executive and a Project Manager

4.4.3 Process description

The objectives of this sub-process are to:

- Identify the Executive from the project's stakeholders

- Identify the most appropriate Project Manager for the project

- Confirm the selected people's availability, their acceptance of these roles and their commitment to carry them out

- Appoint them to their respective roles.

A prerequisite of this first sub-process is the existence and availability of a Project Mandate. Because this is the process that precedes the whole of the project, it will be very variable in application, depending particularly on the quality of the Project Mandate information. The following steps will be involved:

- Ratify the key elements of the Project Mandate

- Establish any missing information

- Identify candidates for Executive and Project Manager

- Establish the responsibilities for each role

- Appoint Executive

- Appoint Project Manager

- Confirm appointments via agreement to job descriptions by corporate or programme management and appointees.

The Project Mandate should indicate the general type of project, its size and complexity and its political and business sensitivity. This information will help to identify appropriate candidates for the Project Manager role.

There may be a draft Project Plan included in the Project Mandate from earlier work. This would give an idea of the time frame of the project – useful when confirming the availability of people to fill the roles.

The outline of the roles of Executive and Project Manager, given in *Project management team roles*, Appendix B, should be used as the basis for discussion between the Executive and the Project Manager on tailoring and agreement of their roles.

4.4.4 Responsibilities

Responsibility for this sub-process lies with corporate or programme management.

4.4.5 Information needs

Table 4.1 SU1 information needs

Management information	Usage	Explanation
Project Mandate	Input/Update	The trigger for the project
Agreed job descriptions for the Executive and Project Manager	Output	Basis for sign-up by the Executive and Project Manager
Appointed Executive and Project Manager	Output	Job descriptions agreed

4.4.6 Key criteria

- If the project is part of a programme, will the programme management team fulfil any roles on the Project Board?

- Does the proposed Executive have the financial and functional authority necessary to support the project adequately?

- Has the availability of candidates been measured against any forecast duration of the project to ensure that individuals are available for as much of the project as possible?

- Are any candidates likely to change jobs in the near future in a direction that would remove them from the project? If so, has this information been taken into consideration when making the appointments?

- Do the appointees have the skills and knowledge required to undertake their tasks?

Hints and tips

Where the size or importance of the project warrants it, agreed job descriptions should be signed by the person or persons undertaking the role, plus, where appropriate, their line management; copies should be held by that person or persons and a signed copy also held in the project files.

For small or low-risk projects it may not be appropriate to have formal job descriptions, but the people should have read and understood the responsibilities contained in the role descriptions.

If the project is part of a programme, programme management will appoint the Executive and may influence the appointment of the Project Manager as well. The programme may leave the appointment of the remainder of the Project Board to the Executive.

4.5 Designing a Project Management Team (SU2)

4.5.1 Fundamental principles

- The project needs the right people in place, with the authority, responsibility and knowledge to make decisions in a timely manner

- The project management team needs to reflect the interests of all parties who will be involved, including business, user and supplier interests

- Project management requires resources and calls for a range of skills, which must be available within the project management team

- It is important that consideration is given to all the activities that are involved in managing the project so that no important aspects are overlooked. It is also important that all the skills needed by the project are made available. All the roles identified in the *Organisation* component must be filled in some way in each project.

4.5.2 Context

Having identified an Executive and the Project Manager, the next job is to review the project size, complexity and areas impacted by the final outcome, then design the project management team with appropriate representation of user, supplier and Project Support.

In practice it is normal that this sub-process and the next, *Appointing a Project Management Team* (SU3), will have considerable overlap.

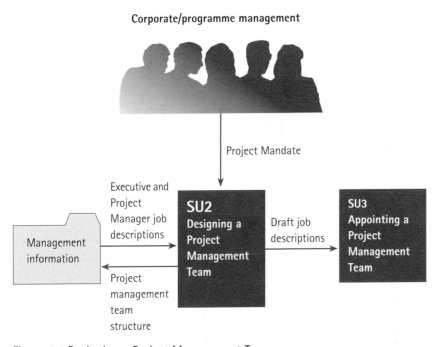

Figure 4.4 Designing a Project Management Team

4.5.3 Process description

The objectives of this sub-process are to:

- Design the project management team structure appropriate to the size and nature of the project and the groups involved

- Identify candidates for each role in order to produce a recommended project management team

- Determine the responsibilities and requisite skills for each position

- Where the project is part of a programme, programme management has responsibility for ensuring the establishment of an appropriate Project Board. If this is done, most of this sub-process will not be required. The programme may, however, leave the appointment of the remainder of the Project Board to the Executive.

The PRINCE2 project management team structure described in *Organisation*, Chapter 14 and *Project management team roles*, Appendix B should be used as a basis for the sub-process. There are certain steps that must be undertaken:

- Identify candidates for the Project Board roles and create their job descriptions

- Assess whether any members of the Project Board are likely to delegate any of their assurance responsibilities; this will assist the Project Manager to advise on the design of any assurance roles and the selection of candidates to fill them; this aspect may need to be revisited after the other Project Board roles are actually appointed

- Consider whether separate individuals are likely to be needed as Team Manager(s) or whether the Project Manager will be filling this role personally; the final decision on this may not be taken until the planning of each stage

- Examine the Project Manager role definition and propose any Project Support roles required; a checklist of potential Project Support responsibilities is shown in *Project management team roles*, Appendix B

- Assign candidate names to all roles identified; the design should state whether each role will be allocated to one individual, shared or combined with another role. Also assess the time and effort required to fill the role

- Identify who will need to approve these appointments in the next sub-process, SU3.

It may be necessary to obtain information from the Project Brief and Project Approach in order to complete this sub-process.

4.5.4 Responsibilities

The Executive and Project Manager are jointly responsible for the design. The Executive will take specific responsibility for the Project Board design.

4.5.5 Information needs

Table 4.2 SU2 information needs

Management information	Usage	Explanation
Agreed Executive and Project Manager job descriptions	Input	Specifies the existing agreed responsibilities to avoid gaps/overlaps
Project Mandate	Input	Indicates the likely user and customer interests
Project management team structure	Output	This forms the basis of discussion with the appointees and with the senior management
Draft job descriptions for the remaining members of the project management team	Output	Ready for discussion and approval in sub-process SU3

4.5.6 Key criteria

- Have the customer and supplier resident quality assurance and internal audit functions been catered for?

- Does the organisation design balance with the overall projected cost, criticality and importance of the project?

- Can the proposed Project Board members make the commitments required of them?

- Have all the roles and responsibilities been allocated? If not, are the exclusions justified?

- Does the design allocate roles and responsibilities to individuals with the requisite knowledge, time and authority to carry them out?

- Are all relevant stakeholders represented in the project management team?

- How should the PRINCE2 model be adapted where the customer or supplier uses methods or technology that call for specific organisation-and-control models?

- Does the project management team structure fit in with, and support, any programme management structure?

- If the project is part of a programme, is there to be programme representation on the Project Board or as some part of the project management team?

- Do any assurance and support roles fit into any overall programme or strategy assurance and support functions?

Hints and tips

If the project is part of a programme, programme management may choose to appoint all members of the Project Board or leave this to the Executive. In the latter case, the Executive should confirm the acceptability of the design with programme management.

The user and operational interests that will be impacted by the project's product(s) should be considered for Project Board representation.

The Project Board is a decision-making body, not a discussion group. For this reason it is not a good idea to allow the Project Board to grow too large. Ideally, it should not grow beyond, say, three to six people, even for a large project. It may not always be possible to restrict it to this size, but, for example, often a separate user group can be set up, which will appoint one of its members to act as the Senior User on the Project Board.

While it is important to give consideration to all the items discussed, it will often not be possible to provide all the information needed to make all appointments during start-up and thus there will often be a need to finish some appointments during initiation, or at the beginning of a stage.

Ensuring that quality testing has appropriate user and/or customer representation is the responsibility of the Senior User. This should be taken into consideration when discussing any delegation of the Senior User's assurance responsibilities.

It is essential to ensure that the project is not adversely affected by delays in customer or supplier management chains. This should be considered when thinking of individuals, particularly when filling the various Project Board roles.

A Project Board member should not delegate his/her role. This usually leads to a deputy who does not have the authority necessary to make the required decisions.

Where a third party is funding the project, it may be necessary for the financier to be extensively involved in the management of the project. Project Board roles should reflect this, but should also emphasise the user's role in specifying what is needed and monitoring the project to ensure that the solution is going to satisfy these needs.

Where the project is part of a programme, this sub-process can be used to design the lines of communication between project and programme. This may mean programme representation explicitly within the project management team.

If the supplier cannot be identified at this time, perhaps due to the Project Approach of tendering the work during the early stages of the project, consider having procurement or purchasing department representatives to take the Senior Supplier role in the interim.

Where there are many suppliers (for example, on a major construction project) consider creating a supplier forum that elects a representative as Senior Supplier to represent their views on the Project Board.

4.6 Appointing a Project Management Team (SU3)

4.6.1 Fundamental principles

- An essential for a well-run project is that every individual involved in the management of the project understands and agrees:
  - who is accountable to whom for what

- who is responsible for what

- what the reporting and communication lines are

● There must be agreement and acceptance by everyone of their roles and responsibilities

● There should be no gaps in responsibilities once the roles have been tailored; someone should be clearly responsible for each given management aspect.

4.6.2 Context

Having created a design for the project management team in sub-process SU2, this now needs discussion and agreement with the individuals identified.

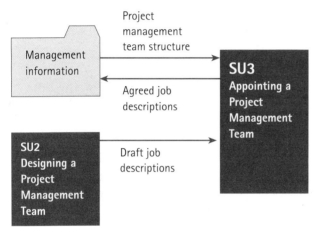

Figure 4.5 Appointing a Project Management Team

4.6.3 Process description

The objectives of this sub-process are to:

● Appoint people to:

- the Project Board

- Project Assurance (where appropriate)

- Project Support (where appropriate)

- team management

● Ensure that these individuals understand their roles and responsibilities in the management and support of the project

● Ensure that the individuals are actively committed to carrying out their roles and responsibilities

● Confirm the reporting and communication lines, and include in management information as this will impact on the Communication Plan.

These objectives are met by a process of consultation and discussion with all the people involved and, if necessary, their line management.

As agreement is reached with Project Board members on their roles, thoughts on the delegation of any of their Project Assurance responsibilities may change from the original project management team design. This may lead to a redesign and a further round of appointments or role modifications.

Each PRINCE2 role definition will need to be tailored to the particular environment and individual. The individual concerned should sign the resulting agreed job descriptions. Copies should be held by that individual and the Project Manager.

For any Project Assurance or support personnel appointed, the Project Manager needs to confirm what their availability to the project will be.

4.6.4 Responsibilities

The Executive is responsible for the appointments, assisted and advised by the Project Manager. The Executive will have to liaise with corporate or programme management to identify the appropriate personnel and negotiate for their availability.

4.6.5 Information needs

Table 4.3 SU3 information needs

Management information	Usage	Explanation
Project management team structure	Input	Identification of the planned allocation of roles, amended if necessary
Draft job descriptions	Input	Appointed and confirmed project management team
Agreed job descriptions	Output	Roles tailored to the project and the individual

4.6.6 Key criteria

- Did final agreement on job descriptions cause any transfer or change of responsibilities that has an impact on another job?

- Have all appointees understood and accepted the responsibilities of their role as described in the job description?

- Have the appointees the appropriate skills for the job? Have they received appropriate training to fulfil their roles? Have they sufficient time to fulfil their roles?

Hints and tips

Thought needs to be given to how the various support processes, such as Project Issue management, will be handled.

The customer or supplier may have a Project Support Office in existence, from which some or all of the Project Support identified may be obtained.

If the project is part of a programme that itself has programme support, thought will have to be given as to how the project will interface with the programme.

4.7 Preparing a Project Brief (SU4)

4.7.1 Fundamental principles

Before proceeding any further, the Project Board needs to satisfy itself that the project is worth doing.

The project needs to start with a reliable statement of requirements and expectations to ensure it is based on consistent and adequate information.

Even if the project is part of a programme and the programme has provided a Project Brief, documentation can become out of date quickly; hence it will need checking before proceeding.

4.7.2 Context

The external trigger for the project is the Project Mandate. This sub-process checks the content of the Mandate to ensure that it is still correct and enhances it, where necessary, into the Project Brief.

Where the project is part of a programme, the programme may create the Project Brief, thus reducing the work of this sub-process. The project team should validate any provided Project Brief and may need to expand on some of the statements in it. If the Project Brief is provided by a programme, the programme management must agree any changes (for example, impacts on constraints, such as delivery dates). Such changes would need impact analysis at programme level and may cause entries in the programme and project Risk Logs.

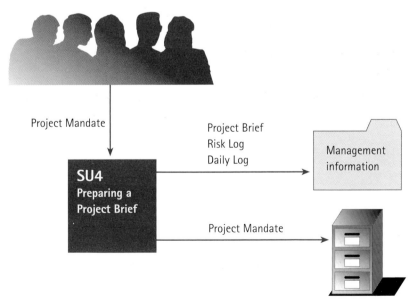

Figure 4.6 Preparing a Project Brief

4.7.3 Process description

The objectives of this sub-process are to:

- Prepare the formal terms of reference for the project

- Establish the customer's quality expectations

- Establish the Acceptance Criteria for the project

- Begin a record of any risks facing the project

- Ensure there is an outline Business Case based on the information provided in the Project Mandate.

The Project Mandate information may not be complete or accurate. This sub-process achieves a stable statement of project requirements in the form of the Project Brief.

The Project Brief needs to include high-level information on **what** needs to be done, **why** (the benefits to be achieved), **who** will need to be involved in the process, and **how** and **when** it will be done. The aim of the Project Brief is to allow the Project Board to decide whether there is sufficient justification to warrant the expenditure proposed by the initiation Stage Plan. The outline for the Project Brief, given in *Product Description outlines*, Appendix A, lists the information needed for this purpose.

The customer's quality expectations need to be agreed at this early stage. They will impact every part of the product development, thus affecting time and cost. Definition of the customer's quality expectations should come from the customer/user community, led by the Senior User, the Executive and other stakeholders. See *Quality in a project environment*, Chapter 18 for further details.

The user requirements should be prioritised. Later, if problems cause reconsideration of the project's scope, funds can then be targeted at those items promising the highest return. Part of the terms of reference should be the Acceptance Criteria, given in *Product Description outlines*, Appendix A. These are based on the customer's quality expectations.

The contents of the Project Brief should be discussed with all stakeholders.

The level of detail needed for each element of the Project Brief will vary with different project circumstances. However, each element needs to be considered, even if the result of that consideration is that the element is not needed.

The Business Case will be refined as part of the Project Initiation Document and throughout the project. However, the basic justification for the project needs to be understood, either defined in the Project Mandate or developed in this sub-process and added to the Project Brief. See *Business Case*, Chapter 13 for further details.

The customer's quality expectations and Acceptance Criteria will also be used in the initiation stage to create the Project Quality Plan.

PRINCE2 suggests that a Project Manager should keep a Daily Log, an informal record of any events, decisions, agreements and monitoring tasks. This will be needed throughout the project, so it is a good idea to create it during this sub-process.

Risks may come to light during this sub-process and therefore a Risk Log should be created as early as practical within this sub-process to hold details of any risks, their analysis and any actions.

4.7.4 Responsibilities

The Executive is ultimately responsible for the production of the Project Brief. In practice, the Project Manager and any appointed Project Support staff will do much of the actual work. The Executive's Project Assurance role should review the outline Business Case and Risk Log.

4.7.5 Information needs

Table 4.4 SU4 information needs

Management information	Usage	Explanation
Daily Log	Output	The Project Manager's informal record of actions, decisions, events and jobs to be done
Risk Log	Output	To record risks, including any noted in the Project Mandate or Project Brief
Project Brief	Output	Submission to the Project Board as part of the justification for initiation
Project Mandate	Input	The external trigger from corporate or programme management containing the reason for the project

4.7.6 Key criteria

- Does the Project Brief contain all the required information?
- Is the information in the various sections of the Project Brief consistent?
- Is the 'ownership' of the project properly defined?
- Is there any potential disagreement on the Project Brief contents from Project Board members?
- Is the Project Brief suitable for a decision to be made on whether to authorise initiation or not?
- If this project is one of a chain of related projects, does the content of the Project Brief conform to any prior projects?

Hints and tips

Check the Project Brief for the project informally with each member of the Project Board before presenting it for formal approval.

Try to determine whether there are any conflicts of interest within the parties to the project.

In small projects the Project Brief may not be produced as a separate document. It may be more appropriate to go straight to producing an outline Project Initiation Document, which would then be refined. In such a case, *Starting up a Project* (SU) and *Initiating a Project* (IP) could combine into one process.

Keep the Project Brief as small and high level as is consistent with the decisions that need to be taken in *Authorising Initiation* (DP1).

4.8 Defining Project Approach (SU5)

4.8.1 Fundamental principles

Before any planning of the project can be done, decisions must be made regarding how the work of the project is going to be approached. For example, will the solution be:

- Bought 'off the shelf'
- 'Made to measure'
- Developed in-house
- Contracted to third parties
- Based on an existing product
- 'Built from scratch'
- Based on specific technologies?

It is also necessary to make sure that the way in which the work is to be conducted is in line with practices and guidelines currently understood between customer and supplier and does not jeopardise the project in any way.

4.8.2 Context

This sub-process takes information from the Project Brief, together with information from a range of customer and supplier sources, to produce the defined Project Approach.

The Project Approach will be used when developing the Project Quality Plan and Project Plan in the next process, *Initiating a Project* (IP).

4.9.6 Key criteria

- Does the initiation Stage Plan show that sufficient resources are available to help the Project Manager develop each of the elements of the Project Initiation Document and the following Stage Plan?

- Has an appropriate level of management reporting been established as required by the size or level of risk of the initiation stage?

- Does the initiation Stage Plan show how each element of the Project Initiation Document will be produced?

- Is there sufficient information for the Project Board to make the decision on whether to start the project or not?

- Have those with Project Assurance responsibilities indicated which parts of the draft Project Initiation Document they wish to be checked, how and by which resources?

Hints and tips

Initiation stages are often short. If communication with the Project Board is frequent enough, formal reporting arrangements will be unnecessary.

While it is always important to plan any work prior to commencement, for some small, low-risk projects it may not be necessary to produce too formal a plan for the initiation stage.

The amount of start-up and initiation work, even for large and complex projects, is dependent on what work has gone on before.

5

INITIATING A PROJECT (IP)

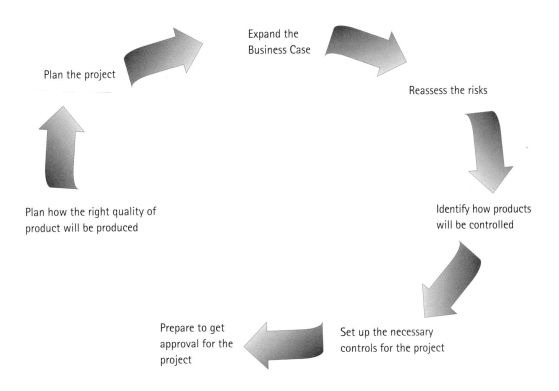

Figure 5.1 Overview of Initiating a Project

5.1 Fundamental principles

A successful project should observe the following principles:

- A project is a finite process with a defined start and end

- All parties must be clear on what the project is intended to achieve, why it is needed, how the outcome is to be achieved and what their responsibilities are, so that there can be genuine commitment to the project

- Well-managed projects have an increased chance of success.

Following these principles will ensure that the project can be successfully scoped and managed to its completion.

5.2 Context

Initiating a Project (IP) is aimed at laying down the foundations for the fulfilment of the principles just described. It follows the pre-project process *Starting up a Project* (SU). It is triggered by *Authorising Initiation* (DP1), leads to *Authorising a Project* (DP2), and invokes the *Planning* (PL) process to create the Project Plan and the *Managing Stage Boundaries* (SB) process to create the next Stage Plan. Initiation should always be the first stage in any PRINCE2 project.

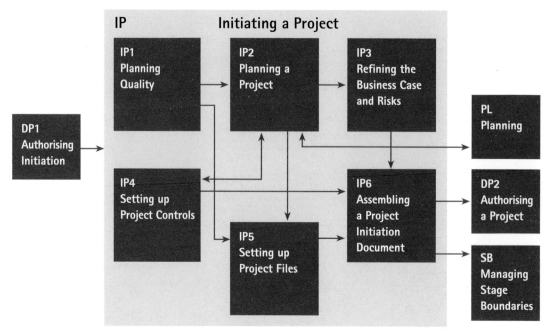

Figure 5.2 Initiating a Project

5.3 Process description

The purpose of *Initiating a Project* is to draw up a 'contract' in the form of a Project Initiation Document between the Project Board and the Project Manager, so that there is common understanding of:

- The reasons for doing the project

- What key products the project will deliver

- How and when these will be delivered and at what cost

- The scope of what is to be done

- Any constraints which apply to the product to be delivered

- Any constraints which apply to the project

- Who is to be involved in the project decision making

- How the quality required will be achieved

- What risks are faced

- How the project is to be controlled

- Who needs project progress information, how and when

- The next commitment that the Project Manager needs (the next Stage Plan).

- Refining the project's Acceptance Criteria
- Establishing the approach to be used within the project for the control of changes.

In order to achieve these objectives, various steps have to be undertaken:

- Establish links to any corporate and/or programme quality assurance function and ensure that all project quality activities support, and are supported by, this function. This may include assigning a quality assurance role for the project (as part of the Project Assurance role)
- Establish whether the customer has a quality management system that should apply to aspects of the project
- Establish whether the supplier has a quality management system that should apply to aspects of the project
- Define what combination of standards from those of the customer and supplier will be used in the project
- Establish any quality assurance needs for the project management products and activities, especially meeting the needs of the quality management system where these are applicable
- Establish the means by which overall success of the project's final product is to be measured, and prioritise them
- Identify quality responsibilities both within and external to the project
- Identify the quality control techniques and procedures to be employed during the conduct of the project
- Create the Configuration Management Plan and the change control procedures to be adopted, including:
  - responsibilities
  - procedures
  - change budget
  - documentation
- Assemble and finalise the above elements into the Project Quality Plan
- Set up a Quality Log to hold details of all planned and actual quality checks. Additions will be made to this as each Stage and Team Plan is created.

See *Quality in a project environment*, Chapter 18; *Configuration management*, Chapter 19 and *Change control*, Chapter 20 for further information on these aspects.

Where the project is part of a programme, the Project Mandate passed down from the programme or the Project Brief may have included statements about quality planning. These would form the basis of the Project Quality Plan. If there is any inconsistency between the desired Project Quality Plan and what is contained within the Project Mandate or Project Brief, this must be resolved with programme management.

Where the project will use standards that are already documented, these should just be referenced, with only variations documented, within the Project Quality Plan.

5.4.4 Responsibilities

The Project Manager is responsible for the sub-process, assisted by those with Project Assurance responsibilities, particularly those connected to business assurance. Where a separate quality assurance function exists within a corporate body, the work of this sub-process must be done in close co-ordination with that function.

5.4.5 Information needs

Table 5.1 IP1 information needs

Management information	Usage	Explanation
Project Brief	Input	This document should contain the customer's quality expectations and the Acceptance Criteria
Quality standards	Input	Standards with which projects must comply
Project Approach	Input	To establish the most appropriate approach to quality, there is a need to know how the project's work is to be approached as this could have a fundamental effect on the methods and resources used
Project management team structure and job descriptions	Input/ Update	To establish quality responsibilities and add them into job descriptions where appropriate
Project Quality Plan	Output	This will contain the results of *Planning Quality (IP1)*, including the (possibly) refined and expanded Acceptance Criteria, and will be an element of the Project Initiation Document output from *Assembling a Project Initiation Document* (IP6)
Quality Log	Output	Created in readiness to record all details of quality checks

5.4.6 Key criteria

- Have all quality standards associated with the project's area of impact been identified and considered?

- Has the customer imposed any Acceptance Criteria on the final product that will require quality-related work beyond normal expectations?

- Have all those, and only those, standards relevant to the successful final product of the project been included?

- Are the approaches to assuring quality for the project appropriate in the light of the standards selected?

- Are the quality criteria measurable or assessable by the quality control mechanisms identified?

- Are the change control and quality assurance methods appropriate for the scale, complexity and risk exposure of the project?

- How will quality assurance be provided on projects where the Project Manager is not technically qualified?

Hints and tips

Much of the information discussed earlier in this chapter, such as standards and quality assurance functions, may already be established and documented. It will usually be sufficient for the Project Quality Plan to refer to this documentation, plus clear identification and justification of any variation from the standards. However, the remainder of the Project Quality Plan's contents must be explicitly stated.

The Project Quality Plan may have to take into account any planned change of suppliers during the project, as they may have different quality standards.

5.5 Planning a Project (IP2)

5.5.1 Fundamental principles

Before committing to major expenditure on the project, the timescale and resource requirements must be established. This information is held in the Project Plan and is needed so that the Business Case can be evaluated and the Project Board can control the project.

5.5.2 Context

This sub-process uses the common *Planning* (PL) process to produce the Project Plan. It includes the implications of the Project Quality Plan from *Planning Quality* (IP1) and *Defining Project Approach* (SU5).

The Project Plan becomes a major element of the Project Initiation Document.

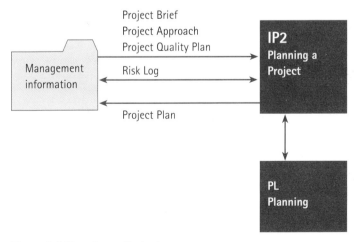

Figure 5.4 Planning a Project

5.5.3 Process description

The objectives of this sub-process are to:

- Understand at a high level the totality of the work that is about to be undertaken by:
  - identifying and, where possible, defining the major products of the project
  - identifying the major activities to be performed to deliver the products
  - assessing the major risks of the project and putting in place countermeasures, as highlighted in *Management of risk*, Chapter 17
  - estimating the effort needed
  - identifying what timescales are achievable, given the project constraints and any key milestones
  - identifying the overall resource requirements and costs
- Identify the key decision and review points for the project, and any implications on these from the Project Approach. From these decide where the management stage divisions should be (as discussed in *Controls*, Chapter 16)
- Use the *Planning* (PL) process to produce the Project Plan.

The Project Approach taken (see SU5) will affect the testing that can be done, the type and amount of development work to be done and other factors influencing the choice of stages, such as whether there will be a large purchasing effort.

It is also necessary to decide on the planning standards to be used for this project, including:

- Tools and techniques
- Content and presentation of plans
- Adoption or otherwise of corporate or departmental standards.

As this sub-process is basically a planning process, the detailed steps needed to carry it out are those explained in *Planning* (PL).

Change budget

At this time it is useful to consider the probable volume of change requests to the objectives or specification that are likely to be submitted during the project. If it is forecast that a number of changes are likely, the Project Manager should suggest to the Project Board that a change budget be set aside to cover the cost of these. This would avoid situations where the Executive is asked to go back to corporate or programme management for an increase in the budget to cover the cost of such changes.

Contingency budget

By this time, the risks (threats or opportunities) to the project will have been analysed in *Analysing Risks* (PL6). If there is a significant exposure to risk, and contingency plans have been prepared, the Project Manager should suggest to the Project Board that a contingency budget be set aside to cover the cost of implementing the plans should the associated risk occur.

5.6.5 Information needs

Table 5.3 IP3 information needs

Management information	Usage	Explanation
Project Brief	Input	Contains high-level views of the anticipated business benefits and risks as identified in Starting up a Project (SU)
Project Approach	Input	Will contain information about the way the work is to be conducted and could provide input to both the Business Case and risk analysis
Risk Log	Update	Add any identified new risks. Modify with details of any changed risks
Project Plan	Update	Update with any significant extra activities and resource requirements to counter risk exposure
Business Case	Update	Extract from the Project Brief and update with the latest (more detailed) information

5.6.6 Key criteria

- Are the risk avoidance costs less than the costs implicit in the threats?

- Is it reasonable that the benefits claimed can be achieved by the anticipated final outcome of the project?

- Has sensitivity analysis been conducted on the Business Case?

- Is the information in a form that is understandable by the Project Board?

- Are plans in place by which the user(s) of the products will realise the benefits?

- Has the Business Case been produced in line with corporate standards?

Hints and tips

Each risk effect is itself a potential cause of another effect in a cause-effect chain. The Project Manager has to decide where and if the chain should be cut to manage risks.

It may be appropriate to use the risk profile model to present a summary of the risks documented in the Risk Log to the Project Board.

Where the project is part of a programme, the programme's risk monitoring mechanism must be used unless there are valid reasons not to do so. It may be sensible to combine the maintenance of all the Risk Logs at programme level.

Funding normally comes from the customer, but there are situations where the supplier fully or partially funds the project (Private Finance Initiative, for example). This may give the customer fewer rights to intervene or control the project and could affect the customer's ability to insist on the inclusion of risk avoidance or reduction activities.

The customer and supplier are likely to have different Business Cases.

The method of payment to suppliers needs to be considered. Payment may be provided on a regular basis throughout the life of the project, staged according to the delivery of particular products, or in a lump sum at the end.

Benefit realisation often requires baselining to be done as part of the project. Once the new product is in place, the old situation has disappeared, making a true comparison impossible. It is sensible to baseline before the project is implemented.

5.7 Setting up Project Controls (IP4)

5.7.1 Fundamental principles

Each decision on the project has to be made in a timely manner by the person or group most appropriate to make that decision, and must be based on accurate information. This sub-process ensures that an appropriate communication, control and monitoring framework is put in place.

5.7.2 Context

This sub-process builds on the information established in the earlier IP processes to produce a statement of project controls.

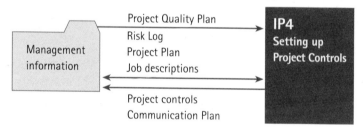

Figure 5.6 Setting up Project Controls

5.7.3 Process description

The objectives of this sub-process are to:

- Establish the level of control and reporting required by the Project Board for the project after initiation

- Develop controls that are consistent with the risks and complexity of the project

- Establish the day-to-day monitoring required to ensure that the project will be controlled in an effective and efficient manner

- Identify all interested parties and agree their communication needs.

In order to achieve these objectives, various steps need to be undertaken:

- Allocate the various levels of decision making required within the project to the most appropriate project management level

- Establish any decision-making procedures that may be appropriate, possibly by tailoring procedures within existing quality management systems or other standard procedures

- Incorporate decision-making authorities and responsibilities into job descriptions where appropriate

- Confirm the stage boundaries to provide the appropriate level of control

- Confirm the tolerances for the project and the escalation processes (from Team Manager to Project Manager, Project Manager to Project Board, and Project Board to corporate or programme management)

- Consider the size of Work Packages to be used, particularly when using external suppliers.

- Establish the information needs associated with each of the decision-making processes

- Establish monitoring mechanisms to satisfy these information needs

- Establish the resource requirements to provide the monitoring information

- Incorporate monitoring mechanisms into plans and job descriptions where appropriate

- Identify all stakeholders outside the project management team and agree with them their information needs, plus any information needed from them by the project. Define the communication content, recipient(s) and sender, method and frequency for all these external communications in the Communication Plan

- Create a Communication Plan as described in the Product Description outline

- Establish the procedures required to produce and distribute the reporting information.

Where the project is part of a programme, the Communication Plan must define how information is to be fed to the programme.

5.7.4 Responsibilities

The Project Manager is responsible, assisted by Project Support and advised by those with Project Assurance responsibilities.

5.7.5 Information needs

Table 5.4 IP4 information needs

Management information	Usage	Explanation
Project Plan	Update	This will need to be updated with activities and resource requirements for monitoring and control
Risk Log	Update	Risk levels will have an impact on the scale and rigour of control activities. New or changed risks may be noted as a result of defining control and monitoring activities. Also there is a need to put in place monitoring devices for risks as they develop
Project Quality Plan	Input	The achievement of quality is one area that must be monitored and controlled. There is, therefore, a need to co-ordinate project controls with the Project Quality Plan
Communication Plan	Output	Identify all communication paths, frequency, methods and reasons
Job descriptions	Update	Incorporate decision-making authorities and responsibilities into job descriptions where appropriate
Project controls	Output	This will form part of the Project Initiation Document

5.7.6 Key criteria

- Are the decisions being allocated to people equipped and authorised to make those decisions?

The next points are there to reinforce the motto 'Not too little, not too much':

- Are the controls appropriate to the risk, scale and complexity of the project?
- Is the level of formality established appropriate to the risk, scale and complexity of the project? This covers such things as reporting, monitoring procedures and job descriptions
- Are all the participants committed to providing the information and acting on it?
- Have the information needs of all people with an interest in the project been considered when creating the Communication Plan?
- Have the tolerances for the project been clearly identified?

Hints and tips

When creating the controls for the project, consider the communications requirements of the project as well as the decisions being made.

Make sure that the level of control is appropriate to the project. Don't over-control for the sake of it.

If the project is part of a programme, make sure that any programme reporting requirements will be satisfied by the defined control structure.

Where information has to be fed back to a programme, this may be done by reports from the project being examined by programme staff or by programme representation within the project.

Programme representation is recommended in estimating the impact of change.

When creating the project schedule, appropriate milestones should be identified to allow any required programme monitoring of project progress, such as the ends of stages and the production of reports required for use by either the programme or other projects.

Try to restrict external communication requests to copies of existing project reports.

In a programme context, each project may operate change management within delegated authority levels.

5.8 Setting up Project Files (IP5)

5.8.1 Fundamental principles

Once the project is under way, it is important to keep track of all the information being produced about the project and the management and specialist products. There is a need to be able to manage different versions of products and to be able to retrieve information quickly and reliably. Establishing a sensible and pragmatic project filing system at the start of the project can ease these problems.

5.8.2 Context

This sub-process takes information from the Project Plan and adds the project filing structure to the Configuration Management Plan. A suggested project filing structure for management documents is given in Appendix E.

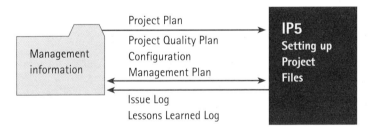

Figure 5.7 Setting up Project Files

5.8.3 Process description

The objectives of this sub-process are to:

● Institute a system of storing and retrieving all information relevant to the management of the project, the quality checking work done and the products themselves, which will provide appropriate support to the project team and to the implementation of change management

- Assign responsibility for managing this filing system.

It may be that a configuration management system is to be used that will provide these facilities for some or all of the project's products.

In order to achieve these objectives, various steps have to be undertaken:

- Establish what information will be produced throughout the project and will need filing

- Establish what products will be produced throughout the project and the need for associated storage

- Establish the retrieval requirements of the people in the Communication Plan

- Establish filing systems that are appropriate for the identified filing and retrieval needs.

The Issue Log and the Lessons Learned Log are also created during this sub-process.

5.8.4 Responsibilities

The Project Manager is responsible for this sub-process, assisted by any Project Support roles and advised by those with Project Assurance responsibilities.

Where the project is part of a programme, the project-level filing structure must be consistent with that at programme level.

5.8.5 Information needs

Table 5.5 IP5 information needs

Management information	Usage	Explanation
Project Plan	Input	Contains all the information about the products that the project is expected to produce
Project Quality Plan/ Configuration Management Plan	Update	Updated with the project filing structure as part of the Configuration Management Plan
Issue Log	Output	Created in readiness to record all Project Issues
Lessons Learned Log	Output	A blank log ready to record aspects of the project that go well or badly

5.8.6 Key criteria

- Is the formality and rigour of the project filing system appropriate for the scale, risk and complexity of the project? Does it fit with corporate culture?

- Will the retrieval system produce all required information in an accurate, timely and usable manner?

- Will the project files provide the information necessary for any audit requirements?

- Will the project files provide the historical records required to support any lessons learned?

Hints and tips

With sensible design, computerised support can avoid the need for multiple copies and ensure that staff have access to only the latest version of information.

The key to success is complete and rigorous naming conventions and version numbering, so that it is at least clear what information is being looked at, and for the Project Manager to have confidence that there is firm control over all master versions of information and products.

Whether paper-based or automated, create a formal configuration management system and appoint a Configuration Librarian as discussed in *Configuration management*, Chapter 19.

Remember that 'files' do not necessarily mean paper. The project files will cover a wide range of media, all of which need to be considered.

Has due consideration been given to the implications of the geographic spread of project personnel?

5.9 Assembling a Project Initiation Document (IP6)

5.9.1 Fundamental principles

There needs to be a focal point at which all information relating to the 'what, why, who, how, where, when and how much' of the project is gathered for agreement by the key stakeholders, and then for guidance and information for those involved in the project.

5.9.2 Context

This sub-process takes all the information from the other IP processes and produces the Project Initiation Document in preparation for the Project Board's decision on whether to authorise the project, covered in *Authorising a Project* (DP2). It also invokes *Managing Stage Boundaries* (SB) to summarise the performance of the initiation stage and prepare the next Stage Plan.

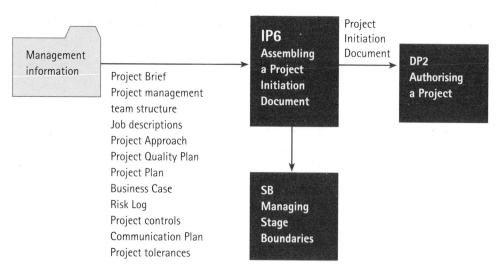

Figure 5.8 Assembling a Project Initiation Document

5.9.3 Process description

The objectives of this sub-process are to:

- Provide a basis for the decisions to be made in *Authorising a Project* (DP2)

- Provide a benchmark for all the other management decisions that need to be made during the life of the project

- Provide an information base for everyone who needs to know about the project

- Prepare a plan for the next stage for Project Board approval.

In order to achieve these objectives, it is important to understand that the information will need to be held and presented in various ways and the Project Initiation Document may not be one physical document.

The steps required to achieve these objectives will include the following:

- Invoke the *Managing Stage Boundaries* (SB) process to prepare the next Stage Plan and draw the initiation stage to a close

- Decide how the information can best be packaged and held so that these objectives can be met for this particular project

- Assemble the information from the previous sub-processes

- Assemble the project organisation structure from the project management team structure and job descriptions; this may include finalising any roles not allocated during SU2 and SU3

- Construct the project definition from the contents of the Project Brief and Project Approach, modified by the Project Plan contents

- Carry out a final cross-check of the information in the various elements to ensure that they are compatible

6.3.3 Stage boundaries

As part of the initiation stage, the Project Board and Project Manager will agree on the division of the project into stages. The division is normally proposed by the Project Manager and approved by the Project Board during informal discussions after production of a draft Project Plan.

Basically the Project Board only authorises the Project Manager to proceed with one stage at a time. At the end of each stage, the Project Board reviews the whole project status and approves the next Stage Plan only if it is satisfied that the Business Case still stands and the project will deliver what is required.

If major problems occur during a stage, the Project Manager will issue an Exception Report and the Project Board may then ask for an Exception Plan to be prepared that will bring the stage (or project) back under control. This is part of 'management by exception'.

6.3.4 Ad hoc direction

The Project Board's main objectives are to provide overall direction and guidance throughout the project, and to ensure that the project and the products remain consistent with business plans. Activities to achieve these objectives are formally defined as part of the Stage Plans, but the Project Board will want to monitor these activities by receiving appropriate reports on key elements from the Project Manager.

There may also be a need for the Project Board to provide advice and guidance to the Project Manager or to confirm some of the decisions he/she needs to make, for example, regarding potential problems.

The Project Board must maintain a feedback on project progress to corporate or programme management during the project.

The Project Board must also be mindful of any changes to corporate strategy or the external environment and reflect the impact of such changes when directing the Project Manager.

6.3.5 Project closure

The project ends with confirmation by the Project Board that everything expected has been delivered to the correct level of quality and that, where applicable, it is in a state where it can be used, operated, supported and sustained.

There may be follow-on actions as a result of the project, about which the Project Board must make decisions and refer to the appropriate bodies.

A date and plan for a post-project review can be agreed. This is a point in the future when the benefits and performance of the end product can be assessed.

Any lessons learned that may be of benefit to other projects are also directed to the relevant body.

Finally, the project's support infrastructure can be disbanded.

The closure process will be modified in situations where the project is terminated prematurely. It is likely that there will be follow-on actions, but not all products may have been produced and there may be little or nothing to support. It is unlikely that there will be a full post-project review, but the review of the End Project Report and Lessons Learned Report may be very important to understand why the project has been prematurely terminated and to determine the best way forward.

6.4 Authorising Initiation (DP1)

6.4.1 Fundamental principles

No one should commit to significant expenditure on the project before verifying that it is sensible to do so.

6.4.2 Context

Authorising Initiation (DP1) is the first major activity for the Project Board. After the process *Starting up a Project* (SU), it must decide whether to allow the project to enter the initiation stage. This may be done at a formal Project Board meeting. The Project Board can, however, choose to make the decision without the need for a formal meeting, as long as all members are in agreement.

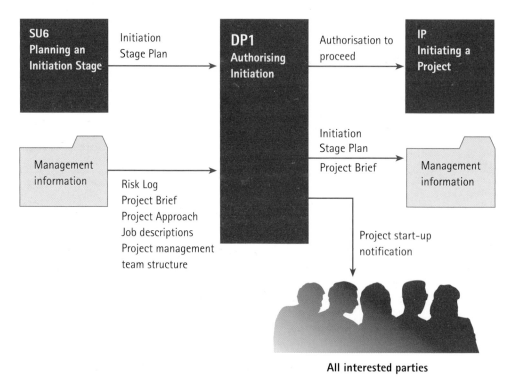

Figure 6.3 Authorising Initiation

6.4.3 Process description

The objective of this sub-process is to ensure that the project is properly initiated by:

● Formally confirming the appointments to the project management team

Project Plan

The Project Plan gives an overall view of the major products, timescale and cost for the project. Any wide variation between this and any previous forecast for the project (for example, one done as part of a feasibility study) should be examined and the Project Board should assure itself of the continued validity and achievability of the plan, and reasons for the variation. The Project Plan needs to be co-ordinated with any relevant strategic and programme management plans.

Project organisation

Most, if not all, of the appointments of the project management team will have been finalised during *Starting up a Project* (SU). These now have to be formally confirmed and any late appointments negotiated. Each member of the team should have agreed their role (as described in *Organisation*, Chapter 14) and this agreement is one of the items that the Project Board has to confirm.

Controls

The Project Initiation Document will include details of the controls that will enable the Project Board to keep overall control of the project. This will include step-by-step approval for the project to proceed via a series of end stage assessments, confirmation of the tolerance level for the project and the stage after initiation, and details of what will happen if any stage exceeds its agreed tolerance. There should be information on the frequency and content of reports from the Project Manager to the Project Board, together with details of how the Project Manager intends to control the project on a day-to-day basis. The Project Board must satisfy itself that these controls are adequate for the nature of the project.

Communication Plan

This should reflect the information needs and timing of communications between the Project Manager, the Project Board and any other interested parties. It includes communication in both directions between the parties. The Communication Plan will contain details of any required co-operation from outside the project, plus links to corporate or programme management. It is the responsibility of the Project Board to obtain this and confirm the availability as part of this sub-process.

6.5.4 Responsibilities

The Project Board is responsible for this sub-process. Most of the input will come from the Project Manager.

6.5.5 Information needs

Table 6.2 DP2 information needs

Management information	Usage	Explanation
Next Stage Plan	Approval	Approval by the Project Board of the next Stage Plan
End Stage Report	Input	Report on initiation stage performance

Request for authorisation to proceed	Input	A request from the Project Manager for authorisation by the Project Board to proceed with the submitted Stage Plan. The Project Board, of course, has the authority to reject the plan. It may ask for a resubmission or decide to close the project. The Project Board also defines the levels of tolerance for the next stage
Project Initiation Document	Approval	Baselined after approval by the Project Board
Authorisation to proceed	Output	Approval by the Project Board to begin the next stage
Stage Plan	Output	Approved by the Project Board
Progress information	Output	The Communication Plan may indicate the need to advise an external group of progress

6.5.6 Key criteria

- Does the project support corporate strategy and programmes?

- Is the Business Case acceptable?

- Are the risks manageable and acceptable?

- Can the Project Manager show that the Project Plan is achievable?

- Is there confidence that the required resources can be made available over the life of the project?

- Are the differing objectives of all parties clear at the point of initiation?

- Do the defined controls ensure that the differing objectives of all parties will be met at each point in the project?

- What happens if one party's decision criteria require cancellation, while others propose continuation? Can contract termination criteria, terms and conditions be agreed to account for this, or should normal contract discharge conditions apply?

- Has PRINCE2 been adapted correctly to account for customer or supplier organisational or control models?

- Do the relevant risks and assumptions clearly identify the impacts on customer and supplier?

- Can or should the supplier have sufficient control over the customer's organisation to be required to bear any of the business risk?

- For each risk and assumption, are each respective customer's management, monitoring and containment responsibilities defined?

- Where a supply-side risk impacts on the customer's Business Case, is it clear whether the supplier or the customer will manage it?

- If the project is based on staged payments, has an appropriately detailed level of identification of product or outcome delivery been identified? Do the Acceptance Criteria reflect the staged payments approach?

- If funding for the project is variable, has adequate consideration been given to how the supplier will ensure that the contracted scope is fully funded?

Hints and tips

Time must be allocated by the Project Board to read and understand the Project Initiation Document and to discuss any points at issue (with the Project Manager and others) so that the decisions taken are well informed.

The process is easier if the Project Board and Project Manager have been working closely together during project initiation. There will be fewer (ideally no) surprises.

The project organisation structure must allow for communication to decision-making forums that already exist within the customer and supplier organisations as well as to temporary ones established to ensure effective management of the project itself. This will normally be a Project Board responsibility. The potential delegation of Project Assurance responsibilities can be used to help achieve the required communication.

In a fixed-funding project, it must still be practical for the customer to pay for any cost increases caused by scope variations requested by the customer.

Where the supplier funds the project there may be implications for the organisation and control of the project. This should be carefully described in the job descriptions of the Executive and Senior Supplier.

Where there is a wide differential between the Business Cases of the customer and the supplier, it is less likely that consistent and compatible decisions and actions will occur. Consider whether knowledge and understanding of the Business Case differentials would assist in assuring compatible behaviour.

Tight time constraints will tend to militate against the type of project relationship that requires extensive, formal controls and communications between customer and supplier. Review the standard PRINCE2 controls and their frequency in the light of any time constraints.

When approving the Project Initiation Document, it should not be forgotten that the next Stage Plan also needs approval.

Where funding for the project is variable, stage approval should include assurance that funds for the stage are set aside. The choice and timing of stages may be done to reflect any need to confirm continued funding.

6.6 Authorising a Stage or Exception Plan (DP3)

6.6.1 Fundamental principles

It is important that work commences on a stage only when the Project Board says it should. This avoids the problem of projects continuing just because no one thinks to stop them.

To enable this to happen, the project should be broken down into manageable sections (stages), at the end of which the Project Board has to approve whether work is to continue or not.

It is also important to spot problems early and react to them.

6.6.2 Context

This sub-process authorises every stage (except the initiation and the first stage) plus any Exception Plans that are raised.

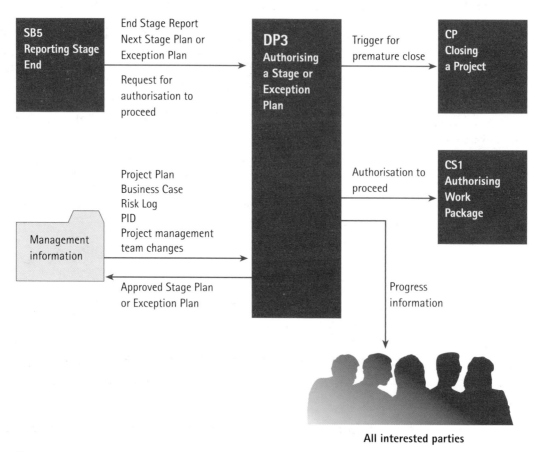

Figure 6.5 Authorising a Stage or Exception Plan

6.6.3 Process description

The objective of this sub-process is to decide whether to authorise the next stage of work and hence commit the required resources, based on:

- A view of the current status of the project

- A detailed forecast of the commitment of resources required by and the products to be created from the next stage of the project

- A reassessment of the likely project end date

- A reassessment of the risk situation

- A reassessment of the Business Case and the chances of achieving the expected benefits.

The Project Manager usually presents the current status of the project, including the results of the previous stage compared with expectations.

The detailed forecast comes from the plan for the next stage, for which the Project Manager is seeking approval. The detailed forecast should match the updated or revised Project Plan.

The updated Project Plan and Business Case are compared with what they were at the start of the project (and at the start of the current stage) to check that the project is still viable.

Any changes to the Business Case defined in the Project Mandate or Project Brief must be communicated to corporate or programme management.

The Project Board sets the tolerances for the next stage as part of giving approval for the Stage Plan.

The sub-process may also be invoked when the stage or project is forecast to exceed its tolerance levels. Early warning of such a situation should have been given to the Project Board via, possibly, Highlight Reports followed later by an Exception Report, which is considered by the Project Board in *Giving Ad Hoc Direction* (DP4) (see *Controls*, Chapter 16 for a full explanation). An Exception Report explains the cause of the deviation and the current situation, the options, the Project Manager's recommendation and the impact on the Project Plan, Business Case and risks.

In the case of a stage being forecast to exceed its tolerances, the Project Board may have instructed the Project Manager to produce an Exception Plan for the Project Board's approval. (There are other options.) An updated Project Plan, Business Case and Risk Log should accompany the Exception Plan.

If the forecast is for the project to deviate beyond its tolerances, the Project Board must consider its brief and decide whether the matter has to be referred upwards. As part of the exception process, the Project Board has to secure any necessary decisions from outside the project for any potential deviations beyond project tolerances. For example, if this project is part of a programme, programme management will have to examine the likely impact on the programme and take appropriate action.

Once authorised, an Exception Plan replaces the plan that was in trouble.

Before authorising a Stage or Exception Plan, the Project Board must ensure that changes in the corporate environment, which may impact on the project or its Business Case, are brought to the attention of the Project Manager and dealt with effectively.

In the event that the Project Board decides that the project is no longer viable, it must instruct the Project Manager to terminate the project and close it down in an orderly manner. This will involve the Project Manager triggering the process *Closing a Project* (CP).

6.6.4 Responsibilities

The Project Board has full responsibility for this sub-process, based on information provided by the Project Manager. Advice would be given by any allocated Project Assurance roles.

6.6.5 Information needs

Table 6.3 DP3 information needs

Management information	Usage	Explanation
Next Stage Plan or Exception Plan	Approval	Plan for which the Project Manager is seeking approval

Project Plan	Input	To allow the Project Board to review the whole project status
Business Case	Input	To allow the Project Board to check that the project is still justified
Project Initiation Document	Input	Used to provide a baseline against which to assess the advisability of any deviations
Project management team changes	Input	To allow the Project Board to ratify any appointment changes
Risk Log	Input	Check that the risks are still acceptable
End Stage Report	Input	Report of stage just completed. Helps assessment of current situation.
Request for authorisation to proceed	Input	Usually a stage approval form for the Project Board to sign
Authorisation to proceed or trigger for premature close	Output	Authorisation to proceed with the submitted plan. During project initiation, the Project Board decides how formal or informal it wishes the approval to be. The Project Board, of course, has the authority to reject the plan. It may ask for a resubmission or decide to close the project. The Project Board also defines the levels of tolerance for the next stage or Instruction from the Project Board to the Project Manager to close the project down before its expected end
Stage Plan or Exception Plan	Output	Approved by the Project Board
Progress information	Output	The Communication Plan may indicate the need to advise an external group of progress

6.6.6 Key criteria

- Was everything expected of the current stage delivered? If not, was this with the approval of the Project Board?

- Are there clear statements about what is to be done about anything not delivered? Does a Project Issue cover it? Is its delivery included in the next Stage Plan (or Exception Plan)?

- Is the project still viable and does it remain focused on the same business need?

- Are the risks still acceptable?

- Are the countermeasures still valid, including any contingency plans?

- Does the Project Board want to, and is it able to, commit the resources needed for the next stage of work?

- In projects that have a different supplier for each stage, is it documented and agreed by all suppliers that the key project information will be made available to subsequent suppliers?

> **Hints and tips**
>
> The Project Board members are likely to be busy people. Setting dates for any end stage assessments can be difficult because of diary commitments. Get these meetings into diaries as early as possible (at the previous end stage assessment) and accept that, in the event, they may not fall exactly at the stage end. Make sure that the stage boundary issues are discussed somewhere near the end of a stage rather than risk that no discussion is held because people are not available.
>
> Make sure that there are 'no surprises' from the outset; that is, the project situation should be discussed informally between the Project Manager and Project Board, and any problems sorted out before any formal request for authorisation of the next stage.
>
> Where the project is part of a programme, careful co-ordination with programme management may be necessary to ensure the timely achievement of programme-level approvals.
>
> Although a stage may stay within its tolerances, information may be produced within a stage that shows that at some time in the future the project will exceed its tolerances. An example would be information that the cost of equipment to be bought a year down the line will exceed the project budget tolerance. It is important that these types of Project Issue are discussed as early as possible, so they should still be raised with the Project Board as exceptions.
>
> Where the project deviates significantly from its tolerances, it may be better to stop the current project and restart with a Project Initiation Document that reflects the new situation.
>
> In small projects, the Project Board and Project Manager may agree to an informal end stage assessment and authorisation to proceed to the next stage. But a formal sign-off and authorisation by the Project Board is a useful document to have in the management file if problems come along later and the Project Manager is asked why a stage was undertaken.
>
> It is essential to ensure that the project is not adversely affected by delays in customer or supplier management chains.

6.7   Giving Ad Hoc Direction (DP4)

6.7.1 Fundamental principles

Even when a stage is proceeding according to plan and within tolerance, there may be a need for the Project Board to be consulted. Such occasions might be:

- To receive regular reports
- For advice on direction when options need clarifying
- When the impact of events external to the project needs to be considered
- To resolve resourcing issues that would affect tolerance
- To resolve areas of conflict
- Organisational changes within the project.

It is also possible that, during a stage, the Project Board itself will need to pass information to the Project Manager about external events and its own changing requirements or pass information to external interested parties.

6.7.2 Context

This sub-process may be needed at any point during the project. It could be prompted by an external event or by information or circumstances arising from within the project.

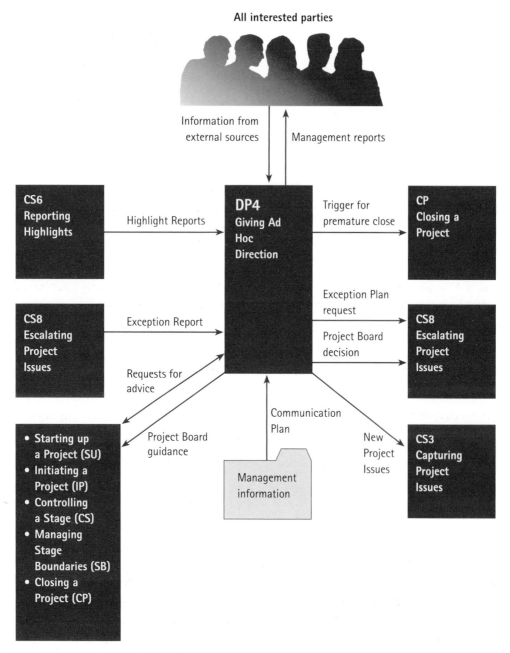

Figure 6.6 Giving Ad Hoc Direction

6.7.3 Process description

The objectives are for the Project Board to:

- Ensure that the project remains focused on the business objectives set and remains justified in business terms

- Ensure that the stage is progressing according to plan

- Ensure that the Project Manager is notified of any changes in the corporate or programme environment that may impact on the project and that appropriate action is taken

- Ensure that the project is kept informed of external events that may affect it

- Make decisions on Project Issues or Exception Reports that are beyond the Project Manager's authority

- Advise the Project Manager of any change to Project Board personnel

- Keep corporate or programme management and other interested parties informed about project progress.

These objectives should be achieved without the need for the Project Board to interfere in the project beyond the controls and reports it has agreed with the Project Manager.

The Project Board should receive regular Highlight Reports from the Project Manager at a frequency agreed for the current stage.

The Project Board should ensure that any serious risk situations are being monitored sufficiently regularly to keep the risks under control. The Project Manager will refer situations to the Project Board via an Exception Report where a stage or the whole project is forecast to exceed its tolerances.

Within its delegated limits of authority, there may be occasions when the Project Board may choose to:

- Ask the Project Manager to submit an Exception Plan for the remainder of the stage to reflect the new situation (see *Producing an Exception Plan* (SB6))

- Reduce the scope of stage or project expectations to bring it back within tolerance using change control (see *Producing an Exception Plan* (SB6))

- Abandon the project (see *Decommissioning a Project* (CP1)).

Project Issues may arise on which the Project Manager needs guidance. The Project Board provides this guidance based on the impact of the Project Issue in question on the Business Case and risks. Project Issues include all questions, Requests for Change and Off-Specifications raised. As these may represent changes to the agreed Project Initiation Document, it is a Project Board function to approve or reject any changes. Agreed changes may need extra time and/or funds.

Where a Project Issue goes beyond the brief held by the Project Board, the Project Board has the responsibility of seeking a decision from corporate or programme management.

The Project Board has the responsibility to obtain any extra or changed resources that occur as a result of agreements with the Project Manager on Project Issues raised.

The Project Board must ensure that external events that could impact the project are monitored adequately and dealt with effectively. Any new information from external sources should be passed to the Project Manager to raise a Project Issue.

The Communication Plan may contain details of external interested parties, such as programme management, who need to receive (or are required to provide) information on project matters at given frequencies from/to the Project Board. The Project Board must make itself aware of any such requirements and how, when and by whom such information is to be either given or received.

There will be times when a Project Board has to be changed. This may be because a current member changes job or extra customers or suppliers may be found and they need representation on the Project Board. It is the Project Board's job to notify the Project Manager. The Project Board must then agree a job description with the new member(s).

6.7.4 Responsibilities

This sub-process is a Project Board responsibility. It may look to share some of the activities with those with Project Assurance responsibilities.

6.7.5 Information needs

Table 6.4 DP4 information needs

Management information	Usage	Explanation
Highlight Report	Input	Regular feedback on progress from the Project Manager
Exception Report	Input	Early warning of a deviation. May trigger the creation of an Exception Plan
Request for advice	Input	Situations where a decision is needed that is beyond the authority of the Project Manager
Communication Plan	Input	Details of any interested parties
Information from external sources	Input	Collection of information pertinent to the project from outside sources
Corporate or programme management reports	Output	Feedback on project progress to outside sources
Project Board guidance	Output	Guidance and instruction to the Project Manager following request for advice or as a result of information from corporate or programme management
Exception Plan request	Output	Request in reaction to the inputs noted above, particularly the Exception Report
Trigger for premature close	Output	Possible closure of the project before its expected end
New Project Issues	Output	Information from the Project Board or via them from external sources may trigger the creation of new Project Issues in *Capturing Project Issues* (CS3)

6.7.6 Key criteria

- Does the Project Manager know how to contact Project Board members in the event of problems arising?

- Are Project Board members aware of the need to react quickly to Project Issues raised?

- Are Project Board members committed to prompt reading of Highlight Reports and to a timely response to them?

Hints and tips

There are projects that are so dynamic that there will be many Requests for Change. The Project Board and Project Manager should agree change authority responsibilities, a procedure and possibly a separate budget (change budget) to handle these.

Expected external changes that can pose a threat to the project should be documented as risks.

The Project Board may delegate among its members responsibility for monitoring particular external sources for any potential impact on the project. Each individual Project Board member will have prime responsibility for monitoring a particular area to which the project might be sensitive – for example, changing interest rates.

The Project Manager may seek Project Board guidance if any risks materialise.

Where the project is part of a programme, if there is to be a change in the composition of the Project Board, the advice and approval of programme management should be sought.

6.8 Confirming Project Closure (DP5)

6.8.1 Fundamental principles

There needs to be a formal handover of responsibility and ownership of the project's products to the ultimate user(s).

For most final products there must be a reliable operational and support environment in place.

Every effort should be made to pass on any lessons that have been learned from the project.

6.8.2 Context

This sub-process is triggered by the Project Manager carrying out the activities and producing the management products of *Closing a Project* (CP). It is the last work done by the Project Board prior to its disbandment.

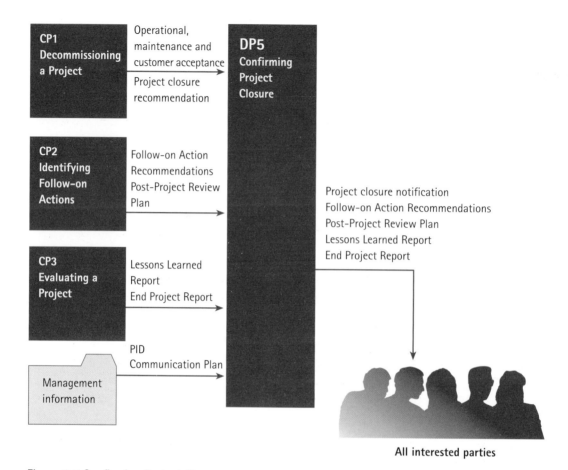

Figure 6.7 Confirming Project Closure

6.8.3 Process description

The project needs to be closed down in an orderly manner.

The objectives of this sub-process are to:

- Ensure that the project has a clearly defined end and an organised handover of responsibility to the group(s) who will use, support and sustain the products
- Release the resources provided to the project
- Gain formal acceptance from the customer that the Acceptance Criteria set down at the outset have been met adequately
- Direct any changes that have not been implemented to an appropriate authority for attention and any lessons learned to the people who best benefit from them
- Establish a future method for verifying that the project has produced the desired benefits
- Notify all interested parties of the closure of the project.

To achieve these objectives, various steps need to be undertaken:

- Ensure that all the completed products have been approved by the customer or are covered by approved concessions (if there have been any concessions, these may also be covered in Follow-on Action Recommendations)

- Ensure that, where appropriate, the resulting changes in the business are supported and sustainable

- Ensure Follow-on Action Recommendations have been recorded correctly and that the appropriate groups have been made aware of their responsibility for taking them forward. These recommendations will have listed all the follow-on actions from the project, those Project Issues that were classified as pending by the Project Board and any proposals for new work emanating from the project. These have to be directed to the appropriate body. They may be given to the support team to implement, or they may go to programme management or a strategy group for consideration as projects in their own right

- Where applicable, ensure the handover of the products and configuration management method to the appropriate support group for ongoing control

- Approve the Lessons Learned Report for distribution. A number of lessons may have been learned during the project about weaknesses or strengths of the processes, procedures, techniques and tools used, when they were used, how they were used and by whom. If there is anything that could benefit other projects within the remit of the corporate body, the Project Board has the responsibility to ensure that this information is passed on to the relevant people, such as quality assurance

- Approve the contents of the End Project Report for distribution to any interested parties, for example corporate or programme management

- Prepare a project closure notification. The Project Board advises those who have provided the support infrastructure and resources for the project that these can now be withdrawn. This should indicate a closing date for costs being charged to the project

- Publish and distribute the plans for the post-project review.

6.8.4 Responsibilities

This sub-process is the responsibility of the Project Board, supported by those with Project Assurance responsibilities.

It is the responsibility of the Executive to ensure that the person who will conduct the post-project review is properly briefed and that accountability is passed to that person.

Where the project is part of a programme, it may be necessary to obtain programme management approval for project closure.

Programme management may also wish to direct the handover of any follow-on work from the project.

6.8.5 Information needs

Table 6.5 DP5 information needs

Management information	Usage	Explanation
Project Initiation Document	Input	Used as the baseline against which to assess how far the project deviated from its initial basis. Also contributes some of the information against which to judge the success of the project
Communication Plan	Input	Used to identify all recipients of information on project closure
Operational and maintenance acceptance	Input	Confirmation that the final product(s) can be used and supported
Customer acceptance	Input	Confirmation that the customer accepts the products
Project closure recommendation	Input	Assurance from the Project Manager that facilities, support and resources can be withdrawn
End Project Report	Approval	More information on which to judge the success of the project. Approved for distribution to all interested parties
Follow-on Action Recommendations	Approval	Recommendations for all Project Issues classified as pending and other future actions
Post-Project Review Plan	Approval	Suggested plan for assessing the achievement of project benefits. Ratified by the Project Board to be passed on to the people responsible for carrying it out
Lessons Learned Report	Approval	Project lessons that have been learned that might be useful to pass on to other projects
Project closure notification	Output	Notification to all interested parties that facilities, support and resources can be withdrawn

6.8.6 Key criteria

- Have the results and products of the project been accepted and are they no longer dependent on work that is part of this project?

- Is the business ready to support, sustain and further develop the environment and products delivered?

- Are the customers content with the results and products?

- Have any necessary programme management requirements been met?

7.3 Process description

The objectives of *Controlling a Stage* are to:

- Deliver the right products
- Ensure that quality is achieved as planned
- Deliver products on time and to cost within agreed tolerances
- Correctly direct and conduct work on products
- Keep control of products via configuration management
- Properly direct and utilise resources
- Update plans with actuals, enabling progress to be checked against the plan
- Correctly cost resource usage
- Correctly manage any deviations from Stage or Project Plans
- Inform all interested parties about project progress in a timely manner
- Ensure that projects are stopped or redirected if the reasons for setting them up have been invalidated by internal or external events.

Central to the ultimate success of the project is the day-to-day control of the work that is being conducted. Throughout a stage, this will consist of a cycle of:

- Authorising work to be done (CS1)
- Monitoring progress information about that work (CS2 and CS9)
- Watching for and assessing Project Issues (CS3 and CS4)
- Reviewing the situation and triggering new Work Packages (CS5)
- Reporting (CS6)
- Taking any necessary corrective action (CS7).

If changes are observed that are forecast to cause deviations beyond agreed Stage and/or project tolerances, *Capturing Project Issues* (CS3), *Examining Project Issues* (CS4), *Reviewing Stage Status* (CS5) and *Escalating Project Issues* (CS8) cover the activities of bringing the situation to the attention of the Project Board.

Other factors that must be borne in mind are as follows:

- The current stage contains work and involves resource expenditure that has been authorised by the Project Board. It is therefore important to give the Project Board feedback on progress against its expectations
- All individual items of work in a stage should be authorised (see the format of the Work Package in *Product Description outlines*, Appendix A)
- Project work can be adequately controlled only against a plan
- If the project is to be successful, the Project Manager and Project Board must react quickly to changes and deviations from the agreed Stage Plan.

7.3.1 Scalability

The core activities of the process can be summarised as:

- Allocate work
- Check on progress
- Ensure that the quality is appropriate for the project's needs
- Ensure that Project Issues are controlled
- Monitor risks
- Report on progress
- Watch for plan deviations.

There should be nothing in this list to alarm the manager of a small project. In even the smallest of projects, the Project Manager must have sufficient time to manage the project activities and resource usage.

The process suggests a number of reports, the inference being that these should be written reports – for example, Work Packages, Highlight Reports and Exception Reports. In small projects a decision may be taken to make some or all of these oral. Even here, the Project Manager must think of what events should be recorded in writing, in case of later disputes. Part of the reason for documenting events and decisions is continuity if the Project Manager is suddenly unavailable.

Some projects may have no separate Team Manager(s) and only one team whose members are directly responsible to the Project Manager. In this case the Project Manager and the Team Manager will be one and the same person and Work Packages will be negotiated between the Project Manager and individual team members. This point should be borne in mind when reading the rest of the section, which will refer to a Project Manager/Team Manager interface.

> **Hints and tips**
>
> The emphasis within this process is on the processes and techniques of controlling a management stage. However, much of the ultimate success of the project will be just as dependent on the handling of the people and 'politics' of the project.

7.4   Authorising Work Package (CS1)

7.4.1 Fundamental principles

It would be chaotic to have the people who are working on the project starting activities whenever they think fit. There must be a level of autonomy within the project team(s), but there will be wider issues involved of which they cannot be expected to be aware. It is therefore important that, in broad terms, work only commences and continues with the consent of the Project Manager.

7.4.2 Context

This sub-process will be running constantly throughout a stage. It interfaces with the process *Managing Product Delivery* (MP), which handles the production of the products involved and provides plan updates to *Assessing Progress* (CS2) during the project. Also *Taking Corrective Action* (CS7) may trigger new Work Packages or require modifications to existing Work Packages.

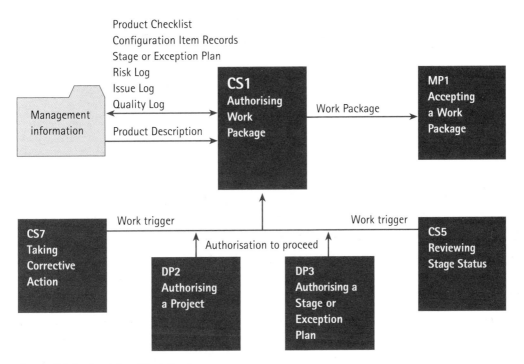

Figure 7.3 Authorising Work Package

7.4.3 Process description

The objective of this sub-process is to keep control over the work of the team(s) by:

- Issuing work instructions (work triggers) to the Team Manager(s) to commence work

- Revising the instructions as required following management decisions.

The set of instructions issued to the Team Manager(s) is known as a Work Package.

In order to achieve this objective, various steps have to be undertaken:

- Review the Product Description(s) for the product(s) to be delivered, ensure that they describe what is required and add any constraints and responsibilities required

- Brief the Team Manager(s) and hand out the Work Package with all relevant documentation and information, including terms of reference covering:

  - the cost and effort that the work is expected to consume

  - the timescale for completion

  - the progress reporting arrangements

- any individuals, groups or products with whom it is necessary to interface in the performance of the work

  - Product Descriptions

- Update the status information to 'under development' in any affected Configuration Item Records

- Ensure that the Team Manager has a valid Team Plan covering the Work Package requirements and the correct resources to carry out the work

- Identify any problems or risks associated with the work and incorporate any necessary changes or other measures to handle these

- Ensure the Team Manager is committed to completion of the work within the terms of reference laid down

- Instruct the Team Manager to proceed via an appropriate form of Work Package

- Confirm the entries made in the Quality Log during *Planning a Stage* (SB1) for planned quality checks and who will chair these checks.

The 'work' discussed in this overview could be by people and resources within the customer organisation, by outside suppliers or by a combination of the two. It could also cover the supply of products or services that do not involve any actual effort. The objectives and steps outlined apply in all circumstances. The formality of the Work Package will depend on the project situation. The suggested contents of the Work Package are given in *Product Description outlines*, Appendix A, together with an explanation of each entry.

This sub-process must be done in conjunction with *Accepting a Work Package* (MP1). The overlap covers the negotiation with the Team Manager on dates and other parameters.

If this is the first Work Package agreed with the Team Manager, a check should be made to ensure that the Team Manager is aware of the project's change control procedure.

7.4.4 Responsibilities

The Project Manager is responsible for this sub-process, assisted by any Project Support roles, and in agreement with the relevant Team Managers. The Configuration Librarian will update the Configuration Item Records. Project Assurance might wish to confirm that suitable quality checking arrangements have been planned.

7.4.5 Information needs

Table 7.1 CS1 information needs

Management information	Usage	Explanation
Authorisation to proceed	Input	Authorisation from the Project Board to proceed with the stage
Product Description(s)	Input	Description of the required product(s), including quality criteria
Work trigger	Input	Information from *Authorising a Project* (DP2), *Authorising a*

		Stage or Exception Plan (DP3), *Taking Corrective Action* (CS7) or *Reviewing Stage Status* (CS5) requiring the creation or modification of a new Work Package
Stage or Exception Plan	Update	The Stage Plan may need to be updated as a result of discussions between the Project Manager and the Team Manager during *Authorising Work Package* (CS1) or because of changes generated in *Taking Corrective Action* (CS7)
Configuration Item Records	Update	Change the status of any products allocated as part of the Work Package
Work Package	Output	Formal handover of responsibility for the detailed conduct of the work and delivery of any products from the Project Manager following agreement with the Team Manager
Risk Log	Update	Updated with any new or modified risks after negotiation with the Team Manager
Quality Log	Update	The Quality Log may need to be updated as a result of discussions between the Project Manager and the Team Manager during *Authorising Work Package* (CS1) to reflect any modification of entries for any planned quality checking to be done
Product Checklist	Update	(If used) The Product Checklist may need to be updated as a result of discussions between the Project Manager and the Team Manager during *Authorising Work Package* (CS1) or because of changes generated in *Taking Corrective Action* (CS7)
Issue Log	Update	Updated with any actions taken on Project Issues

7.4.6 Key criteria

- Is the Team Manager clear what is to be produced and what has to be done to produce it?

- Is the Team Manager clear about the effort, cost and timescale expectations in connection with the work involved?

- Is the Team Manager clear about the expected quality of the work and products and also clear about how that quality is to be checked, as defined in the relevant Product Descriptions?

- Have the quality checking procedures been put in place and resourced?

- Is the work achievable within the terms of reference laid down?

- Is the Team Manager committed to the achievement of the work?

- Has the Stage Plan been updated as required, based on the agreement on the Work Package?

- Should any Project Assurance involvement be planned, especially in quality checking?

Hints and tips

In a simple, low-risk project, Work Package authorisation may be reasonably informal, although thought should be given to recording an individual's work and performance for appraisal purposes.

If a third party is involved, Work Package authorisation should always be formally documented.

Ideally, a Work Package should not spread over more than one stage. If there is any danger of this, it should be broken down so that its intermediate parts fit into one management stage or another.

It is good practice for the people who will receive the resulting products of a Work Package to be involved in writing the relevant Product Descriptions, especially the quality criteria. If this is done, other people should review the Product Descriptions.

If there is a contract in operation between customer and supplier, this may have an impact on the terms of the authorisation. The reverse is also true, so the authorisation of Work Packages should be considered during contract preparation.

When the first Work Package is negotiated with a Team Manager or a team member, the Project Manager should ensure that the change control process is understood.

7.5 Assessing Progress (CS2)

7.5.1 Fundamental principles

In order to make informed decisions and exercise rational control, it is necessary to know what has *actually* happened, to be compared with what it was *hoped* would happen. 'Fire fighting' and day-to-day problem solving can dominate project management. This can result in Project Managers losing sight of the overall goal. It is vital that this is countered by a steady flow of information that provides an overall view of progress and simple, robust monitoring systems to supply the information.

7.5.2 Context

Assessing Progress (CS2) monitors the status of resource utilisation and product development, as documented in the sub-process *Executing a Work Package* (MP2), and reviews the Quality Log, as updated by the quality checks carried out by the team(s). It also receives information on completed and approved products from *Receiving Completed Work Package* (CS9), and keeps the Stage Plan and Product Checklist (if used) up to date.

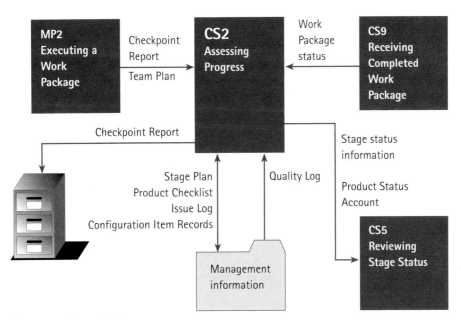

Figure 7.4 Assessing Progress

7.5.3 Process description

The objective of this sub-process is to maintain an accurate and current picture of:

●   Progress on the work being carried out

●   The status of resources.

The main data-gathering control for the Project Manager is the checkpoint, described in *Controls*, Chapter 16. The information is captured in a Checkpoint Report. A Product Status Account may also be requested from configuration management to provide information on the status of the stage's products.

In order to achieve the objectives, various steps have to be undertaken:

●   Collect in all of the progress information for all work currently being undertaken

●   Collect feedback on recent quality checking activities carried out

●   Assess the estimated time and effort to complete any unfinished work (including that not yet started)

●   Assess the utilisation of resources in the period under review and their availability for the remainder of the stage (or project)

●   Review Team Plans with the Team Manager(s) to ascertain whether work will be completed on time and to budget

●   Review entries in the Quality Log – are any checks delayed? What are the results from the latest checks?

●   Update the Stage Plan with actuals to date

●   Identify any points that need attention in *Reviewing Stage Status* (CS5).

7.5.4 Responsibilities

The Project Manager is responsible for this sub-process, assisted by any Project Support roles. The Configuration Librarian would provide any Product Status Account required. If the Team Manager works for a supplier who does not use PRINCE2, the Work Package will still contain a requirement for Checkpoint Reports to be submitted. Project Assurance may review the updated Quality Log.

7.5.5 Information needs

Table 7.2 CS2 information needs

Management information	Usage	Explanation
Checkpoint Reports	Input	Flows of information, either written or oral depending on the need for formality. The update from the information will cover current status of Work Packages against plan
Quality Log	Input	Results of quality checking work done
Issue Log	Update	There may be new Project Issues that affect the status of the stage or vice versa
Work Package status	Input	To update the Stage Plan
Stage Plan	Update	Updated with actuals to date, forecasts and adjustments
Product Checklist	Update	(If used) Updated with actuals to date, forecasts and adjustments
Stage status information	Output	Holds a summary of progress information
Team Plan	Input	Sets out the work to be done and any reporting requirements
Product Status Account	Output	To provide information on the status of the Work Package products
Configuration Item Records	Update	Change the status of any products allocated as part of a Work Package

7.5.6 Key criteria

- Is the level and frequency of progress assessment right for the stage and/or Work Package?

- Is the information timely, useful and accurate?

- Are the estimates of outstanding work objective?

7.8.5 Information needs

Table 7.5 CS5 information needs

Management information	Usage	Explanation
Issue Log	Input	This product will show the current situation regarding all Project Issues. These may be needed for reference when deciding on appropriate action to deal with them
Risk Log	Input	This product shows the current understanding of the problems and threats to the project
Project Plan	Input	Check to establish whether any stage problem (or potential change) would have an impact on the Project Plan
Product Checklist	Input	(If used) This shows the current actual and planned delivery dates for key products
Quality Log	Input	Assess the state of quality checking
Business Case	Input	This is checked for any impact from the current stage progress
Configuration Item Records	Input	These provide information on the current status of products
Stage Plan	Input	The Stage Plan, updated in *Assessing Progress* (CS2), provides the baseline against which progress and the meeting of stage tolerances are measured
Concession	Input	Decision by the Project Board to accept a Project Issue without corrective action
Plan deviation	Output	The information to be passed to *Taking Corrective Action* (CS7)
Tolerance threat	Output	Trigger for an Exception Report
Stage status information	Input/ Output	Information regarding the current progress of the project. This information goes forward to *Reporting Highlights* (CS6)
Stage end notification	Output	Trigger for *Managing Stage Boundaries* (SB) (at the appropriate time near the stage end)
Trigger for project end	Output	Trigger for *Closing a Project* (CP) (at the appropriate time near the end of the final stage)
Work trigger	Output	Trigger for the issue of new Work Packages from *Authorising Work Package* (CS1)

7.8.6 Key criteria

- Have all the aspects of progress, Project Issues and risk been considered?
- Have they been balanced to create a complete picture of the current status of the project?
- Have all reasonable courses of action been considered when deciding on the best way forward?

- Has the project been honest with itself concerning the likelihood of staying within tolerance?

- Do the estimates to complete seem reasonable in the light of all the information available?

Hints and tips

Although this is shown as a discrete sub-process to emphasise the importance of regular progress checking, it will often happen concurrently with other processes. For instance, in parallel with this sub-process, highlights could be produced (*Reporting Highlights* (CS6)) and the following period's work authorised (*Authorising Work Package* (CS1)).

Reviewing Stage Status is a cyclic/iterative process.

Stage status should be reviewed regularly – the frequency of the reviews being related to the length of activities in the plan and the need (or otherwise) for close control. Small-to-medium projects might be reviewed weekly; large projects might be reviewed each fortnight or monthly.

The status of items on or near the critical path (see *Planning* (PL)) may need to be monitored more frequently than other elements of the plan.

Where the project is part of a programme, any new or changed risks must be fed to the programme support office to check for possible impact on other parts of the programme.

7.9 Reporting Highlights (CS6)

7.9.1 Fundamental principles

The Project Board has overall responsibility for the outcome of the project, while delegating day-to-day management to the Project Manager. Good reporting structures keep the Project Board (and all other interested parties) informed and involved.

7.9.2 Context

This sub-process produces Highlight Reports to be passed to the Project Board (see *Giving Ad Hoc Direction* (DP4)) containing progress plus any other information to stakeholders defined in the Communication Plan.

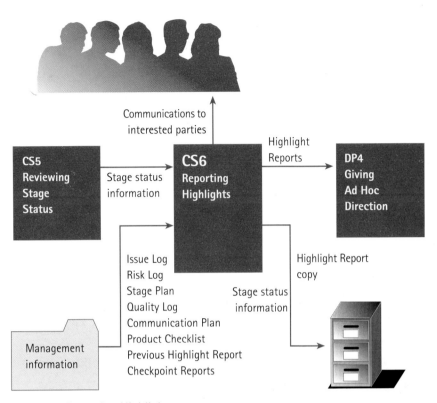

Figure 7.8 Reporting Highlights

7.9.3 Process description

The objectives of this sub-process are to:

- Provide the Project Board with summary information about the status of the stage and project at the frequency defined by the Project Board

- Pass out any other information required by the Communication Plan.

In order to achieve these objectives, various steps have to be undertaken:

- Assemble the information from the Checkpoint Reports and any significant revisions to the Stage Plan or Product Checklist (if used) from *Taking Corrective Action* (CS7)

- Identify any current or potential problems from *Reviewing Stage Status* (CS5)

- Produce the Highlight Report

- Distribute the Highlight Report to the Project Board

- Review the Communication Plan for any other agreed recipients and send these out.

7.9.4 Responsibilities

The Project Manager is responsible for this sub-process, assisted by any Project Support roles. Project Assurance may wish to assess what is being reported to the Project Board.

7.9.5 Information needs

Table 7.6 CS6 information needs

Management information	Usage	Explanation
Stage Plan	Input	Information on products delivered, tolerances and the status of schedule and budget, including any deviations reported from CS2
Product Checklist	Input	(If used) Status of actual and planned product deliveries
Previous Highlight Report	Input	Have all products forecast to be delivered been delivered? Have earlier problems been resolved?
Checkpoint Reports	Input	Progress information from the team(s)
Stage status information	Input/ Output	Information about progress on the project against the plan
Risk Log	Input	Have any risks changed?
Issue Log	Input	Information about any potential problems which need to be brought to the attention of the Project Board
Quality Log	Input	Status of quality checks planned and carried out
Communication Plan	Input	Identification of interested parties who may need information at this time
Highlight Report	Output	Information formatted as required by the Project Board
Communications to interested parties	Output	Content as defined in the Communication Plan

7.9.6 Key criteria

- Has the information been produced in the form requested by the Project Board?

- Is the report being distributed with the agreed frequency?

Hints and tips

The report should be kept as short as possible, consistent with the information needs of the Project Board. A suggested target is a one or two page report.

Where some form of operational support group will pick up responsibility for the end product, this group should be included in the list of those receiving the Highlight Report.

7.10 Taking Corrective Action (CS7)

7.10.1 Fundamental principles

Changes and adjustments to the project need to be made in a considered and rational way, even when they appear to be sufficiently manageable to be absorbed within tolerance.

7.10.2 Context

This sub-process is triggered by the identification of a deviation and instigates corrective action. Input may be needed from other members of the project management team.

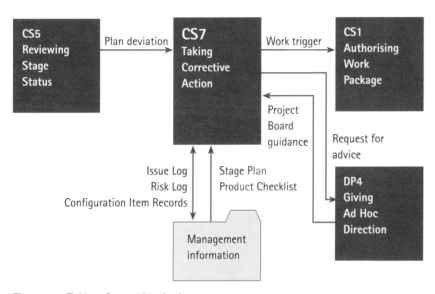

Figure 7.9 Taking Corrective Action

7.10.3 Process description

The objective of this sub-process is to select and (within the limits of the stage and project tolerances) implement actions that will resolve deviations from the plan. Decisions may be required from the Project Board via *Giving Ad Hoc Direction* (DP4). The Project Manager has to decide when to seek the advice of the Project Board.

In order to achieve this objective, various steps have to be undertaken. If the input comes from *Examining Project Issues* (CS4), some of these steps may have already been taken. The steps are:

● Collect any pertinent information about the deviation

● Identify the full cause and effect of the deviation

● Identify the potential ways of dealing with the deviation

● Select the most appropriate option

● Where direction from the Project Board is sought, assemble all information about the problem (it may already be a Project Issue) plus any recommendation

- Make available any baselined products from the configuration library

- Trigger corrective action (via *Authorising Work Package* (CS1)).

Where the actions are small and the problem can be remedied without changing the plan or modifying a Work Package, the Daily Log can be used to note what actions are needed, by whom and by what date. The Project Manager can then use this to speak to the people involved and follow up to ensure that the actions are taken. Where this does not lead to the desired result, more formal action can be taken, such as plan and Work Package adjustments, Exception Reports or maybe just a note in the next Highlight Report.

7.10.4 Responsibilities

The Project Manager is responsible for this sub-process, supported by Project Assurance and Project Support roles and in consultation with Team Managers if appropriate. The Configuration Librarian, where appointed, will make any necessary products available and update Configuration Items as required.

7.10.5 Information needs

Table 7.7 CS7 information needs

Management information	Usage	Explanation
Plan deviation	Input	The plan problem that requires corrective action
Project Board guidance	Input	Response to request for advice
Configuration Item Records	Update	Records updated to show any new product copies issued and any status changes required
Issue Log	Update	This contains details of any Project Issues that could be causing deviations from plan. Updated with any change in status caused by corrective action
Risk Log	Update	The change in a risk may be causing the need for corrective action. Risks in the log may affect the choice of action. Updated with any change in status caused by corrective action
Stage Plan	Input	May show the problem or the spare effort and time available to address the problem. Updated with any change caused by corrective action
Product Checklist	Input	(If used) May show the problem or the spare effort and time available to address the problems. Updated with any change caused by corrective action
Work trigger	Output	Corrective action
Request for advice	Output	Request for advice on corrective action

7.10.6 Key criteria

- Have all sensible options for corrective action been considered?

- Is there confidence that, after the corrective action has been taken, the stage and project will still stay within tolerance?

- Were the impacts on the Business Case and risks fully considered?

- Has the Stage Plan been updated to reflect the corrective actions?

Hints and tips

Beware the cumulative effect on the budget, and the costs of small changes.

Beware the direction in which some small changes may be taking the project.

7.11 Escalating Project Issues (CS8)

7.11.1 Fundamental principles

A stage should not go outside the tolerances agreed with the Project Board.

The Project Manager should always present a recommendation when escalating Project Issues.

7.11.2 Context

This sub-process can be an advance warning to the Project Board of a deviation that may lead to the need for an Exception Plan. The Project Manager can only take corrective action or maintain the status quo while the stage is forecast to stay within the tolerances set by the Project Board. *Escalating Project Issues* (CS8) applies where any corrective action would not save the stage or project from going beyond the tolerance margins.

The decision by the Project Board in response to the escalation may lead to the removal of the problem, the production of an Exception Plan, where cost and/or time targets are adjusted, the approval of a concession or the premature close of the project.

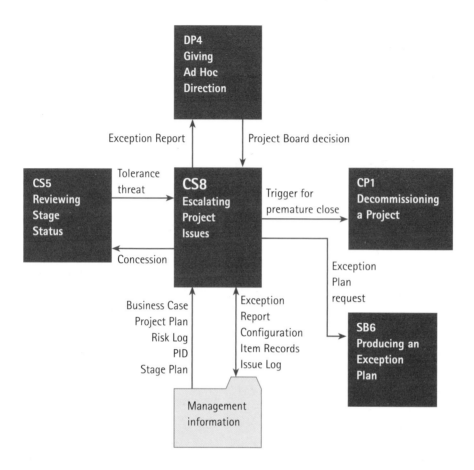

Figure 7.10 Escalating Project Issues

7.11.3 Process description

One of the major controls available to the Project Board is that it sets tolerances for each stage. (Tolerance is fully described in *Controls*, Chapter 16.) The Project Manager only has authority to proceed with a stage while it is forecast to stay within the tolerance margins. If the stage is forecast to go outside the tolerance margins (possibly as a result of a corrective action), the Project Manager must bring the situation to the attention of the Project Board.

One item likely to cause a deviation is a Project Issue. Project Issues are fully described in *Change control*, Chapter 20. There may be one or more Project Issues, the implementation of which would take the stage (and possibly the entire project) beyond the agreed tolerances.

Other causes may be poor estimation, a change in resource availability, resources under or over performing, unplanned tasks, tasks not needed and rework.

The Project Board must make the decision on which (if any) changes to approve for action.

In order to retain the Project Board's overall control, the following steps are taken:

- Assemble the results of the full impact analysis of the deviation; the analysis should cover specialist, user and business impacts (completed in *Examining Project Issues* (CS4))

- Assemble and evaluate options for recovery (or to take advantage of good news) (again, completed in *Examining Project Issues* (CS4))

- Make a recommendation

- Put the situation, options and recommendation to the Project Board in an Exception Report

- The Project Board indicates support or otherwise for the Project Manager's recommendation (in *Giving Ad Hoc Direction* (DP4))

- Update the information in the Configuration Item Records for any affected products.

The suggested content of an Exception Report is given in *Product Description outlines*, Appendix A.

In the Exception Report the Project Manager will advise the Project Board of the impact of the deviation on the Project Plan, Business Case and risks. Various options should be identified and a course of action recommended to the Project Board. After the Exception Report is considered by the Project Board (in sub-process DP4), the Project Board will approve the report and advise the Project Manager of its decision. This may take the form of a request for an Exception Plan to replace the plan that is in exception (usually the remainder of the current Stage Plan), produced in *Producing an Exception Plan* (SB6). The Exception Plan either recovers a situation that is outside tolerance or proposes a new plan with new targets for cost, time, scope, benefit, risk and quality as appropriate, plus new tolerances around these targets. The Project Board's advice should be sought before devising the Exception Plan. All current constraints should be investigated with the Project Board to see if they still stand in the light of the new situation.

Another option that may be taken in response to an Exception Report is to remove the problem (for example, defer the Request for Change). Alternatively the Project Board may decide to grant a concession and continue with the current plan, in which case the appropriate corrective action should be triggered via *Reviewing Stage Status* (CS5). A final and more drastic decision would be to take the project to premature close, in which case the Project Manager will instigate *Decommissioning a Project* (CP1).

The parts of a plan that can be varied in response to an exception situation are:

- Cost

- Delivery date

- Scope

- Quality

- Benefits

- Risk appetite.

Speed is an important factor in notifying the Project Board of an exception situation.

It will often be necessary to revise the Project Plan, as described in *Updating a Project Plan* (SB2).

7.11.4 Responsibilities

The Project Manager is responsible for escalating Project Issues. Those with Project Assurance responsibilities should also be monitoring any situations that could cause a deviation and should bring the matter to the Project Manager's attention. The Configuration Librarian will update Configuration Item Records where necessary.

7.11.5 Information needs

Table 7.8 CS8 information needs

Management information	Usage	Explanation
Tolerance threat	Input	Trigger for the Exception Report
Project Initiation Document	Input	This baseline allows comparison of any change against original expectations
Business Case	Input	The latest version allows examination for impact of the Project Issue on the Business Case
Stage Plan	Input	Updated with the actuals so far, this shows the likely impact on the stage of the deviation in question
Project Plan	Input	This indicates the project status and the overall effect of any deviation
Issue Log	Input/ Update	Details of the change(s) that may have caused the exception situation. Update the Issue Log with the current status when the Project Board's decision has been received
Risk Log	Input	Details of the risk exposure that may have caused the escalation
Exception Report	Output/ Input	Description of the exception situation, its impact, options, recommendation and impact of the recommendation for the Project Board. Subsequent Project Board Approval of the Exception Report, which should be filed for audit purposes
Project Board decision	Input	May be a request for an Exception Plan, cause a premature close of the project, result in deferring the change, or cause a concession to be granted, depending on the decision
Trigger for premature close	Output	As a result of the Project Board's decision to close the project prematurely
Exception Plan request	Output	As a result of the Project Board's decision to request an Exception Plan
Concession	Output	As a result of the Project Board's decision to grant a concession
Configuration Item Records	Update	Fields such as status may be updated, plus the addition of links to the relevant Project Issue

8.4.4 Responsibilities

The Team Manager is responsible for the agreement with the Project Manager. Project Assurance will want to confirm that suitable quality checking arrangements and personnel are included in any Team Plans.

8.4.5 Information needs

Table 8.1 MP1 information needs

Management information	Usage	Explanation
Work Package	Input	Package put together by the Project Manager in Authorising Work Package (CS1) for the Team Manager's agreement. May be revised in coming to an agreement
Team Plan	Output/ Update	A Team Plan is created or details of the Work Package are added to the team's existing plan
Risk Log	Update	The Team Manager adds any risks identified in the Team Plan to the Risk Log
Quality Log	Update	Add any extra information on quality checks
Authorised Work Package	Output	The Work Package is agreed by the Team Manager

8.4.6 Key criteria

- Has there been full consultation on the Work Package between the Project Manager and Team Manager?

- Is there a cost and time allowance for the quality checking work and any rework that may be required?

- Are the reporting requirements reasonable?

- Are any interfacing requirements achievable within the constraints?

- Are any links to the project's configuration management method clear and consistent with the way in which the products will be controlled in the team?

- Has any required interface to Project Assurance been made clear and the interface with the team established?

- Are any risks and the means of managing them identified?

- What is the resource availability over the period covered by the Work Package?

- What skills and experience are needed by the Work Package elements?

- Does the individual or group agree with the work allocated?

- Is there adequate description of the quality required?

- Are any standards and techniques to be used defined?

Hints and tips

Where the project has no Team Managers and the Project Manager hands work directly to a team member, the individual can use this process informally. On small projects it may only be documented via the Daily Log.

This sub-process 'matches' *Authorising Work Package* (CS1) and the two will be done together.

8.5 Executing a Work Package (MP2)

8.5.1 Fundamental principles

The fundamental principles of this sub-process are that:

- Whatever the type of project, the actual task of creating the required products needs to be managed

- In the same way that work is delegated to a Team Manager, so the tracking of that work is also delegated.

8.5.2 Context

This sub-process may occur at a level that is not using PRINCE2 – for instance, when a non-PRINCE2 third party is involved. There is, therefore, no definition of specific standards or procedures to be used, just a statement of what must be done in order for the Team Manager to liaise within the project.

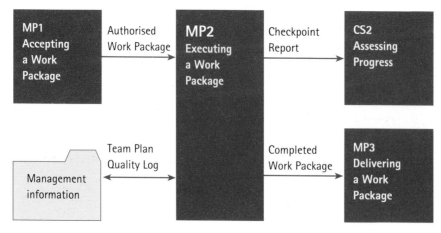

Figure 8.4 Executing a Work Package

8.5.3 Process description

The work on an authorised Work Package has to be monitored at the depth required to provide feedback to the Project Manager as defined in the authorised Work Package. The necessary steps are to:

- Manage the development of the required products/services

- Capture and record the effort expended

- Determine the status of each product in the Work Package

- Monitor and control the risks associated with the Work Package

- Evaluate with the creator(s) the amount of effort still required

- Feed the progress and status information back to the Project Manager in Checkpoint Reports, in the manner and at the frequency defined in the Work Package

- Ensure that the required quality checking procedures are carried out and that the product(s) satisfy the quality standards defined in the Work Package

- Update the Quality Log with details of all quality checks carried out

- Advise the Project Manager of any problems that might impact the agreed tolerance levels for the Work Package. (Formally, this would be done via a Project Issue.)

It is useful for a Team Manager to use a Daily Log, as described in *Controls*, Chapter 16. It can be used to remind the Team Manager to follow up on quality checks still not done or those revealing too many errors or errors taking too long to remedy. Items on the critical path due to start or complete can also be put in the Daily Log to remind the Team Manager to check that everything is on course.

8.5.4 Responsibilities

The Team Manager is responsible for this sub-process. Project Assurance or their representatives will be involved in much of the quality checking.

8.5.5 Information needs

Table 8.2 MP2 information needs

Management information	Usage	Explanation
Authorised Work Package	Input	Work agreed with the Project Manager
Team Plan	Update	Record allocation, planned effort, actual effort and progress, plus any modifications required, are all used to update the Team Plan
Quality Log	Update	Details of the checks carried out on the product to ensure conformance to quality standards are added to the Quality Log
Checkpoint Reports	Output	Progress reports to the Project Manager at the frequency defined in the Work Package
Completed Work Package	Output	Completed Work Package

8.5.6 Key criteria

- Is the work divided into sufficiently small segments to facilitate the required level of control?

- How will progress be monitored?

- How will the final product(s) be checked?

- Does the Team Plan include the quality checking work?

- Are the team members' progress-recording and reporting procedures at the right level for the project reporting requirements?

- Is work being done to the requirements and constraints of the Work Package?

- Are progress-recording and reporting in sufficient detail to give early warning of any threat to the tolerance margins?

- Were the quality checks fully carried out?

Hints and tips

The Team Manager may need to add extra information to the Work Package to indicate version control or configuration management methods to be used within the team.

Procedures must be put in place to keep the Project Manager up to date on progress.

Even if the team is not using PRINCE2, it must provide the Project Manager with the required information in the format stipulated in the Work Package. Therefore, it would be sensible to have recording and reporting procedures that match those of the project (or even use the respective PRINCE2 reports).

8.6 Delivering a Work Package (MP3)

8.6.1 Fundamental principles

Just as the Work Package was accepted from the Project Manager, notification of its completion must be returned to the Project Manager.

8.6.2 Context

The configuration management system used by the project may handle the return of the actual products of the Work Package. The essence of this sub-process is that the Team Manager must ensure that the products are handed over correctly and advise the Project Manager that the handover has occurred.

The sub-process may trigger *Authorising Work Package* (CS1) for the next Work Package or may overlap with it.

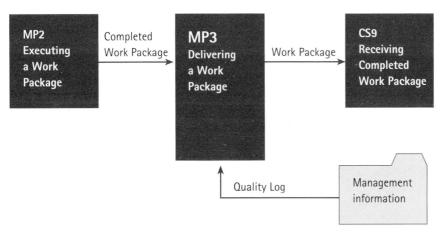

Figure 8.5 Delivering a Work Package

8.6.3 Process description

This sub-process has three elements:

- Obtain acceptance for the products developed

- Hand over the completed products

- Advise the Project Manager of completion of the Work Package.

The methods of achieving these elements should have been defined as part of Work Package authorisation. The acceptance should come from two sources: the person or group identified as the recipient and the Configuration Librarian.

Before advising the Project Manager of the completion, the Team Manager should check that the Quality Log entries are complete for the product(s).

8.6.4 Responsibilities

The Team Manager is responsible for this sub-process, liaising with the Configuration Librarian.

8.6.5 Information needs

Table 8.3 MP3 information needs

Management information	Usage	Explanation
Completed Work Package	Input	Details of the work agreed with the Project Manager updated with actual information
Quality Log	Input	Confirmation of successful quality checks
Work Package	Output	Work Package ready for approval by the Project Manager

8.6.6 Key criteria

- Has the identified recipient accepted the product(s)?

- Has handover been completed, including any configuration management aspects?

- Are any agreed statistics available for the Project Manager to record in the Stage Plan?

- Did anything happen during execution of the Work Package that is worthy of addition to the Lessons Learned Log?

Hints and tips

If the Work Package contains a number of products to be developed, they may be handed over to the project's configuration management system as they are approved. This may imply a period of time before the Project Manager is notified that the whole Work Package has been completed.

The level of formality required will vary according to the project: formal when third parties are involved, informal when the Project Manager manages the work directly.

9

MANAGING STAGE BOUNDARIES (SB)

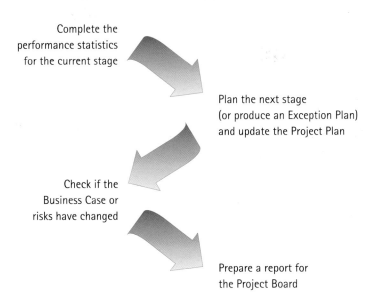

Complete the performance statistics for the current stage

Plan the next stage (or produce an Exception Plan) and update the Project Plan

Check if the Business Case or risks have changed

Prepare a report for the Project Board

Figure 9.1 Overview of Managing Stage Boundaries

9.1 Fundamental principles

Projects, whether large or small, need to be focused on delivering business benefit, either in their own right or as part of a larger programme. The continuing correct focus of the project should be confirmed at the end of each stage. If necessary, the project can be redirected or stopped to avoid wasting time and money.

9.2 Context

Before the end of each stage except the final one, the next stage is planned, together with a review and update of the Business Case, risk situation and overall Project Plan.

This process is normally triggered by *Reviewing Stage Status* (CS5), uses the *Planning* (PL) process to develop the next Stage Plan (or Exception Plan), and its output triggers the Project Board sub-process, *Authorising a Stage or Exception Plan* (DP3).

The steps of this process will also be used when creating an Exception Plan.

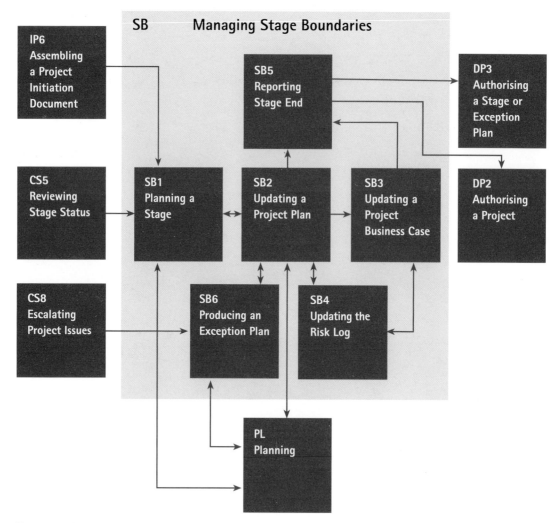

Figure 9.2 Managing Stage Boundaries

9.3 Process description

The objectives of the process are to:

- Assure the Project Board that all products in the current Stage Plan have been completed as defined

- Prepare the next Stage Plan

- Provide the information needed for the Project Board to assess the continuing viability of the project

- Obtain authorisation for the start of the next stage, together with its delegated tolerance margins

- Record any information or lessons that can help later stages of this project and/or other projects.

There could be changes of personnel and management, needing changes to the project management team.

There is also a requirement to review the Project Quality Plan and Project Approach to check whether they need changing or refining.

The stage that follows initiation is normally approved at the same time as the Project Initiation Document. If so, this process would need customising for that situation.

9.3.1 Scalability

As can be seen from the following list, the process has a simple purpose and can be done as informally as the Project Board and Project Manager wish. The reporting and approval may be informal, if the Project Board is agreeable. However, it is advisable to document the major decisions, even if it is only in the Project Manager's Daily Log.

- Gather the results of the current stage
- Plan the next stage
- Check the effect on:
    - the Project Plan
    - the justification for the project
    - the risks
- Report and seek approval.

9.4 Planning a Stage (SB1)

9.4.1 Fundamental principles

Planning each stage of the project ensures that:

- There is sufficient detail for day-to-day control to be exercised against the plan
- Each Stage Plan has the commitment of the Project Board and Project Manager
- The Project Board is fully aware of what it is approving at the start of each stage.

9.4.2 Context

The approaching end of the current stage triggers this sub-process.

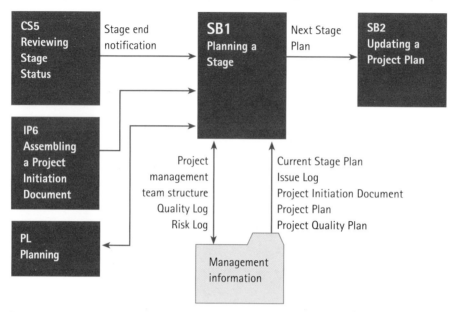

Figure 9.3 Planning a Stage

9.4.3 Process description

The main objective of this sub-process is to prepare a plan for the next stage of the project. The high-level summary of the next stage is expanded from the Project Plan into sufficient detail that the Project Manager will be able to control progress against it on a day-to-day basis. The *Planning* (PL) process is used to develop the plan.

The plan should include all products – not only the specialist ones but management products as well. A typical management product would be the next Stage Plan, which will require preparation towards the end of the stage. Quality activities and products should also appear in the plan and the Quality Log should be updated with the new information. Quality activities will be based on the standards defined in the Project Quality Plan. Whoever is providing Project Assurance should be consulted about the timing and resourcing of quality activities before the Stage Plan is presented to the Project Board.

The Project Manager will normally propose stage tolerances, based on the overall project tolerances and the degree of uncertainty about the Stage Plan's activities and/or resourcing.

The management structure of the next stage must be specified and any new or changed job descriptions prepared.

9.4.4 Responsibilities

The Project Manager is responsible for this sub-process, assisted by Project Support. Those with Project Assurance responsibilities should check out the plan, with respect to it continuing to meet customer and business expectations. Any Team Managers who will be providing products in the stage will normally develop the relevant Team Plans at this time and assist the Project Manager in creating the Stage Plan.

9.4.5 Information needs

Table 9.1 SB1 information needs

Management information	Usage	Explanation
Stage end notification	Input	Indication from Reviewing Stage Status (CS5) that the end of a stage is approaching
Current Stage Plan	Input	The results of the current stage may affect the planning of the new stage activities
Project Plan	Input	This shows the products required from the next stage
Project Initiation Document	Input	Contains the 'what' and 'why' of the project and is the document that specifies the Project Board's terms of reference
Issue Log	Input	May contain information that affects the next stage or Project Issues marked for reassessment at stage end
Project Quality Plan	Input	Provides details of standards to be used in development and quality checking
Quality Log	Update	Add details of any new quality checks planned
Risk Log	Update	Current risks may affect the next Stage Plan and the next Stage Plan may create or modify risks
Project management team structure	Update	This should be updated with any changes for the coming stage
Next Stage Plan	Output	Produced via *Planning* (PL)

9.4.6 Key criteria

- Are the major products shown in the Project Plan for the next stage reflected in the next Stage Plan?

- Are all user, customer or other resources required to check the quality of products identified?

- Are the resources used to check quality in line with the requirements of the Project Quality Plan?

> **Hints and tips**
>
> Ensure that any externally produced products are shown in the Stage Plan, together with sufficient monitoring points to assure the Project Board that these products are both on schedule and to the required quality.
>
> Check any external dependencies to ensure that there has been no change in the scope or constraints of products expected from them.

The Stage Plan will need to be prepared in parallel with any relevant Team Plans.

Ensuring that quality control procedures are used correctly is jointly the responsibility of the Senior Supplier and Senior User. Does the Stage Plan show how this responsibility will be carried out, particularly by the Senior User? The plan needs user involvement in checking products delivered by the supplier.

Where the project is part of a programme, it is unlikely that programme staff will want to record this level of detail, except for any inter-project dependencies. The Project Plan is a more appropriate level. However, the programme may wish to hold a copy of the Stage Plan for reference.

9.5 Updating a Project Plan (SB2)

9.5.1 Fundamental principles

The Project Board uses the Project Plan throughout the project to measure progress. As stages are completed or planned in detail, the Project Plan must be updated to reflect the latest understanding of the project and to allow the Project Board to revise its expectations.

9.5.2 Context

The Project Plan is updated from information in the Stage Plan for the stage that is finishing, the next Stage Plan (from SB1), and any Exception Plan (from SB6) triggered by *Escalating Project Issues* (CS8). Actuals are taken from the first, and the forecast duration and costs from the last two. Details of any revised costs or end dates are passed to the next sub-process, *Updating a Project Business Case* (SB3).

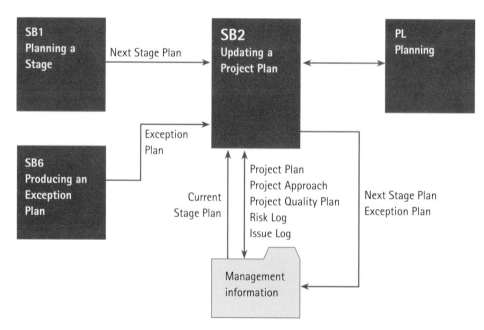

Figure 9.4 Updating a Project Plan

9.5.3 Process description

The Project Quality Plan and Project Approach are reassessed and refined to reflect the current understanding of the project and to form a basis for updating the Project Plan.

The Project Plan is updated based on the actual costs and schedule from a completed Stage Plan or Exception Plan, the new detail of activities and costs from the next Stage Plan and any acquired knowledge about the project. The last might be information about changes that have been agreed by the Project Board and that will cause activities in the next Stage Plan.

The Project Manager should describe in the End Stage Report why any change to the Project Plan has occurred.

9.5.4 Responsibilities

The Project Manager is responsible for this sub-process, assisted by Project Support, and the work checked out by those with Project Assurance responsibility.

9.5.5 Information needs

Table 9.2 SB2 information needs

Management information	Usage	Explanation
Current Stage Plan	Input	The results of the current stage may affect the project planning
Next Stage Plan or Exception Plan	Input	The extra detail in the Stage Plan or Exception Plan may reveal the need to modify the Project Plan
Project Approach	Update	Events may have occurred that modify the approach
Issue Log	Update	There may be Project Issues that need to be addressed at this point
Project Quality Plan	Update	Quality results so far may show the need to adjust the Project Quality Plan
Project Plan	Update	Revised with actuals from the current stage and the forecast from the next Stage Plan. Also updated to reflect any changed or extra products sanctioned by the Project Board
Risk Log	Update	Changes to the Project Plan may affect risks

9.5.6 Key criteria

- How reliable are the figures for cost and schedule for the stage just being completed (especially if fed information from Team Plans)?
- How do the results of the stage impact the Project Plan?
- How does the next Stage Plan impact the Project Plan, Business Case and risks?

- Did any other information come out of the last stage that will impact later stages of the project?

Hints and tips

If the Project Plan is being updated because the scope of the project has changed, make sure that there is an audit trail between cause and effect – for example, ensure that the changes are recorded as Project Issues.

9.6 Updating a Project Business Case (SB3)

9.6.1 Fundamental principles

Projects do not take place in a static environment. The environment external to the project changes, as do the nature and timing of the project's products. The Business Case needs to reflect these changes and must be reviewed and amended to keep it relevant to the project.

9.6.2 Context

The update of the Business Case and the Project Plan is a cyclical process during stage-end activities throughout the project.

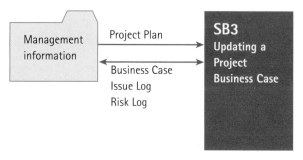

Figure 9.5 Updating a Project Business Case

9.6.3 Process description

The objective of this sub-process is to revisit and revise, where necessary, the costs, benefits, risks and timings stated in the Business Case. These may have been affected by internal or external events.

Various factors will affect this sub-process:

- The final implementation date of the project may have changed, for better or worse, which might affect some or all of the benefits

- The cost of delivering the product might have changed, thus affecting the cost side of the cost/benefit analysis

- Approved changes will have affected products, hence benefits

- Externally the corporate or programme environment into which the product will be delivered may have changed

- The situation with regard to external resources or suppliers may have changed beyond the control of the project

- An Exception Plan may have caused the Business Case to be revisited.

A revised version of the Business Case is created. The Risk and Issue Logs are examined to see if anything has changed that might affect the Business Case.

It is worth noting that changes may improve the Business Case, as well as weaken it.

The Project Board is ordinarily only authorised to continue while the project remains viable (that is, the benefits will be realised within the cost and time parameters set out in the currently agreed Business Case). If costs and/or time are to be exceeded or if it becomes clear that benefits will be substantially lower than those set out in the Business Case, the Project Board needs to have the revised Business Case approved again by corporate or programme management.

9.6.4 Responsibilities

The Project Manager is responsible for this sub-process, assisted by Project Support. Those with Project Assurance responsibilities should check out the work.

The project's benefits are a prime responsibility of the customer.

9.6.5 Information needs

Table 9.3 SB3 information needs

Management information	Usage	Explanation
Project Plan	Input	Have any changes to the Project Plan been made that affect the Business Case?
Issue Log	Update	Are there any new Project Issues that threaten (or could improve) the Business Case? Do Business Case changes raise new Project Issues?
Business Case	Update	Revised to account for any changes to the project that may affect it
Risk Log	Update	Are there any new risks that threaten the Business Case?

9.6.6 Key criteria

- Has anything happened outside the project that affects the Business Case?

- Has the Project Plan changed in a way that impacts the Business Case – for example, in terms of overall cost or the date of the scheduled outcome?

- Has it become impossible to achieve some or all of the identified benefits?

Reviewing the Business Case is best done after the Project Plan has been brought up to date.

It is sensible to review the Business Case after any activities caused by reaction to risks have been added to the new Stage Plan. These activities or their cost may have an effect on the Business Case.

9.7 Updating the Risk Log (SB4)

9.7.1 Fundamental principles

Risks change during the life of the project. New risks arise. Old risks change their status. The exposure of the project to risk should be regularly reviewed.

9.7.2 Context

The update of the Risk Log is a cyclical process during stage-end activities throughout the project. This is the *minimum* number of times to review risks. Lengthy or risky projects will need to review risks more frequently.

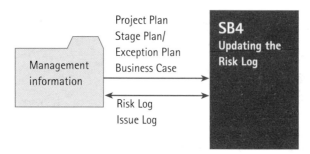

Figure 9.6 Updating the Risk Log

9.7.3 Process description

The objective of this sub-process is to revisit and revise, where necessary, the risks in the Risk Log. These may have been affected by internal or external events.

Each risk should be examined to see if it has increased, disappeared, decreased, happened or stayed the same.

The next Stage Plan or an Exception Plan may raise new risks or change existing risks. This sub-process should therefore be carried out in conjunction with *Planning a Stage* (SB1) and *Producing an Exception Plan* (SB6).

Updates to the Project Plan and Business Case may also contain changes that affect items in the Risk Log. The Business Case update may also have raised new Project Issues, which in turn raise new risks or affect risks already recognised.

For further guidance on risk, see *Management of risk*, Chapter 17.

9.7.4 Responsibilities

The Project Manager is responsible for this sub-process, assisted by Project Support. Those with Project Assurance responsibilities should check out the work.

Each major risk should have an 'owner' – the person best placed to observe the risk and the factors affecting it. This person will often be a member of the project management team but not necessarily.

9.7.5 Information needs

Table 9.4 SB4 information needs

Management information	Usage	Explanation
Business Case	Input	Needs to be referenced in case it has new information regarding risks
Project Plan	Input	Revised Project Plan may provide information as a basis for risk actions and impacts
Stage/Exception Plan	Input	New plan may contain new risks or alter existing ones
Issue Log	Update	Are there any new Project Issues that are caused by (or could improve) the new risks?
Risk Log	Update	Has anything changed?

9.7.6 Key criteria

- Has the situation changed with respect to any of the identified risks?

- Have any new risks been identified?

- Have contingency plans been put in place, where possible, for any risks now regarded as serious?

9.8 Reporting Stage End (SB5)

9.8.1 Fundamental principles

The results of a stage should be reported back to those who provided the resources and approved its execution so that progress is clearly visible to the project management team.

9.8.2 Context

Reporting Stage End involves a review of the impact of the stage on the Project Plan, the Business Case and the identified risks. It follows the earlier *Managing Stage Boundaries* (SB) sub-processes and consolidates their information in a report that is assessed by the Project Board in the sub-process *Authorising a Stage or Exception Plan* (DP3).

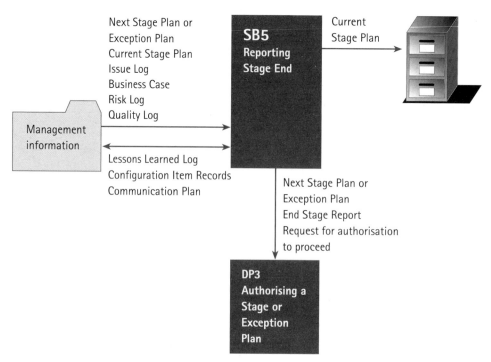

Figure 9.7 Reporting Stage End

9.8.3 Process description

This sub-process should happen as close as possible to the actual end of a stage. The results of the stage are presented in an End Stage Report. The report compares the actual results of the stage in terms of costs, target dates achieved and products produced with the original Stage Plan. A statement is made comparing the results with the agreed tolerances for the stage. The Project Manager gives a view on the continuing ability of the project to meet the Project Plan and Business Case, and assesses the overall risk situation. Feedback is given of the quality control activities undertaken and the results of that work.

A summary is given of all Project Issues received during the stage and what has happened to them.

A configuration audit is performed to check the information in the Configuration Item Records against the actual status of all products and to rectify any discrepancies.

The report is modified if an Exception Plan has triggered it, but it is still needed. Such a report would describe the results to date of the current stage, the tolerance and Project Issue situation and then summarise the Exception Report and discussions that led to the Exception Plan.

The next Stage Plan and the revised Project Plan (if there is a revision) accompany the End Stage Report. The report identifies any variations from the previous versions of these plans and assesses any changes to the risk situation. If the project is still viable in the Project Manager's view, a request to proceed to the next stage will accompany the End Stage Report.

Any lessons learned during the stage are added to the Lessons Learned Log. Any lessons from the current stage are summarised in the End Stage Report.

The Communication Plan is examined and information created and sent as required.

9.8.4 Responsibilities

The Project Manager has the responsibility for this sub-process, with assistance from Project Support. Informal agreement to the report's data and conclusions should be obtained from those responsible for Project Assurance. The Configuration Librarian will assist Project Assurance in performing the configuration audit.

9.8.5 Information needs

Table 9.5 SB5 information needs

Management information	Usage	Explanation
Current Stage Plan	Input	Contains information about the products, cost and dates of the current stage
Business Case	Input	Used to review the contribution of the current stage towards achievement of the benefits
Issue Log	Input	Identifies the Project Issues raised during the stage and reports on how they were dealt with
Risk Log	Input	Source of information about the status of current risks
Quality Log	Input	Source of information about the quality checking activities and results from those who reviewed products for quality
Communication Plan	Update	May contain a requirement to send information to an external interested party at this time. May need updating for new interested parties, for example new suppliers or new Project Assurance
Next Stage Plan or Exception Plan	Input/ Output	Future impact on the project for the End Stage Report
Lessons Learned Log	Update	Updated with any new lessons learned during this stage
Configuration Item Records	Update	Checked to establish that all products are complete and approved. Also checked to ensure details such as version number are correct. Updated where the information in the records does not match the real state of the products
Request for authorisation to proceed	Output	This may be formal or informal according to the project's situation
End Stage Report	Output	Performance of the stage against plan

9.8.6 Key criteria

- Have all products identified in the Stage Plan been produced?

- Have they all been checked for quality?

- Has the customer accepted them all?

- What was the actual resource usage and cost in the stage?

- How many Project Issues were received during the stage?

- How many changes were approved and implemented, in part or completely, during the stage and what was their impact on the Stage Plan?

- Have any changes been carried over into the next stage?

- Does the project still look viable?

- Is the Project Plan still forecast to stay within tolerance margins?

- Did the management of risk correctly identify and handle the risks on the project during this stage?

- Are there any strengths, weaknesses or omissions in the standards and practices used that should be noted for corporate quality management?

- Can any useful measurements be noted from the stage that would benefit the planning of future stages or other projects?

- Were there any discrepancies found when performing the configuration audit? Have the implications of these been addressed and any appropriate entries made in the Lessons Learned Log?

Hints and tips

Following the motto 'No surprises', the Project Manager should informally keep the Project Board aware of what the End Stage Report will say. Any problems should, wherever possible, be resolved before presentation of the report.

The level of formality or informality in the presentation of the End Stage Report depends on factors such as the project size and the desires of the Project Board.

Where the project is part of a programme, the programme support office must examine the End Stage Report, the next Stage Plan and the updated Project Plan to ensure that the project stays in line with the programme.

9.9 Producing an Exception Plan (SB6)

9.9.1 Fundamental principles

A stage is deemed to be in exception as soon as current forecasts for the end of the stage deviate beyond the delegated tolerance boundaries. The project is in exception if the whole project is likely to go beyond tolerance boundaries.

If either a stage or the project is forecast to deviate beyond its agreed tolerance boundaries, it no longer has the approval of the Project Board. A new plan must be presented to take the place of the current plan.

9.9.2 Context

The deviation should have been recognised during *Controlling a Stage* (CS). The Project Manager will have brought the situation to the attention of the Project Board through an Exception Report. The Project Board will have requested that the Project Manager produce an Exception Plan. The Exception Plan will then be presented to the Project Board at an Exception assessment.

- Ensure that all expected products have been handed over and accepted by the customer or relevant subsequent project

- Ensure that the Acceptance Criteria have all been met and get the customer's confirmation of this

- Ensure that arrangements for the support and operation of the project's products are in place (where appropriate)

- Request formal acceptance of the products from the Project Board

- If the project has been closed prematurely, document what has been achieved and recommend the way forward

- Identify any Follow-on Action Recommendations

- Capture and document lessons resulting from the project

- Prepare an End Project Report

- Plan any post-project review required

- Prepare notification to the host location of the intention to disband the project organisation and resources

- Arrange secure and orderly archiving of the project's records.

This process covers the Project Manager's work to close the project either at its end or at premature close. Most of the work is to prepare input to the Project Board to obtain its confirmation that the project may close. If the project is being brought to a premature close, this process will have to be tailored to the actual project situation. It will be a case of what can be saved for use by another project or what remedial work is now required to fill any gaps left by the cancellation of this project.

The Project Initiation Document is examined to check the actual results of the project against the original expectations (or as modified by the Project Board). All planned products should have been approved and delivered to the customer or be ready for handover. There must be documented confirmation from the customer that all Acceptance Criteria, defined at the outset of the project, have been met.

The Project Manager prepares an End Project Report that comprehensively evaluates the actual project result versus that envisaged in the Project Initiation Document.

There may be a number of Project Issues that were put in suspension by the Project Board. These may lead to new projects or enhancements to the products of the current project during its operational life. The Project Manager sorts these out into appropriate Follow-on Action Recommendations.

The Lessons Learned Log, which has been developed during the project, is now turned into a report and made available outside the project.

Notification to the host location that any provided facilities and resources will no longer be required is prepared for Project Board approval, including release dates.

Archiving of the management documents should be arranged, such that any later audit or retrieval can be done conveniently.

Suggested contents of the management products described in this process can be found in *Product Description outlines*, Appendix A.

10.3.1 Scalability

For small projects, the essentials of this process can be summarised as:

- Check that everything has been delivered

- Check that the product is accepted

- Make sure there are no loose ends

- Record any Follow-on Action Recommendations

- Store the project records for audit

- Release resources as required.

Hints and tips

Where the Project Approach indicates a phased handover or implementation of the product(s) it may be worth giving consideration to undertaking some aspects of *Closing a Project*, in particular customer acceptance, operational and maintenance acceptance, outstanding Project Issues and risks associated with the implemented elements, and possibly a review of the Lessons Learned. In this event these elements would form part of the phased implementation work, which may well coincide with a stage boundary.

10.4 Decommissioning a Project (CP1)

10.4.1 Fundamental principles

The main principles are that:

- Every project should come to an orderly close

- Customer and supplier should be in agreement that the project has delivered what was expected; this expectation should have been defined at the outset of the project

- Everyone who has provided support for the project should be warned of its close, so that they can plan for the return of the resources provided for that support

- Project records should be retained to assist with possible audits or the production of estimating metrics.

10.4.2 Context

This sub-process is normally triggered by *Reviewing Stage Status* (CS5), when the Project Manager recognises that the project is nearing the end of the final stage. CP1 is part of the work leading to the Project Board sub-process, *Confirming Project Closure* (DP5). *Closing a Project* (CP) will cycle round the three sub-processes for which there is no specific sequence.

In exceptional cases the sub-process may be used because the Project Board directs the Project Manager to close the project before its planned end.

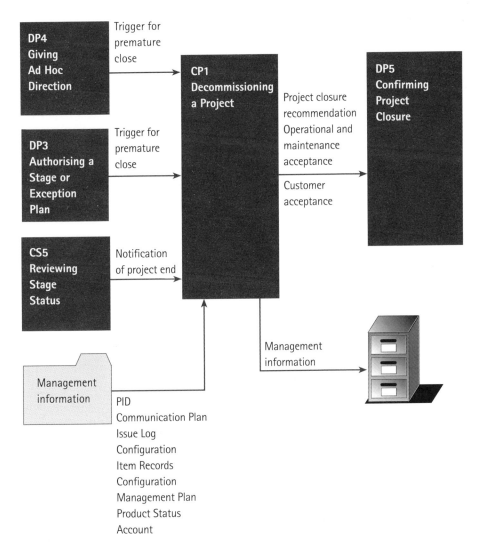

Figure 10.3 Decommissioning a Project

10.4.3 Process description

The objectives of this sub-process are to:

- Ensure that all the project's products have been approved and handed over to the customer or user

- Confirm that the delivered products meet any needs defined in the customer's specification for operation and support (where applicable)

- Confirm that the correct operational and maintenance environment is in place (where applicable)

- Confirm that all Acceptance Criteria have been met

- Complete and store all project information

- Prepare a recommendation to all involved organisations and interested parties that the project is to be closed, and facilities and resources disbanded.

The Project Manager prepares the project closure recommendation to the Project Board that the project resources and the support services can be disbanded. The Project Manager should consult the Communication Plan to ascertain whether any other parties require a copy of the project closure recommendation and act accordingly. The project closure recommendation has to be confirmed by the Project Board.

Before closure of the project can be recommended, the Project Manager must ensure that the expected results have all been achieved and delivered (or have been told by the Project Board that the project is to be closed prematurely).

Configuration Item Records are reviewed and a configuration audit is carried out to confirm that all products have been approved and the Configuration Management Plan consulted on how to hand over products.

Where a product has to be supported and sustained during its useful life, there must be confirmation in the form of operational and maintenance acceptance by the people who will use and support it that they have received the product in a state that allows them to carry out their duties.

The Project Manager must go through the Acceptance Criteria with the customer and obtain agreement that all criteria have been met.

To permit any future audit of the project's actions and performance, the project files should be secured and archived. This entails an important task of weeding out documents that would not be useful to those who may need to access the archived files, for example, audit, the Project Support Office, future Project Managers (for planning models) and those who later carry out the post-project review. It is wise to have the weeding done by a group consisting of the Project Manager, Project Assurance and Project Support.

10.4.4 Responsibilities

The Project Manager has responsibility for this sub-process, but may need assistance from Project Support (including the Configuration Librarian) to gather the necessary input. The Project Manager should have informal contact with Project Assurance during this time for their views on the completeness of work to ensure that there will be no problems with Project Board confirmation of the project closure in *Confirming Project Closure* (DP5).

10.4.5 Information needs

Table 10.1 CP1 information needs

Management information	Usage	Explanation
Project Initiation Document	Input	Contains a statement of the project's Acceptance Criteria
Configuration Item Records	Input	To be checked for completeness and input to the Product Status Account

Product Status Account	Input	Confirmation from the customer's configuration management records that all products are approved
Configuration Management Plan	Input	To confirm how products are to be handed over to the configuration library of those who will maintain the product in its operational life
Configuration audit	Output	Confirm that all products have been approved
Issue Log	Input	Check if all Project Issues have been closed
Trigger for premature close	Input	Instruction from the Project Board to close the project before its expected end
Notification of project end	Input	The trigger from stage monitoring that the normal end of the project is near
Communication Plan	Input	Identification of any other interested party who needs to know
Customer acceptance	Output	Confirmation that the customer accepts the products
Operational and maintenance acceptance	Output	Confirmation that the product can be operated and supported
Project closure recommendation	Output	A note to be sent to the Project Board stating that the project is about to close and that supplied facilities and resources will no longer be needed. The Communication Plan should be consulted to ascertain any other recipients
Management information	Archive	Preserve the important and useful project records for future use by auditors or other enquirers

10.4.6 Key criteria

- Have all products in the Project Initiation Document been approved and delivered?

- Have the operational and support teams formally agreed that they are ready to accept handover (if appropriate)?

- Are the project resources and support services (if any were provided) no longer required?

- Are there any contractual implications when decommissioning the project?

Hints and tips

The configuration management system used on the project to control and record the status of products should check that all products are complete and handed over.

Where the final product will require a lot of potentially expensive maintenance, the Project Manager should ensure that a suitable service agreement or contract has been drawn up between the support group and the end users. In such instances, it may be correct to include the agreement as a project product. This will probably lead to a small team from the operations group being part of the final stages of the project, leading to the delivery of a signed agreement.

The support group would need full information about the product as it is developed (see the Communication Plan in *Product Description outlines*, Appendix A) to understand the support and maintenance implications of the product and its working environment.

10.5 Identifying Follow-on Actions (CP2)

10.5.1 Fundamental principles

If there is any unfinished business at the end of the project, it should be formally documented and passed to those who have the authority and responsibility to take action.

10.5.2 Context

Most of the input will be those items on the Issue Log that were held back by the Project Board.

The output is submitted to the Project Board as Follow-on Action Recommendations.

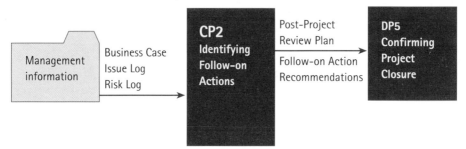

Figure 10.4 Identifying Follow-on Actions

10.5.3 Process description

The aims of this sub-process are to:

- Check that all Project Issues and risks are closed or transferred to Follow-on Action Recommendations. Establish actions required following the project

- Document any Follow-on Action Recommendations

- Recommend a date and produce a plan for any post-project review(s) considered necessary.

A number of actions may be required after the project. The input will come mainly from those Project Issues that were put into 'pending' status by the Project Board during the project. The Risk Log may also contain risks that may affect the product in its useful life.

All unfinished work is documented in Follow-on Action Recommendations.

Many project products should be re-examined after a period of use to check on their quality, effectiveness in use and achievement of benefits. Examination of the updated Business Case will identify whether there are any expected benefits whose achievement cannot be measured until the product has been in use for some time. If this is the case, a recommended date and plan should be made for a post-project review, the benefits to be measured at that time and the measurements to be applied. These benefits should have been defined in the Business Case.

It is not a project activity to produce the post-project review, only to plan it. In summary, the post-project review is to assess achievement of the benefits claimed in the Business Case. The following questions are a sample:

- To what level has the product achieved the benefits expected?
- Is there an identifiable trend of improving benefits?
- Are the user(s) happy with the product?
- Is the product proving to meet quality expectations?
- Is the product as well supported as was expected?
- Are the support staff happy with what they have been given to support the product?
- Have there been any unexpected problems in the introduction?
- Has the product caused new problems?

The Post-Project Review Plan will make use of the information contained in the Business Case (see its *Product Description outline* in Appendix A). This should have stated how the achievement of benefits was to be measured. The plan should be defining:

- What benefit achievements are to be measured
- When benefit achievement can be measured
- How the achievement can be measured
- The pre-delivery situation against which achievement is to be compared
- Who is needed to carry out the measurements (individuals or skill types).

10.5.4 Responsibilities

The Project Manager has responsibility for this sub-process.

10.5.5 Information needs

Table 10.2 CP2 information needs

Management information	Usage	Explanation
Issue Log	Input	Unactioned Project Issues will form the basis of any Follow-on Action Recommendations
Business Case	Input	This will reveal benefits whose achievement cannot be measured immediately and will therefore need a post-project review
Risk Log	Input	Check for any risks to the operational use of the end product(s)
Post-Project Review Plan	Output	Suggested plan for a post-project review for ratification by the Project Board

need to be measured after operational use of the final product is passed to *Identifying Follow-on Actions* (CP2) for inclusion in the Post-Project Review Plan.

The report should also take into consideration the effect on the original Project Plan and Business Case of any changes that were approved. The End Project Report should give final statistics on changes received during the project and the total impact of approved changes. Any outstanding changes should match up with follow-on actions defined in *Identifying Follow-on Actions* (CP2). Statistics may also be appropriate for all quality work carried out.

The End Project Report is concerned with how well the project fulfilled its objectives or, in the case of a premature close, did not fulfil its objectives. The Lessons Learned Report, by way of contrast, is concerned with how well the project was managed and with the project's use of project management processes and techniques – that is, PRINCE2 and any local standards used – and what can be learned from this implementation. This report will be approved by the Project Board and issued to interested parties as part of *Confirming Project Closure* (DP5)

Lessons Learned Report

At the start of the project, a Lessons Learned Log should be created. A note should be added to this every time the project management team spot something about the management or specialist processes, products, techniques or procedures that either made a significant contribution to the project's achievements or caused a problem. This includes the performance of all the project management team, the success of any scaling, the use of the specialist processes and any tailoring of them, change control and quality results.

In this sub-process, all the notes should be collated and turned into a report, including any views with hindsight on the project's management. The report should aim to answer the question: 'What should be done differently next time?' A configuration audit should have been done at the end of the project, as part of sub-process *Decommissioning a Project* (CP1), to look for discrepancies. The cause of any discrepancies might justify an entry in the Lessons Learned Report.

The report is also the repository of any useful measurements and quality statistics collected during the project that will help in the planning and estimation of subsequent projects.

It is important to identify at the beginning of the project who should receive the Lessons Learned Report and make sure that the Project Board knows where it should go. There is little point in preparing the report, only to find that it will not be used.

If a project is brought to a premature close, the reasons should be documented in the Lessons Learned Report, focusing on any failure in the methodology, specialist tools and techniques or staff that caused or contributed to the premature close. Conversely, if the premature close was caused by successful application of the PRINCE2 method, for example, identification that the project was no longer viable or had exceeded its project tolerances, this should also be documented.

10.6.4 Responsibilities

The Project Manager bears overall responsibility for this sub-process, but additional information could come from anyone involved in the project.

10.6.5 Information needs

Table 10.3 CP3 information needs

Management information	Usage	Explanation
Project Initiation Document	Input	Original statement of project objectives, scope and constraints
Issue Log	Input	The reasons for Off-Specifications may provide lessons for future projects
Risk Log	Input	What risks were considered and what happened to them may provide lessons for future projects
Project Quality Plan	Input	This will indicate whether the quality policy and procedures were adequate, and correctly stated
Quality Log	Input	Statistics of the number of quality checks made and the errors found are useful to a quality assurance function
Configuration Item Records	Input	Are there any discrepancies between the records and reality? These may inform the conduct of future products
Lessons Learned Log	Input	This should be an ongoing document from the start of the project, completed with relevant notes on the good and bad lessons learned about management and specialist procedures, forms, other documents, tools and techniques
Project Plan	Update	Updated with the figures from the 'final' stage. Will be reviewed when producing the End Project Report. It may also be useful when preparing the Lessons Learned Report
Daily Log	Input	This may contain useful information which can be analysed as part of the End Project Report or the Lessons Learned Report
Business Case	Input	Any benefits realised already should be described in the report
Lessons Learned Report	Output	This takes the Lessons Learned Log and writes it up into a report to be passed via the Project Board to the group charged with maintaining such quality standards
End Project Report	Output	Evaluation of the achievement of objectives as defined in the Project Initiation Document and of the management performance of the project

10.6.6 Key criteria

- Which management processes or procedures have worked well?
- Which management processes have had problems?
- Was it easy to achieve the required quality?
- Which quality procedures have worked well?

- Were there any weaknesses in quality procedures for specific types of product?

- How well did risk strategies work?

- Were there any unforeseen risks?

- How well were the risks managed?

- Was the contingency used?

- Was training in the management, quality and delivery processes and procedures adequate? Were there recognisable benefits from the level of training given or recognisable problems caused by lack of training?

- How well did any support tools work?

- Could anything have been done to improve skill levels before the relevant work was done?

- If there has been deviation from the Project Initiation Document, is the Project Board still prepared to accept the project closure? Are those deviations reflected in the End Project Report and Lessons Learned Report? Where appropriate, are any deviations reflected in the Follow-on Action Recommendations?

Hints and tips

Concentrate on items that can be of use to future projects.

Observations on successful elements can be as useful as identification of failures and omissions.

Deviations documented in the End Project Report, the Lessons Learned Report and the Follow-on Action Recommendations should, as far as is sensible, avoid overlap – in other words, the same deviations should not be unnecessarily recorded in several places.

Consider whether there are any lessons about the quality procedures that should be directed to any quality assurance function. These might be weaknesses in current standard practices, new quality testing requirements from the products of the project that are not currently covered by standards or new ways of testing quality that the project has pioneered.

Where the project is part of a programme, the programme support office should review the Lessons Learned Report for applicability to the programme or to individual projects within the programme.

There are a number of possible recipients of the Lessons Learned Report. The aim is to identify the group that will distribute the report to other projects, not just current ones but any that may be starting up in the future. Ideally, this should be a group that has the responsibility to maintain project management standards. Some organisations have a project management office; others make the responsibility part of the duties of a quality assurance group. Elsewhere it may be known as management services or the central Project Support Office.

11
PLANNING (PL)

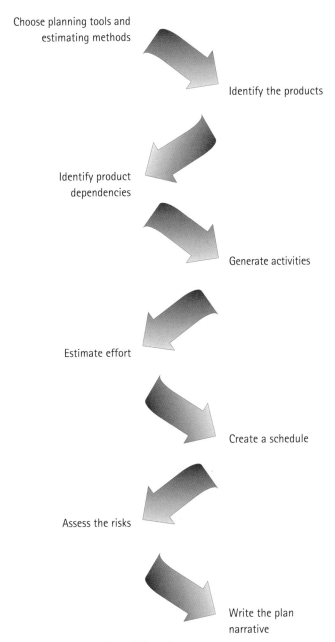

Choose planning tools and estimating methods

Identify the products

Identify product dependencies

Generate activities

Estimate effort

Create a schedule

Assess the risks

Write the plan narrative

Figure 11.1 Overview of Planning

11.1 Fundamental principles

Effective project management relies on an effective planning and control process. Even small projects require planning.

Planning provides all personnel involved in the project with information on:

- What is required
- How it will be achieved and by whom, using what specialist equipment and resources
- When events will happen.

The *Planning* (PL) process is where the technique of product-based planning (described in Chapter 22) is used. Product-based planning is a key technique of PRINCE2 and provides a comprehensive platform for effective planning. It is the technique that enables the Project Manager to:

- Define what the project has to deliver
- Provide descriptions of the required products, the skills needed to develop the products, plus measurable statements of the quality required and how the presence of that quality is to be tested
- Objectively monitor and control progress.

11.2 Context

Planning is a repeatable process and plays an important role in other sub-processes, the main ones being:

- *Planning an Initiation Stage* (SU6)
- *Planning a Project* (IP2)
- *Planning a Stage* (SB1)
- *Updating a Project Plan* (SB2)
- *Accepting a Work Package* (MP1)
- *Producing an Exception Plan* (SB6).

Planning is also an iterative process. There will be a series of loops through the planning steps as extra information becomes available or adjustments are made.

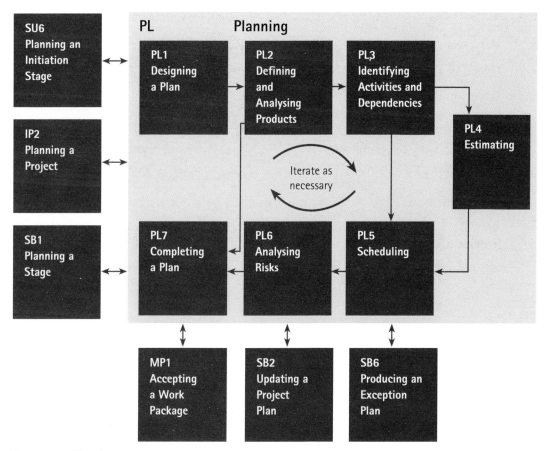

Figure 11.2 Planning

11.3 Process description

The philosophy behind producing plans in PRINCE2 is that:

- Plans are constructed by identifying the products required, and then the activities and appropriate resources necessary to deliver them

- Plans should cover management needs as well as the customer's products

- There should be assurance that all activities are thought through in advance and to a level consistent with the control requirements identified in the Project Initiation Document.

The product-based planning technique provides a start to the planning activity and a planning framework. It involves:

- Establishing what products are needed for the plan

- Describing those products and their quality criteria

- Determining the sequence in which each of the products should be produced and any dependencies.

After these initial steps, the normal steps of planning are:

- Identifying the activities needed to produce the products

- Deciding when the activities should be done and by whom

- Estimating how much effort each activity will consume

- Estimating how long the activities will take

- Agreeing what quality control activities and resources are needed

- Producing a time-based schedule of activities

- Calculating how much the overall effort will cost

- Producing the budget from the cost of the effort plus any materials and equipment that must be obtained

- Assessing the risks contained in the plan

- Identifying the management control points needed

- Agreeing tolerance levels for the plan.

The steps involved are the same for all levels of plan.

Several iterations of the *Planning* process are normally needed.

The Project Approach is a prerequisite for planning. This should have been defined as part of *Starting up a Project* (SU).

11.3.1 Scalability

Planning is essential, regardless of the type or size of project. The amount of detail varies according to the needs of the project.

The Product Checklist is optional in a project. It can be a useful tool for the Project Board to use to review the project's progress, rather than a Gantt chart. It may also be used to clarify the information contained within the Gantt chart.

The first sub-process *Designing a Plan* (PL1) is done only once in a project. Where the project is part of a programme, all the design decisions will probably have been taken at programme level. In a small project it may be just a matter of deciding on a planning tool (if any).

Hints and tips

Keep plans relevant. Be aware of the audience for the prepared set of plans and aim to provide an appropriate level of detail.

Time must be allowed for planning because it is a time-consuming exercise. Planning for the next stage should start towards the end of the current stage.

It is easier and more accurate to plan short stages than long ones.

Past Lessons Learned Reports are an excellent source of information and guidance for planning at all levels, and should be referenced where appropriate.

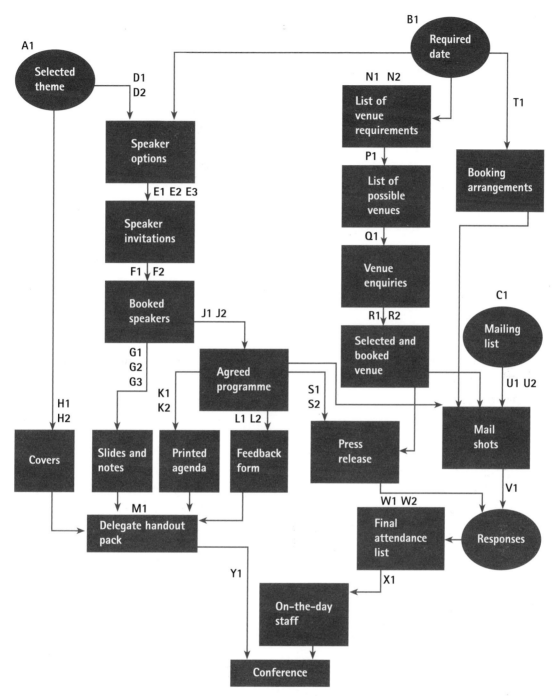

Figure 11.3 Product Flow Diagram for organising a conference

Product	Product ID	Activity ID	Associated Activities	Predecessor
Selected theme	A	A1	Receive theme	–
Required date	B	B1	Receive date	–
Mailing list	C	C1	Receive mailing list	–
Speaker options	D	D1	Identify possible speakers	A1
		D2	Prepare speaker database	D1
Speaker invitations	E	E1	Prepare speaker invite letter	D2
		E2	Merge invite letter	E1
		E3	Post invite letters	E2
Booked speakers	F	F1	Receive replies	E3
		F2	Confirm speaker booking	F1
Slides and notes	G	G1	Prepare slides	F2
		G2	Put into show order	G1
		G3	Print slides	G2
Covers	H	H1	Design covers	A1
		H2	Print covers	H1
Agreed programme	J	J1	Draft programme	F2
		J2	Agree programme	J1
Printed agenda	K	K1	Agree agenda	J2
		K2	Print agenda	K1
Feedback form	L	L1	Agree feedback form	J2
		L2	Print feedback forms	L1
Delegate handout pack	M	M1	Assemble material	H2, G2, K2, L2
List of venue requirements	N	N1	Prepare list	B1
		N2	Agree list	N1
List of possible venue	P	P1	Build venue list	N2
Venue enquiries	Q	Q1	Contact venues	Q1
Selected and booked venue	R	R1	Choose venue	Q1
		R2	Book venue	R1
Press release	S	S1	Prepare release	J2, R2
		S2	Place material	S1
Booking arrangemnets	T	T1	Compile arrangements	B1
Mail shots	U	U1	Prepare merge letter	C1, T1
		U2	Merge/post letters	U1
Responses	V	V1	Receive replies	S2, U2
Final attendance list	W	W1	Compile list	V1
		W2	Finalise list	W1
On-the-day staff	X	X1	Recruit staff	W2
Conference	Y	Y1	Hold conference	M1, X1

Figure 11.4 List of activities for organising a conference

The list of activities should include management and quality checking activities as well as the activities needed to develop the specialist products.

Any constraints should also be identified. External constraints may be:

●   The delivery of a product required by this project from another project

●   Waiting for a decision from programme management.

Wherever possible, external constraints should be described as a dependency on the availability of an external product. Resource-based constraints – for example, 'Is the resource available to do the work?' – are not considered here. They are a question for the scheduling process.

The activities should include any that are required to interact with external parties – for example, obtaining a product from an outside source or converting external products into something that the plan requires.

11.6.4 Responsibilities

The Project Manager is responsible for this sub-process for Project and Stage Plans. Team Plans are the responsibility of the Team Manager(s). There should be support from any Team Managers whose team contributes to execution of the plan in question. Help should also be found from any Project Assurance or Project Support staff allocated to the project. The checking of the work is part of the responsibility of the Project Assurance roles.

11.6.5 Information needs

Table 11.3 PL3 information needs

Management information	Usage	Explanation
Product Flow Diagram	Input	The products and their dependencies are the basis of defining the required activities and their dependencies
Product Descriptions	Input	The derivation section of the description may contain information helpful in identifying dependencies
Risk Log	Input	The Risk Log may contribute risk monitoring activities that need to be added to the plan
List of activities	Output	All the activities required to produce the products
Activity dependencies	Output	Any dependencies between the activities in the preceding list

11.6.6 Key criteria

●   Can any activities be carried out in parallel?

●   Can any activities overlap?

●   Are any gaps needed between certain activities?

- Have sufficient quality checking activities been included? (This question would be at too low a level for the Project Plan.)

Hints and tips

Guard against an explosion of activities at this stage beyond the detail appropriate to the level of plan.

Keep things simple. If in doubt, don't overlap activities.

11.7 Estimating (PL4)

11.7.1 Fundamental principles

Estimating cannot guarantee accuracy but when applied provides a view about the overall cost and time required to complete the plan. Estimates will inevitably change as more is discovered about the project.

11.7.2 Context

Estimating follows identification of the activities in sub-process PL3 and precedes scheduling in sub-process PL5.

11.7.3 Process description

This is an iterative sub-process. The objective is to identify the resources and time required to complete each activity. This will include not only people but also all other resources that will be required.

Since the type of estimating will vary according to the type of project and level of plan, the guidance is of a general nature.

A Project Plan will normally require top-down estimating (that is, an estimate for the total project, broken down across the normal stages for a project of this type), whereas a Stage Plan or Team Plan would use bottom-up methods (an estimate for each product, built up into a figure for the whole plan).

The two major steps in a typical estimating process are:

- *Identify resource types required.* Specific skills may be required depending on the type and complexity of the project. Requirements may include non-human resources, such as equipment, travel or money.

  It is important to agree a definition of resource types. For staff this should include:

  - the skills and experience level(s) required
  - where these skills can be found so that the commitment required of different parts of the organisation can be identified

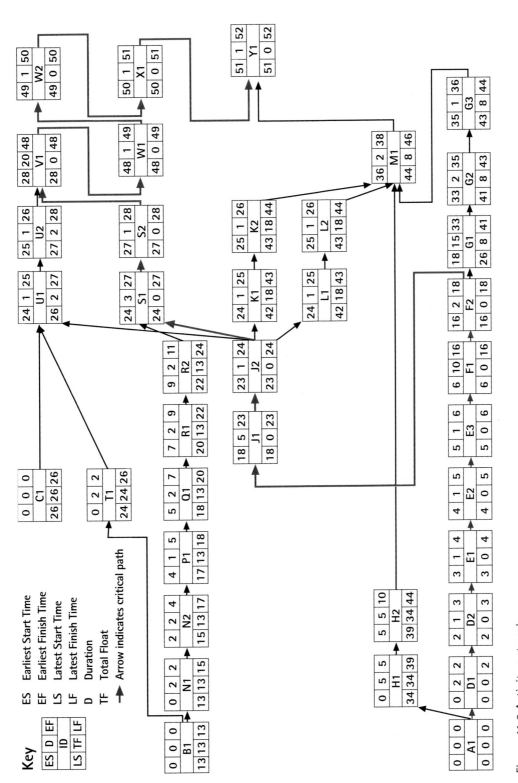

Key

ES	D	EF
	ID	
LS	TF	LF

ES   Earliest Start Time
EF   Earliest Finish Time
LS   Latest Start Time
LF   Latest Finish Time
D   Duration
TF   Total Float
→   Arrow indicates critical path

Figure 11.6 Activity network

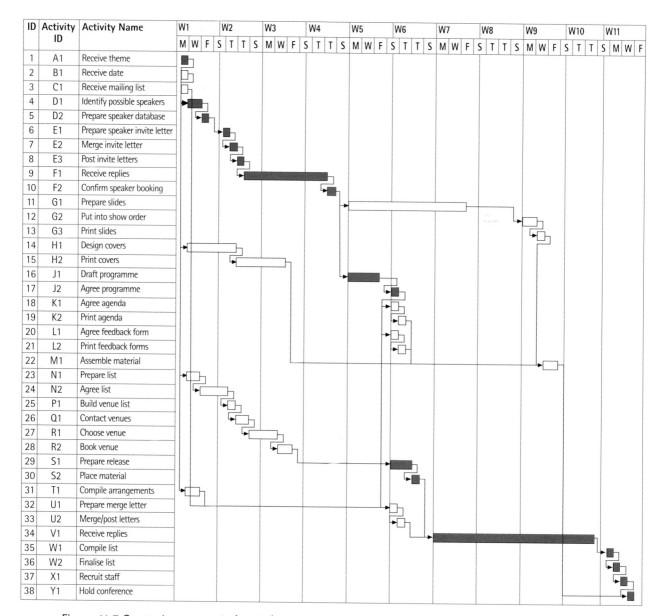

ID	Activity ID	Activity Name	W1	W2	W3	W4	W5	W6	W7	W8	W9	W10	W11
1	A1	Receive theme											
2	B1	Receive date											
3	C1	Receive mailing list											
4	D1	Identify possible speakers											
5	D2	Prepare speaker database											
6	E1	Prepare speaker invite letter											
7	E2	Merge invite letter											
8	E3	Post invite letters											
9	F1	Receive replies											
10	F2	Confirm speaker booking											
11	G1	Prepare slides											
12	G2	Put into show order											
13	G3	Print slides											
14	H1	Design covers											
15	H2	Print covers											
16	J1	Draft programme											
17	J2	Agree programme											
18	K1	Agree agenda											
19	K2	Print agenda											
20	L1	Agree feedback form											
21	L2	Print feedback forms											
22	M1	Assemble material											
23	N1	Prepare list											
24	N2	Agree list											
25	P1	Build venue list											
26	Q1	Contact venues											
27	R1	Choose venue											
28	R2	Book venue											
29	S1	Prepare release											
30	S2	Place material											
31	T1	Compile arrangements											
32	U1	Prepare merge letter											
33	U2	Merge/post letters											
34	V1	Receive replies											
35	W1	Compile list											
36	W2	Finalise list											
37	X1	Recruit staff											
38	Y1	Hold conference											

Figure 11.7 Gantt chart example (partial)

- *Level resource usage*: the scheduling of any allowances should be considered and built into the plan.

  The first allocation of resources may result in uneven resource usage, maybe even over-utilisation of some resources at certain times. Responsibilities are reassigned, activities moved about within any 'float' they may have, and activity durations changed from the original estimate to reflect resource constraints. The end result of this step is a final schedule in which all activities have been assigned and resource usage equates to resource availability.

- *Confirm control points*: the first draft schedule enables the control points identified earlier (in the Product Flow Diagram, Figure 11.3) to be confirmed by the Project Board. End of stage activities (for example, drawing up the next Stage Plan, producing an End Stage Report) should be added to the activity network and a new schedule produced.

- *Calculate resources and costs*: the resource requirements can now be tabulated and the cost of the resources and other costs calculated to produce the plan budget. Remember to consult Project Assurance personnel in case they wish to add specific resources to quality checking activities.

11.8.4 Responsibilities

The Project Manager is responsible for this sub-process. For Team Plans, the Project Manager would involve the person responsible for the work contained in the plan, for example, a Team Manager. Help may be provided by Project Support staff allocated to the Project.

11.8.5 Information needs

Table 11.5 PL5 information needs

Management information	Usage	Explanation
Activity estimates	Input	When studied with the resource numbers, these give the activity duration
Activity dependencies	Input	These give the required sequence of work in the schedule
Resource availability	Input	The start and end dates of resource availability, plus the amount of time they are available in this period, are required
Schedule	Output	A list of activities and their allocated resources, plus the dates over which the activities will take place

11.8.6 Key criteria

- Have all types of required resource been considered?
- Has the critical path been identified?
- Has sufficient monitoring been planned for activities on the critical path?
- Have any training requirements been incorporated?
- Has resource availability been realistically assessed?

Hints and tips

At project level, resources need not be identified by name, but the type of skills required to carry out an activity should be identified.

The availability of the resources required (including those required for quality reviews) should be checked with the relevant line managers.

Be realistic about the availability of resources. Allowance should be made for holidays and time that people will spend on non-project activities. The average working week is only four days after allowing for holidays, training, sickness, etc. Of those four days, at least another half-day will be spent on other duties, even by dedicated staff – for example, quality reviewing for other projects, line management and meetings.

The use of a skills matrix may assist a scheduler when using internal resources. This will allow appropriate people to be pinpointed, as well as giving an overall view of the skills available to the project.

When the availability of resources has been discussed with line managers, any agreement reached with them should be documented immediately.

11.9 Analysing Risks (PL6)

11.9.1 Fundamental principles

Commitment to a course of action without consideration of the risks inherent in that course is courting disaster. Risks should be considered and modifications made to the course of action in order to remove or lessen the impact of those risks.

11.9.2 Context

Once the plan has been produced, it should still be considered a draft until the risks inherent in the plan have been identified, assessed and the plan possibly modified.

11.9.3 Process description

Analysing Risks (PL6) runs parallel to all other planning work. It is an iterative process and the results of analysing risks may result in returning to previous steps and repeating the sub-process as necessary.

An overview of the management of risk is given in the *Components* section of this manual in Chapter 17.

Any planning assumptions create a risk. Are the assumptions correct?

Each resource should be examined for its potential risk content. Is the resource a known quantity? Is the quality of work required and the ability to meet deadlines known? Is the level of commitment known? Will the resource be totally under the control of the Project Manager? Where the answer is 'No', there is a risk involved. Countermeasures would include tighter and more frequent monitoring until confidence in the resource is achieved. It might be better to allocate work that is either easy to do or less critical to the schedule until the skill level has been checked.

Each activity should be checked for risk. Is there any spare time or does the entire schedule depend on no slippage for the activity? Everything on the critical path therefore represents a risk. At the very least the countermeasures should include more frequent monitoring to give early warning of any problem.

The Project Manager should discuss a Stage Plan informally with the Project Board and any Project Assurance personnel appointed by the Project Board before formally presenting it for approval.

The presentation of the plan should be appropriate for the audience. In some circumstances it may be necessary to break down into further detail areas of a plan for the use of teams or individuals.

Be wary of producing an over-complex plan containing lots of detail that might be better supplied in narrative form. A confusing or too detailed plan may 'switch off' the reader.

It helps if assumptions are consistent across all the projects of a programme.

12

INTRODUCTION TO THE PRINCE2 COMPONENTS

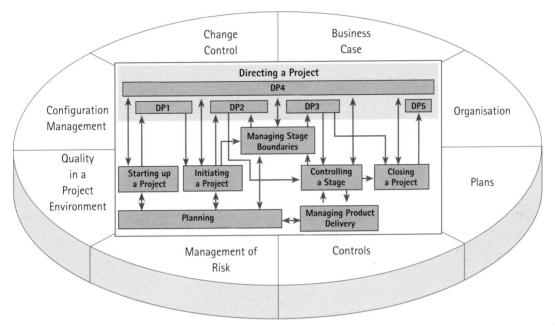

Figure 12.1 The PRINCE2 template

As shown in Figure 12.1, PRINCE2 has a number of components that are used by the processes:

- Business Case
- Organisation
- Plans
- Controls
- Management of risk
- Quality in a project environment
- Configuration management
- Change control.

The following chapters of the manual explain the philosophy of these components and how they should be used.

There are also hints and tips on using and tailoring the components to suit various situations and types of project.

13
BUSINESS CASE

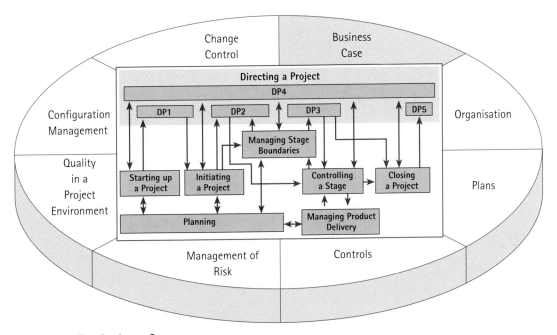

Figure 13.1 The Business Case

This chapter outlines an approach to the development of a project's Business Case. PRINCE2's key philosophy is that its Business Case must drive the project. If a satisfactory Business Case does not exist, a project should not be started. If a Business Case is valid at the start of a project, but this justification disappears once the project is under way, the project should be stopped. The focus of the Business Case should be on the *totality* of business change, not just one element of it – for example, the cost of buying new equipment should take into account the impact on personnel, training, changed procedures, accommodation changes, operational costs, relationships with the public, etc.

In PRINCE2, the Business Case is developed at the beginning of the project and maintained throughout the life of the project, being reviewed by the Project Board at each key decision point, such as end stage assessments.

13.1 What is a Business Case?

- The Business Case is a description of the reasons for the project and the justification for undertaking the project, based on the estimated costs of the project, the risks and the expected business benefits and savings

- The Business Case covers the entire scope of change to the business that is affected by the project

- The Business Case is the most important set of information for the project. It drives the decision-making processes and is used continually to align the project's progress to the business objectives/benefits that are defined within the Business Case

- Business Cases need to be developed according to any organisational standards that might exist and the nature of the project. Some Business Cases will require significant effort in their development and approval because the project will have a major impact on the organisation. Others will require less effort and involvement as the project is self-contained and has minimal impact on other parts of the organisation. Also, the level of investment required will influence the rigour with which the Business Case is developed.

13.2 What should a Business Case contain?

There are many different Business Case formats. Each Business Case should contain sufficient management information such that it can be used effectively throughout the project. The Business Case in PRINCE2 is supported by other documentation such as the Risk Log. As a minimum in PRINCE2, the Business Case should contain information under the following headings. These are the ones that appear under 'composition' in the Business Case Product Description outline in Appendix A.

13.2.1 Reasons

This section provides an explanation of the reasons why the project outcome is needed. This information should be in the Project Mandate. If not, the area needs further investigation during *Starting up a Project* (SU) and the rationale for the project established.

13.2.2 Options

This section should describe in outline the various options that have been considered to deliver the required outcome. The chosen option should be indicated, together with a summary of the reasons why. This information provides assurance that alternatives were considered. 'Do nothing' should always be the starting option to act as a comparison for the other options.

13.2.3 Benefits expected

This section should identify each benefit that is claimed would be achieved by the project's outcome. Each one should be described clearly in measurable terms. It is important to define the current status of each benefit in quantifiable terms so that measurable improvements can be assessed after the project has been completed. Consideration should be given to defining how and when the measurement of improvement can be made. The Executive has the responsibility for defining benefits.

A 'negative' way of assessing benefits may be useful as part of the overall justification for the project. This describes what will happen if the project is not done – for example, the loss of market share, large maintenance costs, heavy legal penalties for non-compliance with new laws.

13.2.4 Risks

This section contains a summary of the key risks facing the project that, if they happen, would seriously affect delivery of the outcome. Details of how these risks will be managed are contained in the Risk Log.

13.2.5 Cost and timescale

This information comes from the Project Plan. If the Project Plan is not yet completed, it may be necessary to outline the project's costs and timescales in the Business Case and refine them when the Project Plan is completed.

13.2.6 Investment appraisal

This illustrates the balance between the development, operational, maintenance and support costs against the financial value of the benefits over a period of time. This period may be a fixed number of years or the useful life of the product.

The baseline for investment appraisal is the 'do nothing' option, i.e. what will the picture of costs and benefits be if the project is not undertaken? This is compared to the picture expected from completing the project.

Wherever possible, benefits should be expressed in tangible ways. To start with, the customer, user or Executive may define many benefits as intangible, for example, 'happier staff'. It is worth making the effort to think carefully about intangible benefits to see if they can be expressed in more tangible ways. In this example, 'happier staff' may translate into less staff turnover and/or less time off for stress-related problems. Both of these can be converted into a likely monetary saving.

13.2.7 Evaluation

There are many ways to evaluate the claimed benefits and investment appraisal. For example, sensitivity analysis can be used to determine whether the Business Case is heavily dependent on a particular benefit. If it is, this may affect project planning, monitoring and control activities, and risk management, as steps would need to be taken to protect that benefit.

Another example is to define three views of the achievement of the benefits, i.e. what are we really expecting, what might we achieve if things went well, what might be the worst-case scenario? The latter might be affected by building into the costs an allowance for estimating inaccuracies, tolerances and risks. This technique is sometimes referred to as GAP analysis (good, average, poor). GAP analysis usually reveals if benefit expectations are reasonable or are really over-optimistic. The result of this analysis can lead to revision of the decision to go ahead with the project, which in turn would form a basis for setting any benefit tolerance.

13.3 Developing a Business Case

- The Executive is the 'owner' of the project's Business Case. It is the Executive's responsibility to ensure the project's objectives, costs, benefits, etc. are correctly aligned with the business strategy or programme objectives

- The Executive may delegate the development of the Business Case to the Project Manager. However, the data upon which the case will be developed will be largely provided by the business and responsibility for an accurate and effective Business Case remains with the Executive. On large projects, the Business Case may require a small team of experts to develop the contents. On small projects, the Business Case may only require one person to develop the information

- During start-up, the information from the Project Mandate is used to develop the information required for the Business Case. Where the project is part of a programme, much of the required information should be available within programme-level documentation. Projects operating within a programme environment may not in themselves deliver business benefits. They may be required to deliver products that are prerequisites for other projects. The Business Case should reflect this

- During initiation, the Business Case is updated to provide more detailed information on the benefits, risks, options and costs. The Project Plan, once completed, gives a much clearer view of risks and costs. This information is used to refine the investment appraisal or GAP analysis. The detailed information on risks is kept in the Risk Log for formal monitoring during the project

- Formal approval of the Business Case is required from the Executive to ensure there is senior management commitment to the project. This approval is part of the formal review done at the end of *Initiating a Project* (IP)

- During each stage of the project, the Business Case is reviewed to confirm that the project remains on track and to check that the Business Case remains valid within the business context. The Business Case requires formal configuration management to ensure any changes to the project's environment are accurately reflected and approved before revising the Business Case. The Business Case remains a 'live' document during the project and all decisions regarding project progress are made using the Business Case as the 'driver'

- The project's Business Case provides all stakeholders with basic information about the project. The Communication Plan for the project should cover how and when the Business Case information is to be communicated to stakeholders and how they can provide feedback and raise issues concerning the Business Case

- At project closure, the Business Case is used to confirm that the project has delivered the required products and that the benefits expected can be realised in an appropriate time frame by the business. The Business Case provides the basis for the Post-Project Review Plan; ensuring that the later assessment of whether the outcome was successful or not is firmly linked to the Business Case.

13.4 Development path of the Business Case

The Project Mandate should contain some basic elements of the Business Case. At this point there may only be some reasons why a solution is being sought. If the project is part of a programme, the Project Mandate may be just a pointer to the programme's Business Case. If the project were preceded by a feasibility study or something similar, the Project Mandate would contain a copy of the Business Case for the preferred option.

Depending on how much information there was in the Project Mandate's Business Case, *Preparing a Project Brief* (SU4) might be required to bring it up to a basic level, containing sufficient justification for the Project Board's *Authorising Initiation* (DP1).

Refining the Business Case and Risks (IP3) is the sub-process that fully develops the Business Case as part of the Project Initiation Document. It now contains the latest information on the costs and time to develop the product, taken from the Project Plan. If not done before, this is also where all benefits will be defined (or revised) and, wherever possible, put into measurable terms. This is needed for the Project Board's *Authorising a Project* (DP2) and also in readiness for the post-project review.

In *Updating a Project Business Case* (SB3) the Business Case is revised for each End Stage Report with information from the stage that is closing and the next stage's plan. This revision is a major input to the Project Board in its decision in *Authorising a Stage or Exception Plan* (DP3).

As part of *Examining Project Issues* (CS4) each Project Issue is reviewed for any impact that it might have on the Business Case.

At the end of a project the Business Case provides the agenda for much of the creation of the Post-Project Review Plan, submitted by the Project Manager as part of *Identifying Follow-on Actions* (CP2).

Hints and tips

It can be useful to hold a stakeholder workshop to help clarify the business objectives and impact of the project. Capturing input from stakeholders to inform the Business Case will help achieve greater commitment to the project.

Thought should be given to baselining benefit measures before the project is implemented so that subsequent measures can be compared to demonstrate that the project has delivered benefit(s).

14
ORGANISATION

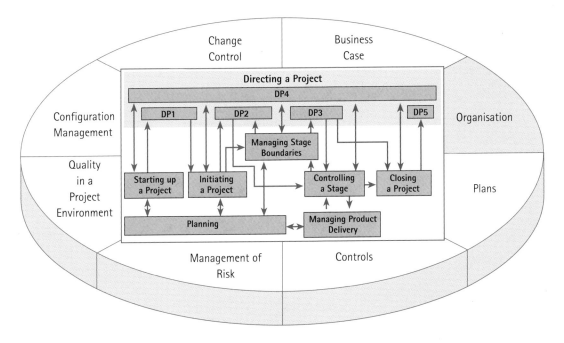

Figure 14.1 Organisation in the PRINCE2 template

14.1 Overview

The PRINCE2 project management structure is based on a customer/supplier environment. The structure assumes that there will be a customer who will specify the desired outcome, make use of the outcome and probably pay for the project and a (prime) supplier who will provide the resources and skills to create that outcome. This assumption has a bearing on how the project is organised.

The customer and supplier may be part of the same corporate body or may be independent of one another.

Establishing an effective organisational structure for the project is crucial to its success. Every project has need for direction, management, control and communication. PRINCE2 offers an approach that provides these elements and is sufficiently flexible to be mapped to any environment.

A project needs a different organisational structure from line management. It needs to be more flexible and is likely to require a broad base of skills for a comparatively short period of time. A project is normally cross functional, an involved partnership.

The project organisation may combine people who are working full time on the project with others who have to divide their time between the project and other duties. The Project Manager may have direct management control over some of the project staff, but may also have to direct staff who report to another management structure.

The management structure of those with a problem to be solved will very often be different from that of those providing the solution. They will have different priorities and different interests to protect, but in some way they must be united in the common aims of the project. The management level that will make the decisions and the commitments on behalf of their interests may be too busy to be involved on a day-to-day basis with the project. But projects need day-to-day management if they are to be successful.

14.1.1 Four layers

PRINCE2 separates the management of the project from the work required to develop the products and concentrates on the former.

A fundamental principle is that the project management structure has four layers, illustrated in Figure 14.2, which undertake:

- Corporate or programme management

- Direction of the project (Project Board)

- Day-to-day management of the project (Project Manager)

- Team management and product delivery (Team Managers).

The first of these instigates a project and defines overall constraints. The project management team, which comprises the other three layers, manages and implements the project.

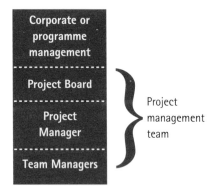

Figure 14.2 The four layers of management

14.1.2 Project management structure

PRINCE2 provides a structure for a project management team that supports:

- Roles for decision makers

- Management by exception for the decision makers

- Full- or part-time project management

- Controlled delegation of some day-to-day management responsibilities, where required, to Team Managers

•   Roles for the independent inspection of all aspects of project performance

•   Administrative support, as required, to the Project Manager and Team Managers

•   Agreement by all concerned on what the various roles and responsibilities are

•   Lines of communication between the project management team members.

The PRINCE2 project management structure (see Figure 14.3) consists of roles and responsibilities that bring together the various interests and skills involved in and required by the project. For the project to be successful, it is important to define these roles at the outset.

A project management structure is a temporary structure specifically designed to manage the project to its successful conclusion to meet the requirements defined in the Project Brief. The structure allows for channels of communication to decision-making forums and should be backed up by job descriptions that specify the responsibilities, goals, limits of authority, relationships, skills, knowledge and experience required for all roles in the project organisation.

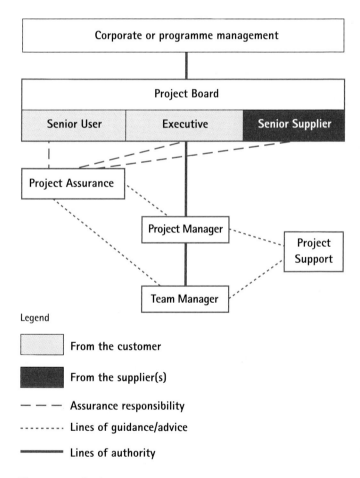

Figure 14.3 Project management structure

All the roles set out in Figure 14.3 have an accompanying role description.

In order to be flexible and meet the needs of different environments and different project sizes, PRINCE2 does not define management *jobs* to be allocated on a one-to-one basis to people. PRINCE2 defines *roles*, which might be allocated, shared, divided or combined according to the project's needs. Associated with this is the concept that some responsibilities for a role can be moved to another role or delegated, but they should not be dropped. If a responsibility is dropped, the risks of doing so must be addressed.

Some of the PRINCE2 roles cannot be shared or delegated if they are to be undertaken effectively. The Project Manager role cannot be shared, neither can the Project Manager or Project Board decision-making roles be delegated. Where individuals have been appointed to Project Assurance roles (see section 14.2.4) by the Project Board, the Project Board still retains accountability for these assurance actions.

Corporate cultures differ; PRINCE2 can be used whatever the culture or corporate organisation structure.

Hints and tips

Contractual and commercial arrangements will often influence the ideal project management organisation.

The project organisation structure should include links with the more permanent, functional or line management structures within both the customer and supplier communities.

14.1.3 Three project interests

Figure 14.4 represents the structure and composition of the Project Board. Three interests must be represented on the Project Board at all times.

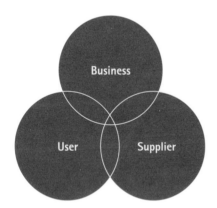

Figure 14.4 The three project interests

Business

The product(s) of the project should meet a business need. The project should give value for money. There should, therefore, be representation from the business viewpoint to ensure that these two prerequisites exist before commitment to the project is made and remain in existence throughout the project. PRINCE2 makes a distinction between the business interests and the requirements of those who will use the final product(s). The Executive role is defined to look after the business interests (representing the customer).

User

There will be an individual, group or groups for whom some or all of the following will apply:

- They will use the final product

- The product will achieve an objective for them

- They will use the end result to deliver benefits

- They will be impacted by the project outcome.

The user presence is needed to specify the desired outcome and ensure that the project delivers it. User management should therefore be represented on the Project Board. They will typically form part of the customer representation.

Supplier

The creation of the end product will need resources with certain skills. Representation is needed from the supplier who will provide the necessary skills. The project may need to use both in-house and external supplier teams to construct the final outcome.

14.1.4 The customer/supplier environment

PRINCE2 is defined in terms of a customer/supplier environment. There are many combinations of customer and supplier that may affect the organisation and control of the project, including:

- A customer with an in-house 'supplier'. Even here they may have separate budgets and therefore need separate 'Business Cases'

- Projects sponsored by a single customer versus those supporting multiple customers

- Those projects that are supplied by a single source versus those with multiple suppliers

- Situations that involve a consortium of equal customers and/or suppliers versus those that involve a 'legal' hierarchy of either:

  - projects supplied by an in-house source (part of the parent organisation)

  - those with a mixture of in-house and external suppliers.

The project's direction set by the Project Board must reflect the agreements and decisions of the three interests as defined in section 14.1.3. It may be difficult in certain business environments to contemplate having the supplier represented on the Project Board, but there must be a common platform for decisions that affect all parties. The Senior Supplier role is needed if the Project Board is to enable full decision making.

At times there may be questions of confidentiality or conflicts of interest. The customer representatives on the Project Board may not wish to discuss everything in front of the supplier and vice versa. There is nothing to prevent either party having private meetings to make internal decisions and/or discuss their position before meeting with the other party. The main objectives are full communication and agreed decisions by all three parties, and the Project Board composition including the Senior Supplier is a powerful aid to achieving these.

If there are problems in identifying an external contractor who could take the role of Senior Supplier (for example, the project involves purchasing and the supplier has not yet been identified) the customer's purchasing manager or contracts manager could take on the role. Whoever is in the Senior Supplier role must have the appropriate authority to deploy supplier resources.

In customer/supplier situations there will always be two Business Cases: the customer's and the supplier's. Unless otherwise stated, in this manual any references to the Business Case mean the customer's Business Case.

14.2 The PRINCE2 project management team

The following is a summary of the project management team. A full description of each role is provided in *Project management team roles*, Appendix B.

14.2.1 Project Board

The Project Board represents at managerial level the business, user and supplier interests of the project. The Project Board members must have authority because they are the decision makers and responsible for the commitment of resources to the project, such as personnel, cash and equipment.

The level of manager required to fill the roles will depend on such factors as the budget, scope and importance of the project. This will often result in people in senior management positions sitting on Project Boards. Their Project Board responsibilities will be in addition to their normal work, which makes it important that PRINCE2 offers them 'management by exception', keeping them regularly informed but only asking for joint decision making at key points in the project.

The Project Board consists of three roles:

- Executive
- Senior User
- Senior Supplier.

These roles should ideally be assigned to individuals who can stay with the project throughout its life.

The Project Board is appointed by corporate or programme management to provide overall direction and management of the project. The Project Board is accountable for the success of the project and has responsibility and authority for the project within the instructions (initially contained in the Project Mandate) set by corporate or programme management.

The Project Board approves all major plans and authorises any major deviation from agreed Stage Plans. It is the authority that signs off the completion of each stage as well as authorising the start of the next stage. It ensures that required resources are committed and arbitrates on any conflicts within the project or negotiates a solution to any problems between the project and any parties beyond the scope of the project. In addition, it approves the appointment and responsibilities of the Project Manager.

The Project Board is responsible for ensuring that the project remains on course to deliver products of the required quality to meet the Business Case defined in the Project Initiation Document. According to the size, complexity and risk of the project, the Project Board may decide to appoint specific additional resources to some or all of the Project Assurance roles. If no additional resources are appointed, assurance remains the responsibility of the Project Board members. Project Assurance is discussed in section 14.2.4.

The Project Board is the project's 'voice' to the outside world and is responsible for any publicity or other dissemination of information about the project.

The Project Board is not a democracy controlled by votes. The Executive is the key decision maker because he/she is ultimately responsible to the business. He/she is supported by the Senior User and Senior Supplier.

Executive

The Executive is ultimately accountable for the project, supported by the Senior User and Senior Supplier. The Executive is responsible for the following key aspects of the project:

Development and continuation of the project Business Case

Overseeing the development of a viable Business Case is part of ensuring that the aims of the planned change continue to be aligned with the business and establishing a firm basis for the project during its initiation and definition. The Executive should be responsible for securing the necessary investment for the business change.

The Executive has the responsibility throughout the project to ensure that the business benefits will be achieved.

Project organisation structure and plans

The Executive ensures that there is a coherent organisation structure and logical plan(s). This will involve being actively engaged with the work of project initiation.

Monitoring and control of progress

Monitoring and controlling the progress of the business change at a strategic level (at an operational level this is the responsibility of the Project Manager). The Project Manager is responsible for regular reports (Highlight Reports) to the Executive (and other Project Board members) on progress of the business change. There will be inevitable Project Issues that arise, requiring the Executive's advice, decision making and communication with senior stakeholders.

Problem referral

Referring serious problems upwards to top management as necessary, in a timely manner. Regular consultation will be required between those delivering the change and its stakeholders and sponsors. The Executive is responsible for ensuring the communication processes are effective and linkages are maintained between the project and the organisation's strategic direction.

Formal closure

Formally closing the project and ensuring that the lessons learned are documented. Closure requires formal sign-off by the Executive that the aims and objectives have been met and that lessons learned are documented and disseminated. Some benefits may already be delivered. However, the activities at closure include the planning of the post-project review when the entire benefits realisation process will be assessed.

Post-project review

Ensuring that the post-project review takes place, which has the purpose of finding out if the benefits, as stated in the Business Case, have been realised. The Executive is responsible for commissioning and chairing these reviews and ensuring that the relevant personnel are consulted and involved in the review process. The output is forwarded to the appropriate stakeholders.

Senior User

The Senior User is accountable for any products supplied by the user(s), such as making sure that requirements have been clearly and completely defined and that what is produced is fit for its purpose, as well as for monitoring that the solution will meet user needs.

The role represents the interests of all those who will use the final product(s) of the project, those for whom the product will achieve an objective, those who will use the product to deliver benefits or those who will be affected by the project. The Senior User role is responsible for:

- Providing user resources

- Ensuring that the project produces products that meet user requirements

- Ensuring that the products provide the expected user benefits.

The Senior User role may require more than one person to cover all the user interests. For the sake of effectiveness, the role should not be split between too many people. The *Hints and tips* section gives guidance on solutions to the problem of too many contenders for the Senior User role.

Senior Supplier

The Senior Supplier needs to achieve the results required by the Senior User. The Senior Supplier is accountable for the quality of all products delivered by the supplier(s). Part of this role is to ensure that proposals for designing and developing the products are realistic. The Senior Supplier aims to achieve the results required by the Senior User within the cost and time parameters for which the Executive is accountable. The role represents the interests of those designing, developing, facilitating, procuring and implementing. The Senior Supplier role must have the authority to commit or acquire the required supplier resources. The Senior Supplier has responsibility for the supplier's Business Case. In some environments the customer might share design authority for specialist solutions, or have a major say in it, along with the suppliers.

The Senior Supplier role may require more than one person to cover all the supplier interests.

For the sake of effectiveness, the role should not be split between too many people. The *Hints and tips* section gives guidance on solutions to the problem of too many contenders for the Senior Supplier role.

Hints and tips

Project Board members are normally very busy outside the project. There is a danger in larger projects that if they don't appoint people to the Project Assurance roles, the Project Assurance responsibilities will not get done. If the Project Assurance roles are not assigned, Project Board members must seriously consider how the work associated with these responsibilities will get done, when they will find the time and how well those responsibilities will be carried out.

Roles may be combined but never eliminated.

It is advisable to avoid combining the roles of Senior User and Senior Supplier if there would be a potential conflict of interest.

Project Boards are the major decision makers. It is important that the business, user and supplier are represented, because they all need to make commitments to the project.

Note: Customer specialists may also be involved in setting the approach and direction of the project, especially in cases where the project is part of a programme.

Both the customer and the supplier may wish to appoint their own Project Assurance roles. In particular, the customer may feel the need for assurance about the specialist aspects of the project, independent of the supplier.

The Senior Supplier may wish to appoint a business assurance role to monitor the supplier's Business Case.

A large Project Board can become unwieldy and inhibit the decision-making process. If there are too many candidates for a Project Board role, they should be encouraged to appoint a spokesperson to carry out that role. In particular, if there are too many wanting to share the Senior User role, a user committee can be formed with a chairperson. The chairperson represents them as Senior User, reports back to the committee and takes direction from it before Project Board meetings.

The involvement of multiple suppliers may necessitate more than a single Senior Supplier representative on the Project Board. Alternatively, if there are many suppliers wishing to share this role, consideration should be given to forming a supplier forum with a nominated chairperson to represent them on the Project Board.

Suppliers should not be in a position to overwhelm the business/user representatives by sheer weight of numbers.

Other interests can be invited to attend Project Board meetings to provide advice, etc. but not to take part in the decision making.

All Project Board members need training in Project Board procedures and responsibilities.

Where the project is one of a string, a decision is needed on who the user is. Is it an end user or is it the next project in the string?

Don't confuse the need for an organisation to manage the project with the need for a communication vehicle.

Project Board members should sign up to their agreed roles and responsibilities before taking the job on.

The authority levels required of Project Board members should match the needs of a project.

Where the project is part of a programme, the programme appoints the Project Board Executive and has the option of appointing the other Project Board members. Alternatively the Project Board Executive may be asked to select the other Project Board members. Where the latter is the case, the advice and approval of the programme should be sought.

There may sometimes be a lack of confidence between a programme and its projects. In order to ensure that a project that forms part of a programme maintains the focus required to fulfil the programme objectives, it will often be appropriate to have programme representation on the Project Board. This may be done either by appointing a programme representative into a Project Board role or by having a representative of programme management attend the Project Board meetings without taking a formal project role. In such cases project decisions that have a programme impact can be made more quickly. The programme representative is more likely to be able to make a decision on the spot, rather than the project having to wait until the programme's managers are consulted. This should lead to a reduction in delays or rework caused by having to wait for crucial decisions.

14.2.2 Project Manager

PRINCE2 provides for a single focus for day-to-day management of the project, namely the Project Manager, who has well-defined responsibilities and accountability. Figure 14.5 gives an idea of the many facets to the role of Project Manager. The Project Manager needs a project organisation structure that will take responsibility for or provide support in addressing these facets and provide support in performing some of the other facets.

The Project Manager is given the authority to run the project on a day-to-day basis on behalf of the Project Board within the constraints laid down by the board.

The Project Manager's prime responsibility is to ensure that the project produces the required products, to the required standard of quality and within the specified constraints of time and cost. The Project Manager is also responsible for the project delivering an outcome that is capable of achieving the benefits defined in the Project Initiation Document.

The Project Manager is responsible for the work of all the PRINCE2 processes except *Directing a Project* (DP) and the pre-project process *Appointing an Executive and a Project Manager* (SU1). The Project Manager would delegate responsibility for the process *Managing Product Delivery* (MP) to the Team Manager(s) in projects using this role. The Project Manager manages the Team Managers and Project Support and is responsible for liaison with Project Assurance and the Project Board.

In a customer/supplier environment the Project Manager will normally come from the customer organisation, but there will be projects where the Project Manager comes from the supplier. In this case, the customer may appoint a 'project director' or 'controller' to be its day-to-day liaison with the Project Manager.

Another example is the regular Project Assurance on behalf of the customer that the project is staying on track to produce an effective and usable solution. A third example is that of assuring on behalf of the Senior Supplier that the correct standards are available, are being used and are being used correctly in the development of the products. This might include Project Assurance that there is an audit trail of all the quality control work being done. Other examples would include security assurance and assurance that the project is staying within programme strategy and guidelines.

If a role is changed during the project, care must be taken to ensure continuity of the work being done by that role.

It is not advisable to combine any Project Assurance roles where there would be potential conflicts of interest.

Anyone appointed to a Project Assurance role should be independent of the Project Manager.

In customer/supplier projects, there may be a need for separate Project Assurance roles to monitor the respective interests of the customer and the supplier.

14.3 Project Support

The Project Manager may need administrative help. This may stem from the sheer volume of work to be done or the mandated use of certain tools where the Project Manager has insufficient expertise, such as in supporting the use of specific planning and control software or configuration management.

The appointment of one or more individuals to Project Support on a formal basis is optional. It is driven by the needs of the individual project and Project Manager. Project Support could be in the form of administrative services or providing advice and guidance to one or more related projects. Project Support can act as a repository for lessons learned and estimating metrics and be a central source of expertise in such things as specialist support tools and project management standards. In smaller projects the Project Support work may be shared between the Project Manager and team members.

One specific Project Support role that must be considered is Configuration Librarian. Depending on the project size and environment, there may be a need to appoint someone to carry out this role. If not, it defaults to the Project Manager together with any other unassigned Project Support functions. See *Configuration management*, Chapter 19 and *Project management team roles*, Appendix B for details of the work.

It is necessary to keep Project Support and Assurance responsibilities separate in order to maintain the independence of Project Assurance.

Hints and tips

The physical location of project staff can present problems if they are geographically remote from each other. If at all possible, choose people at a common location. Alternatively, ensure that suitable communications technology and training in its use is available.

Where the size of projects and number of staff warrant it, the common areas of support may be concentrated into a Project Support Office (PSO). This allows staff to be permanently allocated to this type of work and therefore to become highly skilled at the activities. A PSO can support all projects and set standards, such as the use of planning and control tools, risk management, reporting, change control and configuration management.

15
PLANS

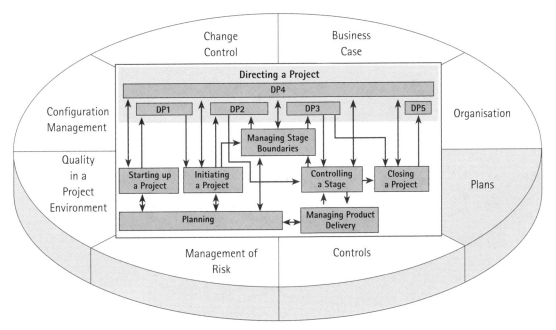

Figure 15.1 Plans in the PRINCE2 template

15.1 Benefits of planning

Effective planning identifies:

- Whether the targets are achievable

- The resources needed to achieve the targets within a time frame

- The activities needed to ensure that quality can be built into the products

- The problems and risks associated with trying to achieve the targets and stay within the constraints.

Other benefits of planning include:

- Avoiding muddle and ad hoc decisions

- Helping the management team to think ahead

- Providing a yardstick against which progress can be measured

- Communication, through the distribution of a plan to all concerned, of what is to be done, how it is to be done, the allocation of responsibilities and how progress will be monitored and controlled

- Gaining commitment from the contributors and recipients

- The provision of personal targets.

Planning is not a trivial exercise. It is vital to the success of the project. A plan must contain sufficient information and detail to confirm that the targets of the plan are achievable.

It is essential to allocate time for the planning activity. Every project should have an initiation stage, in which time is allocated to identify and agree the scope of the project and to plan it in terms of management, resourcing, products, activities, quality and control. Time should also be allocated for the refinement of the Business Case. The initiation stage may or may not be formal, depending on the nature and complexity of the project. In addition, during the initiation stage and towards the end of every stage in the project except the last one, time should be allowed for planning the next stage in detail.

Without effective planning, the outcome of complex projects cannot be predicted in terms of scope, quality, risk, timescale and cost. Those involved in providing resources cannot optimise their operations. Poorly planned projects cause frustration, waste and rework.

15.2 What is a plan?

A plan is a document, framed in accordance with a predefined scheme or method, describing how, when and by whom a specific target or set of targets is to be achieved. A plan is a design of how identified targets for products, timescales, costs and quality can be met.

Plans are the backbone of the management information system required for any project. It is important that plans are kept in line with the Business Case at all times.

A plan requires the approval and commitment of the relevant levels of the project management team, i.e. the Project Board and Project Manager for the Project Plan and all Stage Plans, the Project Manager and a Team Manager for a Team Plan.

15.3 What are the elements of a plan?

When asked to describe a plan, many people think only of some sort of bar chart showing timescales. A PRINCE2 plan is more comprehensive. It should contain the following elements (making maximum use of charts, tables and diagrams for clarity):

- The products to be produced

- The activities needed to create those products

- The activities needed to validate the quality of products

- The resources and time needed for all relevant activities (including project management and quality control) and any need for people with specific skills

- The dependencies between activities

- External dependencies for the delivery of information, products or services

- When activities will occur

- The points at which progress will be monitored and controlled

- Agreed tolerances.

Project and Stage Plans need to have the endorsement and approval of the Project Board. This endorsement should relate to the latest version and will emphasise the importance of the plan to the project. Plans should be presented as management reports, with key information documented in a way that the audience can understand, interpret and question. A Stage Plan might, therefore, be held in two forms: a summary plan suitable for presentation to the Project Board (the basis for authorisation) and the more detailed one used for day-to-day control of the stage.

The statement of activities and breakdown of resource requirements must be backed up by text that explains to the reader:

- What the plan covers (for example, a particular stage, the project, specific products)

- The planning approach taken

- The intended approach to implement the plan (for example, the number of stages, the size of Work Packages)

- How the plan will be monitored and controlled and by whom

- What management reports will be issued

- Any included constraints

- Risks contained in the plan and any countermeasures taken

- External dependencies

- Assumptions made, including any planning assumptions

- Tolerances to be applied

- The quality control methods and resources to be used (Stage and Team Plans).

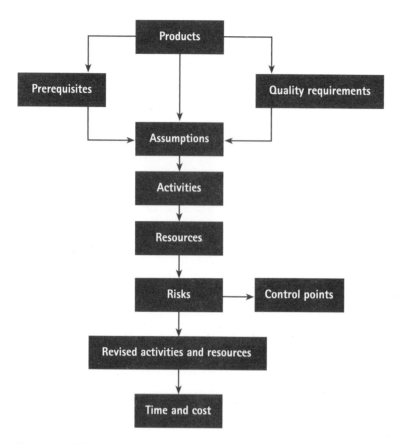

Figure 15.2 The elements of a plan

Figure 15.2 shows the elements of a plan and illustrates how it might be built up starting from a list of the products to be produced. Any prerequisites are identified, together with the quality requirements of the products. These three elements lead to consideration of what assumptions are being made. The next consideration is to define the activities required to generate the products.

The dependencies between the activities are identified and then resources to carry out the activities are added. Risks are then considered, followed by the addition of control points. The last two steps might add to the activities and resources required. Finally, the overall time and cost are calculated.

15.4 The PRINCE2 approach

The PRINCE2 planning structure allows for a plan to be broken down into lower-level plans containing more detail. But all these plan levels, as shown in Figure 15.3, have the same overall structure and are always matched back to the planned requirements, including quality and benefits, before approval.

15.5 Levels of plan

PRINCE2 proposes three levels of plan, the Project Plan, the Stage Plan and the Team Plan, to reflect the needs of the different levels of management involved in the project. Use of the Team Plans illustrated in Figure 15.3 will depend on the needs of the individual project. Team Plans are explained in more detail later in this chapter, but, briefly, a Stage Plan may be broken down into a number of Team Plans (where, for example, a number of teams may be contributing to the work) or a set of sub-contractors' Team Plans may be assembled into a Stage Plan.

Where a Stage or Project Plan is forecast to exceed its tolerances, an Exception Plan will often be put forward that will replace the plan. Where a Team Plan is forecast to exceed its tolerances, a similar procedure should be followed between Project and Team Managers.

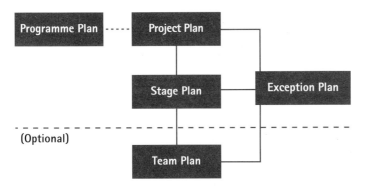

Figure 15.3 Plan levels in PRINCE2

The principal idea behind the levels is that the lower the level, the shorter the plan's time frame and the more detail it contains. The levels and number of plans required by a project will be determined according to its size and extent of risk exposure. Activity durations and resource requirements become more difficult to estimate accurately the further into the future they extend. Regardless of this problem, there is still a need to provide a provisional estimate of the duration and cost of the project as a whole in order to gain approval to proceed.

It is seldom desirable, or possible, to plan an entire project in detail at the start. The reasons for this include:

● Uncertainty about the detail of later elements of work

● A changing or uncertain environment

● Risk factors that could change the situation

● Difficulty in predicting resource availability

● Difficulty in predicting business conditions.

However, if the current elements of work are to be controlled, detailed plans containing firm estimates are needed for the realistically foreseeable future. For these reasons, plans need to be produced at different levels of scope and detail.

Where a project forms part of a programme, the Project Plan will exist within the context of the programme plan. The programme plan may place constraints that will need to be considered as the Project Plan is being prepared or reviewed. There needs to be uniformity between project and programme plans to ensure that the project is working to meet programme objectives and products, especially as the Project Plan should be revised to address Project Issues and risks as they develop.

15.5.1 Project Plan

An overview of the total project is needed. This is the Project Plan. It forms part of the Project Initiation Document. The Project Plan is a mandatory PRINCE2 plan. It provides the Business Case with project costs and is used by the Project Board as a basis against which to monitor actual costs and project progress stage by stage. The Project Plan identifies key products, resource requirements and the total costs. It also identifies major control points within the project, such as stage boundaries. The Project Quality Plan (see *Quality in a project environment*, Chapter 18) for the project is documented separately in another part of the Project Initiation Document.

Once the Project Initiation Document has been accepted, the initial Project Plan is baselined and shows the original plan on which the project was approved. As the project moves through its stages, subsequent versions of the Project Plan are produced and baselined at the end of each stage to reflect:

- Progress already made
- Any agreed changes in circumstances
- Any revised forecast of cost and/or duration of the total project.

The initial and current versions of the Project Plan form part of the information used by the Project Board to monitor how far the project is deviating from its original size and scope.

If the Project Plan is likely to exceed the agreed tolerance levels (see *Controls*, Chapter 16) the deviation must be referred upwards by the Project Board to get a decision on corrective action.

15.5.2 Stage Plan

For each stage identified in the Project Plan, a Stage Plan is required. Each Stage Plan is produced near the end of the previous stage. It will be the basis of the Project Manager's day-to-day control. For a very small project of only two stages (initiation plus the rest), the Project Manager may choose to incorporate the detail of the Stage Plans physically into the Project Plan.

The Stage Plan is similar to the Project Plan in content, but each element will be broken down to the level of detail required to be an adequate basis for day-to-day control by the Project Manager. The validity of assumptions and risk analyses should be reassessed for the stage, as these may have changed since they were previously considered or new risks may have arisen or become apparent when looking in more detail.

Each Stage Plan is finalised near the end of the previous stage as part of *Managing Stage Boundaries* (SB). This approach should give more confidence in the plan because:

- The Stage Plan is produced close to the time when the planned events will take place

- The Stage Plan is for a much shorter duration than the Project Plan

- After the first stage, the Stage Plan is developed with knowledge of the performance of earlier stages.

15.5.3 Team Plan

Team Plans are optional and the need for them will be determined by the size and complexity of the project and the number of people involved. They will often be needed if there are separate teams from different skill groups or from external contractors.

The plans are prepared in parallel with the Stage Plan, either by subdividing the activities of the stage into the tasks for which the teams are responsible or by taking the plans prepared by each of the teams and assembling a Stage Plan from them. The latter will be the case where there are large elements of sub-contracting of the work of the project. The Team Manager would create a Team Plan for input into *Managing Stage Boundaries* (SB) or revise an existing one as part of *Accepting a Work Package* (MP1). In both cases a Team Plan will require the approval of the Project Manager.

15.5.4 Stage and team quality plans

Stage and Team Plans should contain a quality plan which will identify the method(s) to be used to check the quality of each product created/updated during the activities covered by the plan and the resources to be used for the checks. The user and supplier Project Assurance roles have a key part to play here in:

- Identifying products of key interest to their role

- Specifying who should be involved in quality checking these products

- Specifying at what points in the product development quality checking should be done.

For example, for any quality reviews the names of the review chairperson and the reviewers will be given. The timing and resource effort will be shown in the graphic plan (typically a bar chart). The stage and team quality plans will not be separate documents, but an integral part of the relevant plans.

15.5.5 Exception Plan

When it is predicted that a plan will no longer finish within the agreed tolerances, an Exception Plan is normally produced to replace that plan. An Exception Plan is prepared at the same level of detail as the plan it replaces. An Exception Plan picks up from the current plan actuals and continues to the end of that plan. Most Exception Plans will be created to replace a Stage Plan, but a Team Plan or even the Project Plan may need to be replaced.

The format of an Exception Plan is given in *Product Description outlines*, Appendix A.

An Exception Plan to replace a Team Plan needs the approval of the Project Manager. If a Stage Plan is being replaced, this needs the approval of the Project Board. Replacement of a

Project Plan because of a deviation beyond project tolerances must be referred by the Project Board to corporate or programme management.

Hints and tips

When planning, it is easy to forget to add the resources needed to do impact assessment on change requests. Even if a change is subsequently rejected, the assessment will still consume time and effort, probably from the senior team members.

It is important to identify for which products the customer and supplier are responsible. An extra heading can be added to the Product Description to record this information.

Plans need to be at an appropriate level to facilitate control. Will the supplier's and customer's plans be written at the same level of detail?

Often the frequency of Highlight Reports is defined for the whole project in the Project Initiation Document, but the frequency can be varied for different stages. For example, the Project Board may request no Highlight Reports in the shorter initiation stage and a higher frequency for later stages.

A Highlight Report's purpose is to allow the Project Board to 'manage by exception' between end stage assessments. The Project Board is aware of the Stage Plan to which it is committed and of the tolerance margins that it agreed with the Project Manager. The Highlight Reports confirm that progress is being made within those tolerances. Early warning of any possible problems may be reported to the Project Board via the Highlight Report. The Project Board can react to any problems that are reported, as formally or informally as it feels is necessary.

The Project Board can request that copies of the Highlight Report are sent to other interested parties. This should be documented in the Communication Plan.

There is no requirement for the Project Manager to present the Highlight Report formally at a meeting but those with Project Assurance responsibilities may wish to review the content prior to its submission to the Project Board.

Product Description outlines, Appendix A contains a suggested outline for a Highlight Report.

Hints and tips

The Project Manager can use the Highlight Report to convey concern about items that are under the control of any member of the Project Board. As the report is provided to all members of the Project Board, any member whose commitment is the source of the concern will feel pressure from the other members to put the matter right.

The Senior User has part of the responsibility for monitoring project deliverables. This may be difficult to do where a remote supplier or third party is developing or procuring the product. Monitoring can be assisted by Checkpoint and Highlight Reports and by user involvement in checking the quality of such products.

16.4.10 Exception Report

An Exception Report is a warning from one level of project management to the next higher level that a serious problem exists that needs a decision, such as the Team, Stage or Project Plan will deviate outside its tolerance margins. It is a wise precaution for the Project Manager to document the report.

There are situations where it is the tolerance for the whole project that is at risk and not just that for the stage. For example, information may be found that shows that a major equipment expenditure, which is to be made much later in the project, will greatly exceed current expectations and take the project outside tolerance.

An Exception Report describes a forecast deviation, provides an analysis of both the exception and the options for the way forward and identifies the recommended option. There is a suggested content for the Exception Report in *Product Description outlines*, Appendix A. The Project Board considers an Exception Report as part of the sub-process *Giving Ad Hoc Direction* (DP4).

Where the Exception Report describes a forecast deviation from project tolerances the Executive must immediately communicate this to the corporate or programme management.

Where a Team Manager prepares an Exception Report it will be submitted to the Project Manager as a Project Issue and reviewed as part of *Examining Project Issues* (CS4).

Where the project is part of a programme, exception situations may occur because of changes or problems at the programme level. Examples would be a business change or the late delivery of an externally purchased product, which may impact the whole programme or just a single project. Changes to end dates or to the specification of products to be delivered by the project are likely to have a knock-on effect on the programme. To avoid duplication of effort and to save time, those exception situations likely to impact more than a single project within a programme should be co-ordinated at programme level.

16.4.11 End stage assessment

Part of the philosophy of breaking the project into stages is that the Project Board only commits to one stage at a time. At the end of each stage the Project Board takes a good look at the project to decide if it wishes to proceed to the next stage. This review is called an end stage assessment. According to such factors as project size, criticality and risk situation, the end stage assessment may be formal or informal.

However it is done, the end stage assessment is a mandatory control point at the end of each stage. The assessment approves the work to date and provides authority to proceed to the next stage. A stage should not be considered complete until it has received this formal approval.

The specific objectives of an end stage assessment are to:

- Review the project against its Business Case and ensure that the project is still viable
- Review the results of the stage against the Stage Plan
- Satisfy the Project Board about the quality of the products delivered
- Establish that the current stage has been completed satisfactorily
- Check whether any external event has changed the project's assumptions
- Perform a risk analysis and management review of the project and the next Stage Plan and incorporate the results into the next Stage Plan and Project Plan
- Review overall project status against the Project Plan (which may now have been revised)
- Review the next Stage Plan against the Project Plan
- Ensure that a complete and consistent baseline is established for the next stage
- Review the tolerances set for the next stage
- Ensure that the specialist aspects of the project are still sound
- Authorise the passage of the project into the next stage (if the Business Case continues to be viable).

The Project Board has the right to refuse to approve the next Stage Plan if it is unhappy with any of the aspects mentioned in this list. It can either ask the Project Manager to rethink the next Stage Plan, force closure of the project or refer the problem to corporate or programme management if the problem is beyond its remit.

16.4.12 End Stage Report

The End Stage Report is the vehicle through which the Project Manager informs the Project Board of the results of a stage. The Project Board can compare the results in terms of products, cost and time against the Stage Plan that it approved.

The End Stage Report contains all the information necessary to enable the Project Board to achieve the objectives described for an end stage assessment. It forms a record that can be audited at any time in the project, giving a summary of what happened in a stage, the state of the Project Plan, Business Case and risks.

16.4.13 Exception assessment

An exception assessment is held between the Project Board and Project Manager to approve an Exception Plan. If any of the Project Board's assurance responsibilities have been delegated, the people to whom assurance has been delegated would also participate. Its purpose is for the Project Manager to present an Exception Plan covering a revised Stage or Project Plan to the Project Board and obtain its approval for implementation of the plan. As with the end stage assessment, it may be formal or informal according to the size, criticality and risk of the project.

The format of an Exception Plan is given in *Product Description outlines*, Appendix A.

Every Exception Plan presented to the Project Board has an impact on the Business Case and risks. The recommended option will also have an impact on the same items. The Project Board must consider both sets of impact.

16.4.14 Daily Log

A Daily Log can help a Project Manager in controlling the project. It is normally a notebook whose pages consist of the items listed in the *Product Description outlines*, Appendix A.

These can be tailored to the Project Manager's own preferences or needs. Entries can be made at any time. One key time would be when the Project Manager reviews the stage status. Another way of getting into a regular habit of making entries would be to sit down at the end or beginning of a week. Consideration of all the stage documents may lead to entries in the Daily Log. Typical entries might be:

- Check with a risk owner on the current state of a risk

- Note what is on the critical path and check with the producer on the work status

- Note any products due for completion in the next few days and check their status

- Review the Quality Log for any checks that are late in being done

- Make a note to check on any outstanding Project Issue's impact analysis

- Make a note to follow up on any outstanding item on the last Highlight Report that should have caused action from one or more Project Board members

- See if action can be taken on activities that are slipping before the plan has to be modified

- Check on the status of tolerances.

Other entries may come from discussions with Team Managers, team members or Project Board members; these include phone calls to be made, Communication Plan changes, Work Packages to be adjusted, etc.

It is sensible for the Project Manager always to have the Daily Log at hand. Relying on memory is a recipe for disaster.

16.4.15 Lessons Learned Log

A Lessons Learned Log should be set up in *Setting up Project Files* (IP5). It should record any lessons, good or bad, that are learned as the project progresses. A suggested structure is given in *Product Description outlines*, Appendix A. It should cover both management and specialist matters. Its aims are to:

- Provide lessons and advice that can be used to improve future planning and performance
    - in a later stage of this project
    - in future projects
- Improve general company standards.

16.5 Controlled close

Before the Project Board allows the project to close (unless the project has been prematurely terminated), it has the control to ensure that:

- All the agreed products have been delivered and accepted

- Arrangements are in place, where appropriate, to support and maintain the product in its useful life

- Any useful statistics or lessons for later projects are passed to the relevant body

- A plan has been made to enable a check on the achievement of the benefits claimed in the project's Business Case.

At project closure the Project Board must confirm in writing (for the project management file) its acceptance that the project has been completed. If necessary, these statements can be qualified – for example, that the products have been delivered with minor deficiencies that can be rectified later.

The following information is generated at the close of the project, which leads to control actions by the Project Board.

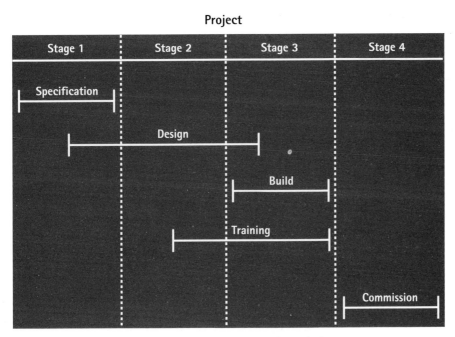

Figure 16.5 Products crossing management stage boundaries

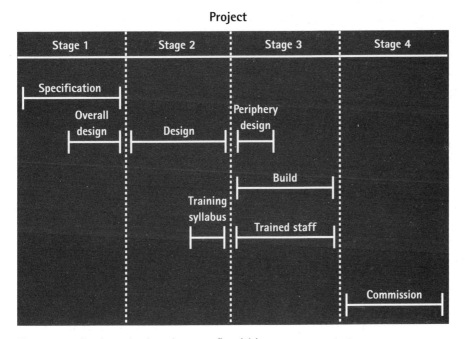

Figure 16.6 Products broken down to fit within management stages

16.6.2 How to define stages

The process of defining stages is fundamentally a process of balancing:

- How far ahead in the project it is sensible to plan
- Where the key decision points need to be on the project
- The amount of risk within a project
- Too many small stages versus too few big ones.

This will be a balance of the factors identified earlier and will be influenced by any Team Plans. However, the Project Manager will have to reconcile the Stage Plan and any relevant Team Plans. This is discussed in *Plans*, Chapter 15.

16.6.3 How to use stages

The primary use of stages is as a basis for dictating the timing of the stage boundary processes covered by *Managing Stage Boundaries* (SB) and by the associated *Authorising a Stage or Exception Plan* (DP3). These processes are used to make decisions regarding the continuation or otherwise of the project.

One element of this decision-making process is whether the stage that has just been completed has been completed successfully. This can be problematic to determine where the management stage ends partway through one or more elements of specialist work, since it can be difficult to establish whether the specialist work is under control. The PRINCE2 technique of *Product-based planning*, Chapter 22 is invaluable here, since by using it the Project Manager can identify the detailed products involved in any element of specialist work and can hence identify all the products that are due to be produced within the confines of any given management stage. This can then be used to assess completion or otherwise of the stage.

Stages can be very useful as a means of bringing Project Board control to risky projects. Stage breaks can be inserted at key points when risks to the project can be reviewed before major commitments of money or resources. Driving this will be *Planning a Project* (IP2).

17
MANAGEMENT OF RISK

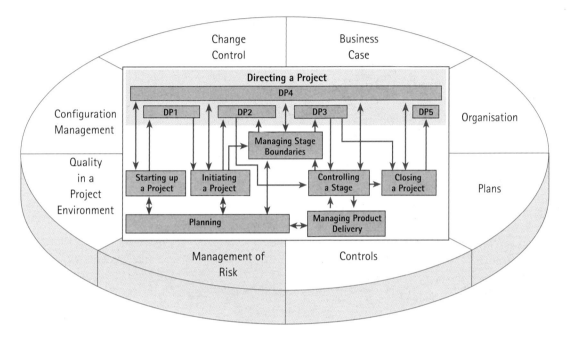

Figure 17.1 Management of risk in the PRINCE2 template

17.1 What is risk management?

Risk is a major factor to be considered during the management of any project. Project management must control and contain risks if a project is to stand a chance of being successful.

Risk can be defined as uncertainty of outcome (whether positive opportunity or negative threat). Some amount of risk taking is inevitable if the project is to achieve its objectives.

The task of risk management is to manage a project's exposure to risk (that is, the probability of specific risks occurring and the potential impact if they did occur). The aim is to manage that exposure by taking action to keep exposure to an acceptable level in a cost-effective way.

Risk management involves having:

- Access to reliable, up-to-date information about risks

- Decision-making processes supported by a framework of risk analysis and evaluation

- Processes in place to monitor risks

- The right balance of control in place to deal with those risks. (This is explained later in this chapter in section 17.2.1, Risk tolerance.)

Risk management at the project level focuses on keeping unwanted outcomes to an acceptable minimum. Decisions about risk management at this level form an important part of the Business Case. Where suppliers and/or partners are involved, it is important to gain a shared view of the risks and how they will be managed.

17.2 Risk principles

Projects bring about change and change incurs risk. Change is usually about moving forward and this often means the use of new methods or new technology. These aspects can increase the risks. There are some essential elements that need to be in place in a project if risk management is to be effective and innovation encouraged, i.e. that:

- The Project Board supports and promotes risk management, and understands and accepts the time and resource implications of any countermeasures

- Risk management policies and the benefits of effective risk management are clearly communicated to all staff

- A consistent approach to risk management is fully embedded in the project management processes

- Management of risks is an essential contribution to the achievement of business objectives

- Risks through working with programmes and other projects are assessed and managed

- There is a clear structure to the risk process so that each element or level of risk identification fits into an overall structure

- Where the project is part of a programme, changes in the state of any project risks that are also identified as programme risks must be flagged to programme management or the designated risk management function in the programme.

17.2.1 Risk tolerance

Another name for this is 'risk appetite'. Before determining what to do about risks, the Project Board and Project Manager must consider the amount of risk they are prepared to tolerate. This will vary according to the perceived importance of particular risks. For example, the view of financial risks and how much the project team is prepared to put at risk will depend on a number of variables, such as budgets, the effect on other parts of the programme or organisation, or additional risks such as political embarrassment. A project team may be prepared to take comparatively large risks in some areas and none at all in others, such as risks to health and safety. Risk tolerance can be related to other tolerance parameters – for example, risk to completion within timescale and/or cost and to achieving product quality and project scope within the boundaries of the Business Case.

Perceptions of risk tolerance have to be considered in detail to establish the optimum balance of a risk occurring against the costs and value for money of limiting that risk. The organisation's overall tolerance of exposure to risk must also be considered as well as a view of individual risks.

17.2.2 Risk responsibilities

The management of risk is one of the most important parts of the job done by the Project Board and the Project Manager. The Project Manager is responsible for ensuring that risks are identified, recorded and regularly reviewed. The Project Board has four responsibilities:

- Notifying the Project Manager of any external risk exposure to the project

- Making decisions on the Project Manager's recommended reactions to risk

- Striking a balance between the level of risk and the potential benefits that the project may achieve

- Notifying corporate or programme management of any risks that affect the project's ability to meet corporate or programme objectives.

The Project Manager modifies plans to include agreed actions to avoid or reduce the impact of risks.

Risk analysis requires input from the management of the organisation. The organisation's management, in turn, is kept informed by the Project Board of the risk analysis results.

Communication is particularly important between the project and programme levels within the organisation. Where the project is part of a programme, the management of risk procedures used by the project must be consistent and compatible with those of the programme unless there are valid reasons not to do so. Where a risk is uncovered in the programme, any affected projects should be involved in the analysis of that risk. Similarly, project risk evaluation should include staff from the programme.

Project risks that threaten programme milestones or objectives must be escalated to programme management.

17.2.3 Risk ownership

An 'owner' should be identified for each risk; this should be the person best situated to keep an eye on it. The Project Manager will normally suggest the 'owner' and the Project Board should make the decision. Project Board members may be appointed 'owners' of risks, particularly risks from sources external to the project. Allocating ownership of the risk process as a whole and the various components is fundamental from the outset. When describing who owns the various elements of risk, it is important to identify who owns the following:

- The risk framework in totality

- Setting risk policy and the project team's willingness to take risk

- Different elements of the risk process, such as identifying threats, through to producing risk response and reporting

- Implementation of the actual measures taken in response to the risks

- Interdependent risks that cross organisational boundaries, whether they be related to business processes, IT systems or other projects.

Overall ownership of the risk management process is likely to lie with the Executive.

However, the Executive will need to ensure that the people who own the various parts of the risk process are clearly defined, documented and agreed, so that they understand their various roles, responsibilities and ultimate accountability with regard to the management of risk.

Normally the risk 'owner' will have the responsibility of monitoring each risk that they own. If the owner is a Project Board member, the actual task of monitoring may be delegated, but the responsibility stays with the owner. The Executive, for example, has ultimate responsibility for monitoring any risks or opportunities facing the Business Case, particularly any external ones, such as changes in company policy. The Project Manager has the job of keeping a watching brief over all risks and checking that the defined actions, including monitoring, are taking place and are having the desired effect.

Risks owned at team level should be reported on in the Checkpoint Reports. The Project Manager includes some form of report on any significant risks in the Highlight Report. The End Stage Report also summarises the risk status.

Where a risk (threat or opportunity) actually occurs, the Project Manager will either instigate contingency action, or deal with the Project Issue under *Change control*, Chapter 20.

17.3 The risk management cycle

Every project is subject to constant change in its business and wider environment. The risk environment is constantly changing too. The project's priorities and relative importance of risks will shift and change. Assumptions about risk have to be regularly revisited and reconsidered; at a minimum, this should occur at each end stage assessment.

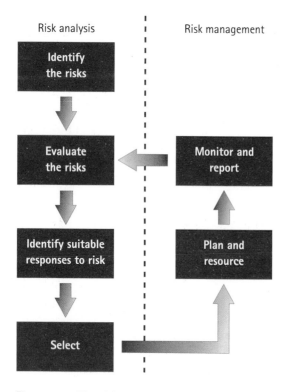

Figure 17.2 The risk management cycle

Figure 17.2 shows the main steps through the risk management cycle. The steps are described in more detail below.

17.3.1 Risk analysis

Identify the risks

This step identifies the potential risks (or opportunities) facing the project. *Risk categories*, Appendix C lists various categories of risk that make a useful start point for risk identification. It is important not to judge the likelihood of a risk at this early time. This is done in a controlled manner in a later step. Attempting to form judgements while identifying a list of potential risks may lead to hurried and incorrect decisions to exclude some risks.

Once identified, risks are all entered in the Risk Log. This contains details of all risks, their assessment, owners and status. A suggested list of contents is given in *Product Description outlines*, Appendix A. The Risk Log is a control tool for the Project Manager, providing a quick reference to the key risks facing the project, what monitoring activities should be taking place and by whom. Reference to it can lead to entries in the Project Manager's Daily Log to check on the status of a risk or associated activities.

Evaluate the risks

Risk evaluation is concerned with assessing probability and impact of individual risks, taking into account any interdependencies or other factors outside the immediate scope under investigation:

- Probability is the evaluated likelihood of a particular outcome actually happening (including a consideration of the frequency with which the outcome may arise). For example, major damage to a building is relatively unlikely to happen, but would have enormous impact on business continuity. Conversely, occasional personal computer system failure is fairly likely to happen, but would not usually have a major impact on the business
- Impact is the evaluated effect or result of a particular outcome actually happening
- Impact should ideally be considered under the elements of:
  - time
  - cost
  - quality
  - scope
  - benefit
  - people/resources.

Some risks, such as financial risk, can be evaluated in numerical terms. Others, such as adverse publicity, can only be evaluated in subjective ways. There is a need for some framework for categorising risks, for example, high, medium and low.

When considering a risk's probability, another aspect is when the risk might occur. Some risks will be predicted to be further away in time than others and so attention can be focused on the more immediate ones. This prediction is called the risk's proximity. The proximity of each risk should be included in the Risk Log.

The results of the risk evaluation activities are documented in the Risk Log. If the project is part of a programme, project risks should be examined for any impact on the programme (and vice versa). Where any cross-impact is found, the risk should be added to the other Risk Log.

Identify suitable responses to risk

Suitable responses to risk break into broadly five types, as shown in Table 17.1.

Table 17.1 Suitable responses to risk

Prevention	Terminate the risk – by doing things differently and thus removing the risk, where it is feasible to do so. Countermeasures are put in place that either stop the threat or problem from occurring or prevent it having any impact on the project or business
Reduction	Treat the risk – take action to control it in some way where the actions either reduce the likelihood of the risk developing or limit the impact on the project to acceptable levels
Transference	This is a specialist form of risk reduction where the management of the risk is passed to a third party via, for instance, an insurance policy or penalty clause, such that the impact of the risk is no longer an issue for the health of the project. Not all risks can be transferred in this way
Acceptance	Tolerate the risk – perhaps because nothing can be done at a reasonable cost to mitigate it or the likelihood and impact of the risk occurring are at an acceptable level
Contingency	These are actions planned and organised to come into force as and when the risk occurs

Any given risk could have appropriate actions in any or all these categories. There may be no cost-effective actions available to deal with a risk, in which case the risk must be accepted or the justification for the project revisited (to review whether the project is too risky), possibly resulting in the termination of the project.

Select

The risk response process should involve identifying and evaluating a range of options for treating risks, and preparing and implementing risk management plans. It is important that the control action put in place is proportional to the risk. Every control has an associated cost. The control action must offer value for money in relation to the risk that it is controlling.

Figure 17.3 Balancing the risk

Selection of the risk actions to take is a balance between a number of things. For each possible action it is, first, a question of balancing the cost of taking that action against the likelihood and impact of allowing the risk to occur, as shown in Figure 17.3. As an example, if a charity carnival is arranged, is it worth taking out insurance for £3,000 guaranteeing £6,000 if the carnival is rained off? Or, since the carnival date is in summer, do we take the risk and not spend the insurance money?

But the selection is usually more complex than that. As Figure 17.4 shows, there are many elements to be taken into consideration.

There may be several possible risk actions, each with different effects. The choice may be one of these options or a combination of two or more. We then have to consider the impact of (a) the risk occurring and (b) the risk action on:

● The Team, Stage and/or Project Plans

● The business or programme

● The Business Case

● Other parts of the project.

The consideration has to be done in the light of the risk tolerances.

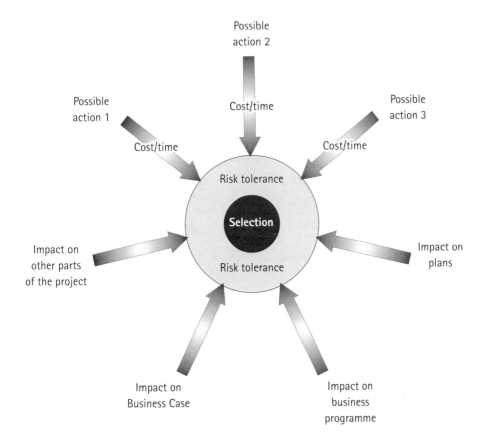

Figure 17.4 Risk action selection

17.3.2 Risk management

Plan and resource

Having made the selection, the implementation of the selected actions will need planning and resourcing and is likely to include plan changes and new or modified Work Packages:

- *Planning*, which, for the countermeasure actions itemised during the risk evaluation activities, consists of:
  - identifying the quantity and type of resources required to carry out the actions
  - developing a detailed plan of action; this will be included in Project and Stage Plans either as additional activities or as a contingency plan
  - confirming the desirability of carrying out the actions identified during risk evaluation in light of any additional information gained
  - obtaining management approval along with all the other aspects of the plans being produced
- *Resourcing*, which will identify and assign the actual resources to be used to conduct the work involved in carrying through the actions
  - these assignments will be shown in Project and Stage Plans
  - note that the resources required for the prevention, reduction and transference actions will have to be funded from the project budget since they are actions that we are committed to carrying out
  - contingency actions will normally be funded from a contingency budget.

Monitor and report

There must be mechanisms in place for monitoring and reporting on the actions selected to address risks.

Some of the actions may have only been to monitor the identified risk for signs of a change in its status. Monitoring, however, may consist of:

- Checking that execution of the planned actions is having the desired effect
- Watching for the early warning signs that a risk is developing
- Modelling trends, predicting potential risks or opportunities
- Checking that the overall management of risk is being applied effectively.

In the event that monitoring indicates that the action is not having the desired effect or the risk tolerance may be exceeded then an Exception Report should be generated.

17.4 Risk profile

This is a simple mechanism to increase visibility of risks and assist management decision making. It is a graphical representation of information normally found in existing Risk Logs.

It is only one possible representation of a project's risk status. The Project Board may choose to have an easy-to-read diagram, as shown in Figure 17.5 for example, included in the Highlight Report.

The profile shows risks, using the risk identifier, in terms of probability and impact with the effects of planned countermeasures taken into account. The Project Manager would update this matrix in line with the Risk Log on a regular basis. In the example, we can see that risk 5 is currently considered to be of high probability and high impact. In particular, any risk shown above and to the right of the 'risk tolerance line' (the thick black line) should be referred upwards. This line is set for the project by agreement between the Executive and Project Manager.

As risks are reviewed, any changes to their impact or probability which cause them to move above and to the right of the 'risk tolerance line' need to be considered carefully and referred upwards for a management decision on the action to take.

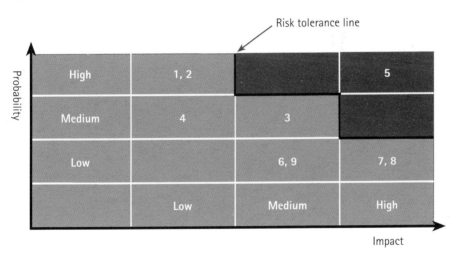

Figure 17.5 Summary risk profile

17.5 Budgeting for risk management

A project needs to allocate the appropriate budget, time and resources to risk management. The risk process must be embedded in the project environment, rather than being tacked on as an afterthought. The cost of carrying out risk management and the level of commitment and time, such as contingency plans, risk avoidance or reduction, need to be recognised and agreed. While the budget may be allocated to actions relating to risk treatment, there is often a failure to provide sufficient budget to the earlier parts of the process, such as risk assessment, which can require a diverse range of skills, tools and techniques. Experience has shown that allocating the correct budget to the risk management process early on will pay dividends later.

17.6 Mapping the management of risk to the PRINCE2 processes

At key points in a project, management of risk should be carried out (Figure 17.6).

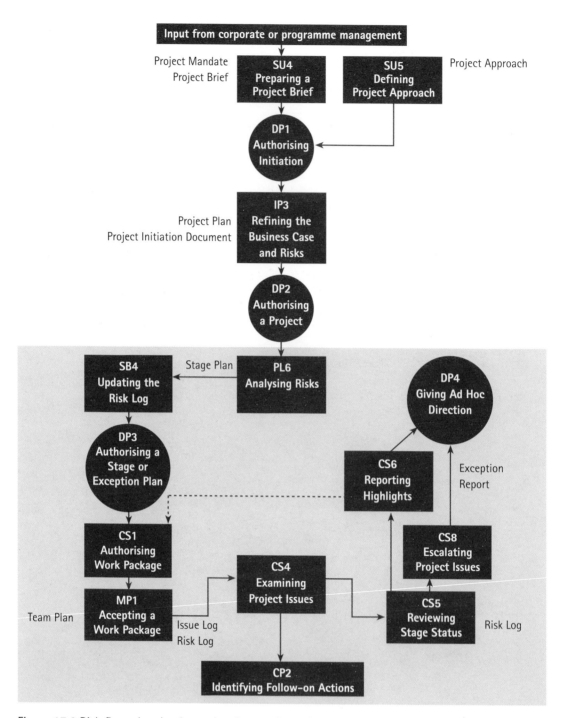

Figure 17.6 Risk flow, showing key points in a project when management is necessary

17.6.1 Preparing a Project Brief (SU4)

The Risk Log needs to be created by this time. A suggested structure for this is given in *Product Description outlines*, Appendix A. The Project Mandate may have referred to a number of risks facing the potential project. These may be such risks as competitor action, impending or mooted legislation, company policy changes, staff reorganisation or cash-flow problems. Certainly, the preparation of the Project Brief should give rise to an early study of such risks.

Creation of the Project Approach (see *Defining Project Approach* (SU5)) may also have introduced some extra risks.

17.6.2 Authorising Initiation (DP1)

This is the first formal milestone when the Project Board can examine the Risk Log as part of deciding whether project initiation can be justified. Pragmatically, the Project Manager should have discussed informally with board members any known risks that seem to threaten the project viability.

17.6.3 Refining the Business Case and Risks (IP3)

The Project Manager examines risks again as part of preparing the Project Initiation Document. At this time the Project Plan will be created and this may identify a number of risks, such as unknown performance of resources, contractor ability and any assumptions being made in the plan. New risks may also come to light as a result of adding detail to the Project Brief. At the same time, all existing risks are reviewed for any new information or change in their circumstances.

17.6.4 Authorising a Project (DP2)

The Project Board now has an updated Risk Log to examine as part of its decision on whether to go ahead with the project. As a result of refining the Business Case, a number of risks may have been identified. Very often the 'owners' of these risks will be members of the Project Board and they should confirm their ownership and the actions required of them.

17.6.5 Analysing Risks (PL6)

Each time a plan is produced, elements of the plan may identify new risks, modify existing ones or eliminate others. No plan should be put forward for approval before its risk content has been analysed. This analysis may lead to the plan being modified in order to take the appropriate risk action(s). The Risk Log should be updated with all such details.

17.6.6 Updating the Risk Log (SB4)

As part of the preparation for a new stage, the Project Manager updates the Risk Log with any changes to existing risks.

17.6.7 Authorising a Stage or Exception Plan (DP3)

Before authorising a plan, the Project Board has the opportunity to study the risk situation as part of its judgement of the continuing viability of the project.

17.6.8 Authorising Work Package (CS1)

Negotiation with the Team Manager or team member may identify new risks or change old ones. It may require the Project Manager to go back and amend some part of the original

Work Package or change the Stage Plan. Examples here are the assignee deciding to use new technology or needing to find special/rare resources.

17.6.9 Accepting a Work Package (MP1)

This is the point when the Team Manager produces a Team Plan to ensure that the products of the Work Package can be delivered within the constraints of the agreed Work Package. Like any other plan, it may contain new risks or modify existing ones.

17.6.10 Examining Project Issues (CS4)

Assessment of a new Project Issue may throw up a risk situation. For example, a proposed change may produce a risk of pushing the stage or project beyond its tolerance margins.

17.6.11 Reviewing Stage Status (CS5)

This brings together the Stage Plan with its latest actual figures, the Project Plan, the Business Case, open Project Issues, the tolerance status and the Risk Log. The Project Manager (in conjunction with the Project Assurance roles) looks for risk situation changes as well as any other warning signs.

17.6.12 Escalating Project Issues (CS8)

As well as Project Issues, a risk change may cause the Project Manager to raise an Exception Report to the Project Board.

17.6.13 Reporting Highlights (CS6)

As part of this task, the Project Manager may take the opportunity to raise any risk matters with the Project Board. Examples here would be notifying the board of any risks that are no longer relevant, warning about new risks and reminders about risks that board members should be keeping an eye on. The suggested format of a Highlight Report is included in *Product Description outlines*, Appendix A.

17.6.14 Giving Ad Hoc Direction (DP4)

The Project Manager advises the Project Board of exception situations via the Exception Report. The Project Board has the opportunity to react with advice or a decision – for example, bringing the project to a premature close, requesting an Exception Plan or removing the problem. The Project Board may also instigate ad hoc advice on the basis of information given to it from corporate or programme management or another external source.

During risk analysis the Project Manager will discuss the countermeasures with the Project Board and obtain its decision through this sub-process.

17.6.15 Identifying Follow-on Actions (CP2)

At the end of the project a number of risks may have been identified that will affect the product in its operational life. These should be transferred to the Follow-on Action Recommendations for the information of those who will support the product after the project.

17.7 Interdependencies

Risks may have additional factors relating to them that increase the complexity of assessing a project's overall exposure to risk. These include interdependencies. It is essential to understand the interdependencies of risks and how they can compound each other. For example, a skills shortage combined with serious technical problems and a requirement to bring the delivery date forward are common examples of risk compounding. Interdependencies can occur at all levels and across different levels.

A project may have interdependencies with other projects. A project may be dependent upon a supplier delivering products or services that have a further interdependency upon another internal project delivering its objectives and so on in the supply chain. These need to be explicitly identified and assessed as part of the process of risk management. Interdependencies often cross different boundaries, such as ownership, funding, decision making, organisational or geographical boundaries. You must be able to assess risk and communicate across these boundaries.

17.8 Further risk management considerations

The relationship between benefit and delivery risks

Often the risk management process is focused primarily on delivery rather than benefit. Changes to delivery dates, costs, quality, etc. are not related back to the benefits. The drive to deliver may continue long after the potential benefits have been significantly reduced or lost. A common cause of this is that the owners of benefit objectives are not the same as the owners of delivery. Decisions taken with regard to delivery must be related back to benefit and vice versa.

Internal versus external risks

Much is made of the difference between internal and external risks. The major differences, however, relate to the ability to apply the risk process to them. Internal risks can be just as difficult to identify, assess and evaluate as external risks and thus be just as complex to manage. The same broad principles of risk management apply to both.

Hints and tips

The cost of setting up a management of risk process for a project depends on the technical, political and organisational complexity involved. There are some general guidelines that can be applied, however. Planners for projects should expect to spend 1–3 per cent of their budget on an initial risk management effort and an additional 2 per cent on monitoring and updating this throughout the development life cycle.

Checklist on assignment of risk ownership:

- Have owners been allocated to all the various parts of the complete risk process and the full scope of the risks being catered for? For example, suppliers may be tasked with ownership of assessing and evaluating risk as part of their contracts

- Are the various roles and responsibilities associated with ownership well defined?

- Do the individuals who have been allocated ownership actually have the authority in practice to fulfil their responsibilities?

- Have the various roles and responsibilities been communicated and understood?

- Are the nominated owners appropriate?

- In the event of a change, can ownership be quickly and effectively reallocated?

- Are the differences between benefit and delivery risks clearly understood and, if required, do they have different owners?

The Project Manager's Daily Log can be very useful in monitoring risks. Entries can be made in it for the Project Manager to check on the status of any risks where he/she is the owner. Other entries can be made to remind the Project Manager to check that other owners are monitoring and controlling their risks and feeding the information back.

Where the project is part of a programme:

- Programme management is responsible for ensuring the management of those risks with interdependencies between projects and programme

- Where appropriate, the programme should take part in the risk management activities at the project level. This can normally be done by attendance at end stage assessments by either a member of programme management or a designated risk management function

- Risks are frequently common across projects and would benefit from being centralised at programme level. The cost of corrective action can be reduced if it is planned, agreed and actioned only once. Also, problems can result from an inconsistent approach being taken by projects.

18
QUALITY IN A PROJECT ENVIRONMENT

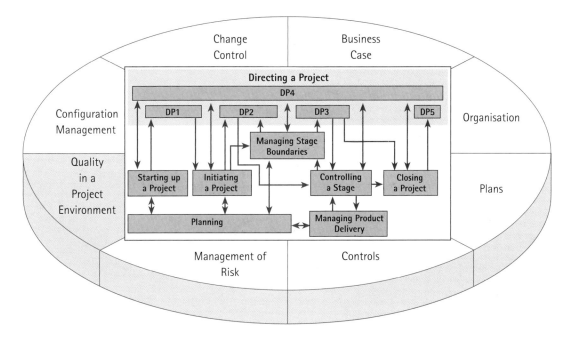

Figure 18.1 Quality in the PRINCE2 template

18.1 Purpose

The purpose of this chapter is to outline the main elements of quality as they apply to a project and to put project quality in context with ISO (International Organisation for Standards) quality standards.

18.2 What is quality?

Within projects, quality is a question of identifying what it is about the project's products or services that makes them fit for their purpose of satisfying stated needs. Projects should not rely on implied needs. These lead to uncertainty and, as such, are of little use.

18.3 Quality management

Quality management is the process of ensuring that the quality expected by the customer is achieved. It encompasses all the project management activities that determine and implement the Project Quality Plan. The various elements of an organisation's quality management interrelate and are as follows:

- A *quality system*, which has an organisation structure, procedures and processes to implement quality management. Both the customer and the supplier may have quality systems. The project may have to use one of these systems or an agreed mixture of both. PRINCE2 itself will typically form part of a corporate or programme quality system where it has been adopted as a corporate or programme standard

- *Quality assurance*, which creates and maintains the quality system and monitors its application to ensure that the quality system is operated and is effective in achieving an end product that meets quality and customer requirements. A quality assurance function should be separate from and independent of the organisation's project and operational activities to monitor use of the quality system across all projects within the corporate body. If such an independent body does not exist, the Project Assurance function will assume the quality assurance role within the project

- *Quality planning*, which establishes the objectives and requirements for quality and lays out the activities for the application of the quality system. In the Project Initiation Document the quality methods for the whole project are defined in the Project Quality Plan. It is important that the customer's quality expectations are understood and documented prior to project commencement. This is done in *Starting up a Project* (SU). Each Stage Plan specifies in detail the required quality activities and resources, with the detailed quality criteria shown in the Product Descriptions. Product Descriptions define the required quality criteria for a product and the quality control method to be used to check for the existence of that quality. The Product Description may need to be updated if a change to the product is agreed. Once approved, a Product Description should not be changed without passing through change control

- *Quality control*, which is the means of ensuring that products meet the quality criteria specified for them. Quality control is about examining products to determine that they meet requirements. Quality reviews are the primary PRINCE2 technique in making project quality work and are fully described in *Quality review technique*, Chapter 24.

18.4 The quality path

The path to quality in PRINCE2 is shown in Figure 18.2. Each element in this figure is explained in the following sub-sections, with cross-references to the areas of PRINCE2 that relate to it. Figure 18.3 shows an alternative representation of this.

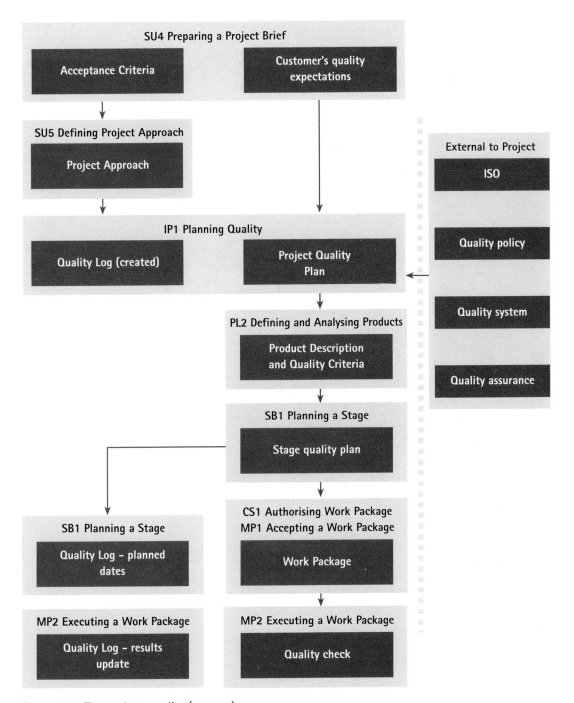

Figure 18.2 The path to quality (process)

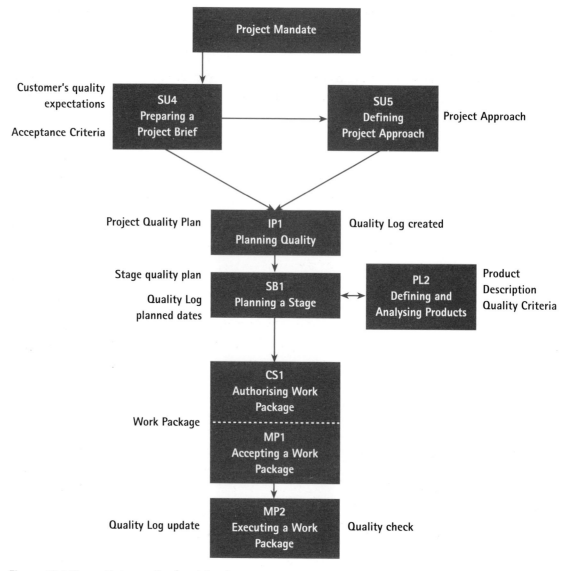

Figure 18.3 The path to quality (workflow)

18.4.1 Elements of the quality path

In PRINCE2, quality considerations begin with discovering what the Acceptance Criteria and customer's quality expectations are. This should be done in the sub-process *Preparing a Project Brief* (SU4). No realistic plan can be made to provide the customer with a quality product until both customer and supplier understand and agree what that quality should be. The customer and supplier need a common understanding of the link between quality, cost and time and must balance these while ensuring that the end product is fit for purpose and built within the other constraints.

Customer's quality expectations

The colloquial use of the word 'quality' implies 'high quality', i.e. the use of the best materials, expert craftsmanship, inspection at all points of the product's development, and thorough testing beyond all its expected limits, but this may not be the case. All products do not have

problem may be found during quality control that requires a lot of time and/or resource to fix. It may even be decided, because of time constraints, to approve a product that contains an error. In both these cases the error may be accepted as a concession. This will be raised as a Project Issue (as an Off-Specification), so that a record exists and the error will not be overlooked.

If a Project Issue requires changes to one or more products, the relevant Product Descriptions should be checked to see if they also need changing.

18.4.3 What is special about quality in the project environment?

It is very difficult, if not impossible, to achieve the business benefits of a product if that product does not meet the customer's quality expectations.

By its nature, a project is a temporary environment created for a particular purpose. As such, any required quality management for the project may have to be created specifically for that project if the organisation does not already have a quality system in place.

18.5 Making project quality work

Project quality planning should cover the following aspects to ensure that the project delivers to an acceptable level of quality:

- How each product will be tested against its quality criteria

- When each product will be tested against its quality criteria

- By whom each product will be tested against its quality criteria

- How acceptance will be notified.

The first aspect is actioned in *Planning Quality* (IP1) at the outset of the project, during *Initiating a Project*. The next two aspects are actioned in the relevant Stage Plans, created in *Planning a Stage* (SB1).

Quality is achieved by a combination of actions. The quality criteria for all levels of product are stated in measurable terms in the Product Descriptions (this is described in *Product-based planning*, Chapter 22). The process of producing the products and services is controlled via *Authorising Work Package* (CS1) and *Assessing Progress* (CS2).

The final aspect is the process of using all the quality checking techniques defined in the quality system. These split largely into two groups:

- Objective methods, where, after applying them, there is a largely definitive 'yes' or 'no' answer as to whether the product is 'to quality'. Examples of these methods are the use of gauges and meters, testing and checklists

- Subjective methods, where the criteria involve either judgement or opinion, such as user friendliness, conformance to business strategy and market acceptability. To control the process of checking conformance to quality in these areas, the quality review technique is available.

Hints and tips

It is almost always possible to define objectively measurable criteria. But it is sometimes not worth it – that is, not cost or time effective.

The Daily Log can be used by either the Project Manager or the Team Manager to note down a check that needs to be made about quality, such as finding out why a planned quality check has not been done (or not recorded in the Quality Log), why so many errors were discovered in a quality check and so on.

Customers and suppliers may have different quality standards. It is important to ensure that appropriate measures are agreed with/between all parties.

19

CONFIGURATION MANAGEMENT

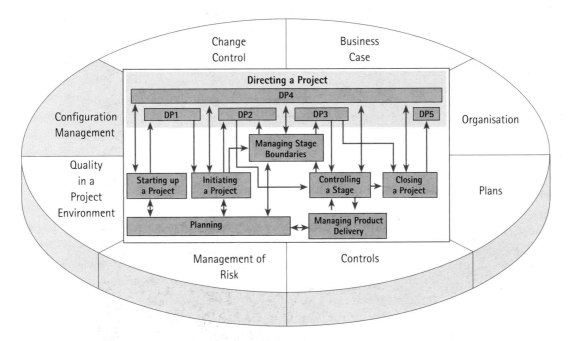

Figure 19.1 Configuration management in the PRINCE2 template

19.1 Purpose

No organisation can be fully efficient or effective unless it manages its assets, particularly if the assets are vital to the running of the organisation's business. The assets of the project are the products that it develops and these also have to be managed. The name for the combined set of these assets is a configuration. The configuration of the final outcome of a project is the sum total of its products.

Within the context of project management, the purpose of configuration management is to identify, track and protect the project's products.

19.2 Definition

Configuration management may be thought of as asset or product control. It is a discipline that gives precise control over the project's products by allowing management to:

- Specify the versions of products in use and in existence and hold information on:

  - their status (for example, in live use, archived, ready for quality checking)

- who owns each product (the individual with prime responsibility for it)
- the relationships between products

- Maintain up-to-date records containing these pieces of information

- Control changes to the products by ensuring that changes are made only with the agreement of appropriately named authorities

- Audit the records to ensure that they contain the authorised products and only these products.

The construction of a car is a good example of the need for configuration management. What components have to be brought together in order to assemble this version of the car? What about that recent change to the fascia – and the redesigned windscreen wipers? How can the assemblers be sure that they have the correct components? The answer is: from the records held by configuration management. If a replacement window winder for a five-year old model is needed, the car's serial number in conjunction with the records kept by configuration management will ensure that the right one is supplied.

From this example it can be seen that configuration management is needed throughout a product's life and will need to continue beyond the life of the project that created it. The creation of the product in a project is only part of the need. Within a project the job of configuration management is to provide:

- The mechanisms for managing, tracking and keeping control of all the project's products. It keeps files and libraries of all the products of a project once they have been quality controlled, controlling access to them and maintaining records of their status

- Safe and secure storage of each product in the way most appropriate for that product. This will include controlling access to the product in such a way as to avoid on the one hand 'damage' to the product and, on the other, to protect against inappropriate access

- The ability to select and package the various components that comprise the final working product. This covers releasing the complete product or updates to it

- A system for logging, tracking and filing all Project Issues.

Configuration management plays a major part in the quality control of a project. Without it, managers have little or no control over the products being produced – for example, what their status is, where they are, whether they can be changed, what the latest version is. Configuration management contributes to the economic provision of quality products:

- By making the management of changes and upgrades to a product cheaper and less error prone

- By helping to identify products that may be affected by problems in related products

- By checking which versions of products the user is using or connected to, whether products in use are authorised, whether products have been affected by changes and which other related products might be the cause of any problems.

Configuration management is not optional. If more than one version of a product has been

- Establishment of baselines (described in section 19.3)

- Performance of configuration audits.

Many of these functions could be incorporated into the role of Configuration Librarian. Apart from the configuration management work, the Configuration Librarian also creates and maintains the project and stage files.

Items can only be amended or deleted through submission of an authorised Project Issue to the Configuration Librarian.

19.5.1 Configuration management coverage

The amount and formality of configuration management needed by a project depends on the type and size of the project and the project's environment. It is a question that needs to be faced at the outset of a project.

The configuration management method should cover all products once they have reached the stage of draft completion.

19.5.2 Configuration management of PRINCE2 management products

One aspect to consider is whether to place the PRINCE2 management products under configuration management. For example, a Stage Plan will be updated with actuals many times. It is sensible to put this under version control. A record must be retained showing the status at various moments during the stage. Each update should be a new version to avoid overwriting the Stage Plan that was agreed by the Project Board, or even the Stage Plan as it stood two weeks ago.

The same argument can be applied to any of the PRINCE2 management products that may change as the project progresses, such as the Project Plan, the Business Case, the project management team and their job descriptions. It is therefore sensible to place such products under configuration management.

The Issue, Risk, Quality and Lessons Learned Logs are not normally put under configuration management. They are simply updated on a regular basis. Similarly, reports that only have one version are unlikely to be placed under configuration management.

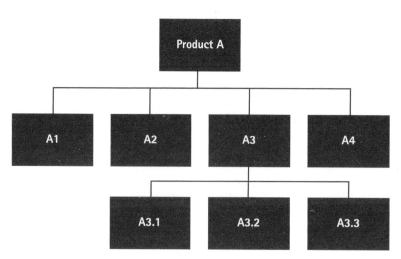

Figure 19.2 Configuration breakdown

19.5.3 Choosing the level of product

An important part of configuration management is deciding the level at which control is to be exercised – with top-level products broken down into components that are themselves products and so on. Figure 19.2 shows Product A, which consists of components A1, A2, A3 and A4. Each of these components can be broken down into smaller components. In this example, A3 is made up of A3.1, A3.2 and A3.3. Each of the components shown is called a product, including the total product.

Normally, products are defined down to the lowest level at which a component can be independently installed, replaced or modified. Each project has to decide on the level at which to stop breaking products down to further levels. As another example, if the product is a training manual, does it make sense to break this product down into sub-products, such as contents page, index, overview chapter, glossary of terms, etc.? Would such a breakdown be better and more simply shown as the 'composition' part of the training manual's Product Description?

Other considerations in choosing the level of product breakdown are cost and effort. A more detailed breakdown gives greater control, but also increases the cost and effort of configuration management.

19.6 Configuration management and change control

There must be a close liaison between configuration management and change control. A key element is the ability to identify and control different versions of a product.

A baselined product can only be changed under formal change control. This means that a Project Issue has been authorised and presented to the Configuration Librarian. Once a product has been approved, that version of it never changes. If a change is required, a new version of the product is created that will encompass the change. The change should be referenced to the relevant Project Issue.

A product should not be issued for change to more than one person at a time. Where there are multiple changes to be applied to one product, they must be combined in some way and the completion of the product encompassing all changes must be delegated to one person. In a large, complex environment, this may not be practical, but the multiple changes must still be co-ordinated by one person/function to avoid clashes between the various changes. Alternatively, subsequent changes must wait until the current change has been implemented. Then, after approval of this change, the next version can be issued for the next change.

Where possible, the master copy of any product should never be issued, only a copy.

19.7 Configuration management and a Project Support Office

Because most final products will exist in operational use long after the project to create them has finished, configuration management is usually carried out on an organisation-wide basis, the same approach being used to look after both project and operational products. This is a good reason for providing configuration management expertise to all projects from a central Project Support Office, which will continue to control the products throughout their operational life.

There may be a requirement for a project to fit in with existing methods of configuration management used by the customer. Most end products from projects will have a long, useful life and will be modified many times during that life. Configuration management is essential to keep track of the changes. If the project has been outsourced, the configuration management method used by the supplier needs to be compatible with that of whichever group will look after the product during its operational life.

20

CHANGE CONTROL

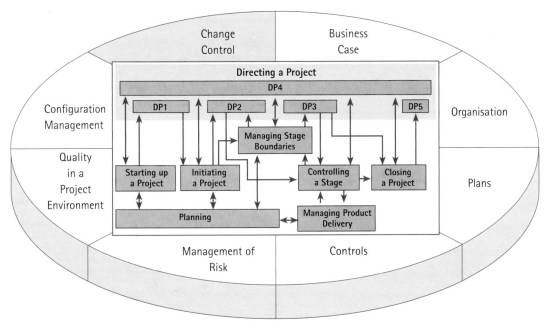

Figure 20.1 Change control in the PRINCE2 template

20.1 Purpose

Changes to specification or scope can potentially ruin any project unless they are carefully controlled. Change is, however, highly likely. The control of change means the assessment of the impact of potential changes, their importance, their cost and a judgmental decision by management on whether to include them or not. Any approved changes must be reflected in any necessary corresponding change to schedule and budget. A technique for the control of change is given in *Change control technique*, Chapter 23.

There is a need in any project to manage all relevant documents. These may be change requests, suggestions or good ideas, or documents relating to problems in fulfilling the requirements, recording external changes to the Business Case or risks, or simply asking questions or making observations about some aspect of the project, such as the likely transfer of someone on the project management team. PRINCE2 uses change control as a common procedure to capture and record all these Project Issues.

20.2 Project Issue management

The objective is to capture, log and categorise all Project Issues. Project Issues may be raised at any time during the project, by anyone with an interest in the project or its outcome.

A Project Issue is anything that could have an effect on the project (either detrimental or beneficial). Project Issues include:

- A change in requirements, however minor (even apparently very minor changes can have major long-term implications)

- A change in the environment applicable to the project, for example:

  - a legislative change

  - a corporate change of direction

  - a new customer

  - a new supplier

  - an unexpected change to a member of the project management team

  - actions by a competitor

  - a programme management directive

  - a corporate reorganisation

- A problem occurring or being identified that was not anticipated during risk analysis

- An anticipated but unavoidable risk occurring

- A problem or error occurring in work completed or currently under way

- Advice of a new risk

- A query about any aspect of the project.

Managing Project Issues will involve:

- Capturing and formally logging the Project Issue (in the Issue Log)

- Assessing the Project Issue to decide on the type and therefore what action is required

- Investigating the required actions

- Documenting the actions and confirming their completion

- Reviewing the Issue Log on a regular basis to monitor progress on outstanding Project Issues.

Project Issues can arise from a very wide range of sources (including other project processes), can come in many forms and can show themselves in many ways. The first requirement of this process is, therefore, to provide a consistent and reliable method of capturing all Project Issues. All Project Issues should be entered into the Issue Log as soon as they have been identified.

An initial assessment needs to be made as to the nature of each issue. Apart from general problems and questions, two specific types of change can result:

- A Request for Change, which, for whatever reason, will cause a change to the specification or Acceptance Criteria of the project or one of the project's products. Any additional cost to carry out the change will normally have to be funded by the customer

- An Off-Specification, covering errors or omissions found in work already conducted or planned for the future, which will result in agreed specifications or Acceptance Criteria not being met. Additional costs to carry out this work will normally fall on any suppliers involved.

The funding implications make it important that the distinction between these two types of Project Issue is made. There is usually more motivation to fix mistakes (Off-Specifications) than make changes (Requests for Change). However, they are both processed in the same way.

Where the Project Issue is advice of a new risk, it should be logged in the Risk Log and analysed in the normal manner within *Examining Project Issues* (CS4). The suggested countermeasure may bring about a change to the project and be examined as such prior to submission to the Project Board for selection.

20.3 Authority levels

One consideration at project initiation should be who is permitted to authorise changes (Project Issues) to what the project is to produce. Because this is a potential change to what the Project Board originally committed to at the start of the project, it is the Project Board's responsibility to agree to each change before it is implemented. In a project where few changes are envisaged, it may be reasonable to leave this authority in the hands of the Project Board. But projects may be in a dynamic environment, where there are likely to be, for example, many requests to change the initial agreed scope of the project. Remember, a Project Issue may be a notification of a failure to meet the specification, not just a request for change by the user. Questions to consider include:

- Is the Project Board prepared to make the time available to review all Project Issues?

- Does it wish to consider only the top priority Project Issues and delegate decisions on minor ones to another body?

The Project Board needs to decide before the project moves out of project initiation where the authority for approving or rejecting Project Issues lies and these responsibilities must be written into the appropriate job descriptions. In some projects the Project Board may choose to delegate decisions on Project Issue action to a group, here called a 'change authority'.

For projects that exist within a programme, programme management will define the level of authority that the Project Board will have to approve changes.

20.3.1 Change budget

As well as considering where authority for decision lies, the Project Board must consider:

- How will changes be funded?

- Will the Project Board go back to corporate or programme management to vary funding, timetable or scope each time a change is desired?

Unless the anticipated level of change on a project is low, it is advisable for the change authority to be given a budget to pay for changes. This arrangement can avoid a number of exception assessments by the Project Board in projects where the frequency of Project Issues is forecast to be high. Where a change budget has been allocated, there must be agreement on how it is to be used, where the responsibilities lie and what constraints there are on its use.

20.4 Integrity of change

Project Issues should not be considered in isolation. Some other considerations are as follows.

20.4.1 Benefit/Business Case driven

Project Issues should be viewed against the benefits they offer and their impact on the Business Case.

20.4.2 The Risk Log

Project Issues should be considered in three ways under the 'risk' heading:

- Would it impact an existing risk?

- Has it already been anticipated as part of the risk management processes, and hence the mechanism for handling it already identified?

- Would it create a new risk?

20.4.3 Time/cost/risk function balance

There must be a balance between the advantage achieved by incorporating the change and the time, cost and risk of implementing it. This is illustrated in Figure 20.2. Can the project afford the delay? Can the extra funds be found? (Or will the change save time and money?) Is this a good way of spending the extra funds? Is it too risky? Should (and can) the change wait until after the current project ends?

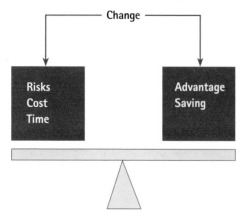

The balancing act between risks, costs and time,
and what the customer gets out of it

Figure 20.2 Balancing the decision to change

22
PRODUCT–BASED PLANNING

The product-based planning technique can be used for all levels of plan required in a project. It is used in the sub-process *Defining and Analysing Products* (PL2).

This technique provides a product-based framework that can be applied to any project to give a logical sequence to the project's work. A 'product' may be a tangible one such as a machine, a document or a piece of software; or it may be intangible, such as a culture change or a different organisational structure. Within PRINCE2, these will all be called 'products'. The technique is demonstrated in section 22.7 with a simple example of organising a conference.

22.1 The four products of product–based planning

Four products are created within the product-based planning technique:

- A Product Description of the final product of the project
- A Product Breakdown Structure
- Product Descriptions of each product
- A Product Flow Diagram.

22.2 The benefits of product–based planning

Product-based planning is an integral part of the PRINCE2 attention to the quality of products. It focuses on the final product and thereby ensures that all breakdowns and activities add value and contribute to that final product.

22.2.1 Product Breakdown Structure

A Product Breakdown Structure is a hierarchical structure that breaks down a final product into its constituent sub-products. It helps the planner to think of what other products are needed to build the final product, and to clarify and identify all necessary work for the creation of that final product. Breaking down products into a lower level of detail makes it easier to:

- Estimate the effort, resources and timescale needed
- Apply quality criteria more specifically
- Avoid omitting products.

22.2.2 Product Descriptions

A clear, complete and unambiguous description of each product is a tremendous aid to its successful creation. A Product Description aids understanding of what the product's purpose is and aids estimation of the effort its creation will require.

A Product Description carries important information about the product. It is a key element in the quality work of a project. It is given to the creator to explain what quality is required of the product when built. It is later given to the quality checkers to identify how the presence of that quality will be tested and to help establish if the required quality has been built into the product.

There should be at least one Product Description per project – that of the final product. It is also advisable to have Product Descriptions for each simple product (see section 22.4.1) on the Product Breakdown Structure. A documented and agreed Product Description for each product helps to:

- Ensure that all personnel affected by that product have the same understanding of the product's purpose

- Provide a pointer to the way in which the product is to be presented

- Define its quality criteria

- Determine how the presence of that quality will be tested.

22.2.3 Product Flow Diagram

Every planner needs to know the answer to the question: 'What comes next?' The Product Flow Diagram shows the sequence of development of the products of the plan and any dependencies between them. It also identifies dependencies on any products outside the scope of the plan. It leads naturally into consideration of the activities required, and provides the information for non-PRINCE2 planning tools, such as network planning and Gantt charts.

22.3   Producing a Product Description of the final product

The first task in product-based planning is to assist the customer to write a Product Description for the final product of the project. Discussion of the various Product Description fields (see *Product Description outlines*, Appendix A) will help clarify what is required.

22.4   Producing a Product Breakdown Structure

The second task in product-based planning is to produce a Product Breakdown Structure (PBS). The objectives of this are to:

- Identify the products to be created or obtained by the planned work

- Identify additional products needed to build and support the final products
- Build a consensus on the best product groupings that should be used to generate ideas on what products have to be created or obtained.

22.4.1 Simple products

Products at the lowest level of any branch of the hierarchy are 'simple products', so called because they are not broken down into more detail in the Product Breakdown Structure. The lowest level on a Product Breakdown Structure is not fixed. It depends on the level of detail required on the plan to allow the Project Board, Project Manager or Team Manager to exercise an appropriate level of control. Simple products should be represented in the Product Breakdown Structure diagrams in a rectangle.

22.4.2 Intermediate products

'Intermediate product' is a term used to describe a product that is broken down into further products, i.e. everything that appears in a Product Breakdown Structure apart from the final product and the simple products at the bottom of the various branches of the hierarchy. Intermediate products are one of two types: integration products or collective groupings. These are defined below.

Integration products

An integration product is one where one or more activities, such as assembly or testing, will need to be applied to that product after its sub-products have been produced. Integration products should therefore appear in the Product Flow Diagram and require a Product Description to be written for them. They should be represented in the diagrams in a rectangle.

Collective groupings

A collective grouping is not a 'product' that itself requires work. Rather, a collective grouping is just a convenient way of grouping a number of products. It is simply used as a trigger to further thoughts by the planner of what actual products are required. An example of a collective grouping might be 'training product grouping' – not a product in itself, but used as a starting point to think of real products, such as lecture notes, student notes, exercises, slides, etc. Collective groupings can appear in the Product Breakdown Structure but should **not** be carried forward into the Product Flow Diagram. A collective grouping should be represented in diagrams in a rhomboid.

The designer of a Product Breakdown Structure should be very clear in the naming of intermediate products to indicate whether they are integration products or collective groupings. A sensible naming convention would be to include the word 'group' or 'grouping' in the name of a collective grouping, and 'integrated', 'tested' or 'assembled' in the name of an integration product.

Planners may use both integration products and collective groupings in the Product Breakdown Structure. Figure 22.1 shows a simple example of the Product Breakdown Structure of the Project Initiation Document (PID). Diagram (a) shows 'Assembled PID' as a simple product under the collective grouping 'PID Product Grouping'. In this case, the rule would be to transfer all the simple products to the Product Flow Diagram, but not the collective grouping. Diagram (b) shows 'Assembled PID' as an integration product; this would be transferred to the Product Flow Diagram.

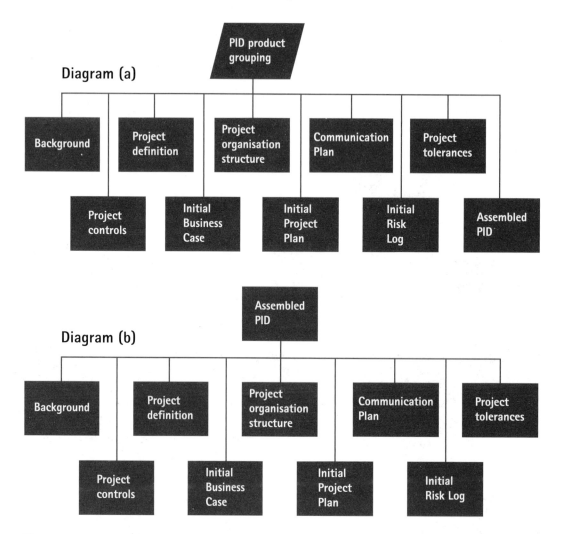

Figure 22.1 An example of using a collective grouping or an integration product

When a team is creating a Product Breakdown Structure, there is likely to be a discussion on which collective groupings should be identified, i.e. how products will be grouped. For example, if the outcome of a project were a computerised accounts system, users might want to break the system down into collective groupings called Accounts Payable, Accounts Receivable, General Ledger, etc. The suppliers might want collective groupings called Screens, Reports, Databases, etc. Neither breakdown is wrong, but the project team must reach a consensus on which approach will be used in the Product Breakdown Structure and hence in the project. Agreement on a common language for use throughout the project will help with team building.

22.4.3 Types of product

A PRINCE2 project has two types of product:

- Specialist products whose development is the subject of the plan

- Management products that will be required as part of managing the project, and establishing and maintaining quality (for example, Highlight Reports, End Stage Reports, Project Issues, etc.).

Figure 22.2 shows the standard PRINCE2 management products in one possible Product Breakdown Structure arrangement (from many alternatives). The management products stay constant, whatever the type of project, and can be used as shown or with any relevant modifications for all projects. To allow a larger font and thus make the diagram more easily readable, the quality products are expanded in Figure 22.3. These diagrams remind the planner to think of the management products that will be needed and that will require effort and time to produce.

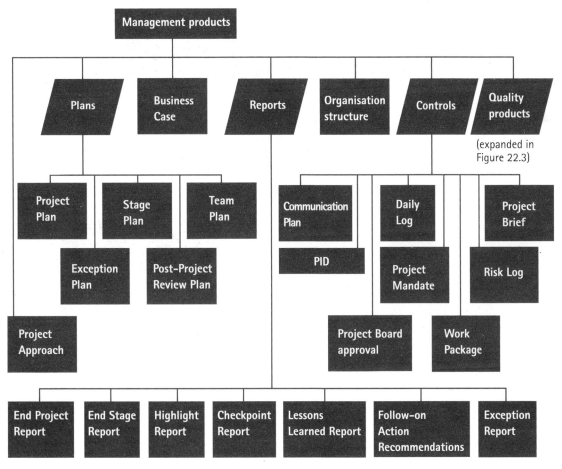

Figure 22.2 Management Product Breakdown Structure

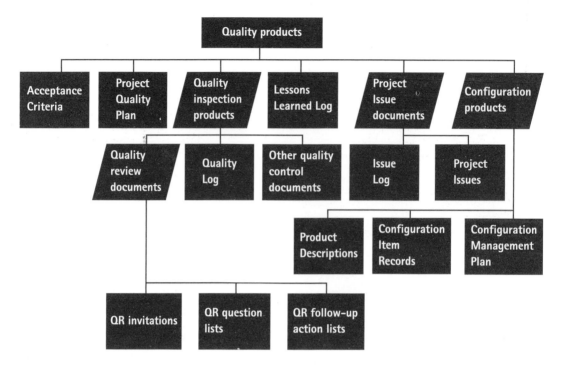

Figure 22.3 Management Quality Products

During a project, there will be many 'versions' of products such as the Business Case. A new 'version' may be created at the end of each stage. There is no value in trying to illustrate multiple versions of a product in a Product Breakdown Structure.

22.4.4 Levels

The key to producing the breakdown of the specialist products is that it should show the scope of the plan. The planner places the final product of the plan at the top of the Product Breakdown Structure hierarchy. This is then broken down into its major products to form the next level of the structure. Each of these is then further broken down until an appropriate level of detail for the plan is reached. Figure 22.2 shows one possible way of depicting a Product Breakdown Structure, but there are others, such as spider diagrams.

22.4.5 Product states

One concern when creating a Product Breakdown Structure is whether to include different states of products. Two examples of product states might be 'mixed plaster, applied plaster and set plaster' and 'dismantled machinery, moved machinery and reassembled machinery'. This is the planner's decision. The key questions are whether the various states of a product require their own Product Description and a set of quality criteria and quality checks. The first example may be better handled as one 'plaster' product in the diagrams with its various states dealt with as activities in the sub-process *Identifying Activities and Dependencies* (PL3). With the example of the machinery, the planner may feel that each 'state' is sufficiently different as to require its own Product Description, and that it is sensible to put all three states in the diagrams as products in their own right. Another reason for defining different states of a product is that responsibility for the respective products may change – for example, one group may dismantle the machinery, a specialist moving company may move it and another team may reassemble it. Each group would require a separate Product Description.

22.4.6 External products

As stated earlier, the key to producing the breakdown of the specialist products is that it should show the scope of the plan. The Product Breakdown Structure should include not only the products to be delivered by the project, but also any products that already exist or are to be supplied from external sources. The Project Manager is not accountable for the creation of external products, but the project does need the product(s) in order to achieve its objectives. A plan must therefore include any external products required to achieve its objectives plus suitable dependencies on these external products.

A different symbol should be used to identify external products. In this manual, an ellipse is used to indicate an external product in both the Product Breakdown Structure and the Product Flow Diagram. It should be noted that it is the *product* that is shown, not the source of the product. For example, if a plan needs the local train timetable, 'rail timetable' would be the external product, not the relevant train company.

In the simple example later in the chapter of organising a conference, the Product Breakdown Structure for the specialist products might be constructed as shown in Figure 22.5. 'Selected theme' is an external product because it exists at the start of the project.

22.4.7 Key criteria

- Have all specialist products required to satisfy the business need been identified?
- Have all management products that must be generated during the project to ensure audit or Project Assurance, guidance and control been identified?
- Does the required plan rely on products that are outside the scope of this project (external products)? If so, have they all been identified?
- Is responsibility for these external products clearly identified and agreed?
- How will progress on external products be monitored by this project?

Hints and tips

The products in a plan include not only those that will be developed within the plan but any 'products' external to the project that are required as input to the work identified in the plan.

If a product is further broken down in the Product Breakdown Structure, there should be a match between the composition content of its Product Description and the breakdown of that product in the Product Breakdown Structure.

The delivery of each external product is a dependency and therefore represents a potential risk.

Higher-level products must be completely defined by the lower-level products to which they are attached. The implication in breaking a product down to a lower level is: 'This product consists of these products and only these products'. It should not be: 'This product is followed by these products'.

It is unnecessary to break a product down into only one simple product. This is not decomposition. It is the equivalent of saying: 'This product consists of only one product' – in which case the breakdown is unnecessary and incorrect.

Arrows should not be used in a Product Breakdown Structure. There is no sequence implied in the positioning of products in this diagram.

Branches in a Product Breakdown Structure should not join up again lower down in the hierarchy.

If there is not enough space on the drawing medium being used to show a breakdown horizontally, it can be shown vertically, but only as in example (a) in Figure 22.4; example (b) implies that it is a series of one-to-one breakdowns, and would therefore be incorrect.

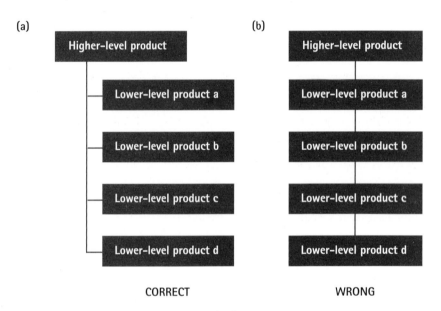

Figure 22.4 Drawing a breakdown vertically

22.5 Writing a Product Description

As stated earlier, product-based planning for a project should begin with writing a Product Description for the final product of the project. It is also recommended that Product Descriptions are written for each significant simple product and each integration product on the Product Breakdown Structure or Product Flow Diagram. Product Descriptions for collective groupings are optional.

Product Descriptions should be written as soon as possible after the need for the product has been identified. Initially, this may only be a 'skeleton' with little more than the title and identifier as information. It will be refined and amended as the product becomes better understood and the later planning steps are done. A Product Description should be baselined when the plan containing the creation of that product is baselined. If the product is later changed, the Product Description must also pass through change control.

22.5.1 Product Description contents

An example of a Product Description for one of the products in the simple example is shown in Figure 22.6.

Detail of the contents of a Product Description can be found in *Product Description outlines*, Appendix A.

Although responsibility for writing Product Descriptions rests officially with the Project or Team Manager, it is wise to involve representatives from the area with expertise in the product and those who will use the product in question. The latter should certainly be asked to define the quality they expect of the product.

22.5.2 Key criteria

- Are the products clearly and unambiguously defined?

- Have all types of quality check for the products been specified, i.e. ones that will check that the quality criteria have been met?

- Are there centrally held standards to which the description can point when it comes to defining the quality criteria, and have they been applied?

- Where there are conflicting customer and supplier standards, has a sensible agreement or compromise been reached?

- Does the user/customer want any specific standards used?

- Have the right people been involved in writing each Product Description?

- Are suitable checklists available to help check the products?

Hints and tips

Writing down the purpose and composition in a Product Description helps clarify how much work is needed to create the product. This can be a big help in estimation.

Product Description outlines, Appendix A contains outlines of all PRINCE2 management products. It should not be necessary for each project to redefine these unless there are local changes to them.

Writing good Product Descriptions is not a trivial undertaking. In particular, quality criteria, aimed at separating an acceptable product from an unacceptable one, need careful thought.

It is essential to involve the user or customer in writing Product Descriptions, defining quality criteria and deciding how the product can be checked against these criteria.

Test the setting of quality criteria by asking the question: 'How will I know when work on this product is finished as opposed to stopped?'

Listing the composition of a product can often remind the planner of other products that are needed.

Very often, the same products are created in many plans. Standard Product Descriptions can be written that can be used by many plans.

Are there any standard checklists that can be used?

Don't try to replace a detailed requirements specification with a Product Description.

If the quality criteria for a product are agreed with the customer, this may assist in the ultimate acceptance of the product.

If Product Descriptions are used as control documents, then additional information, such as estimated and actual dates and effort, may be added.

Identifying who will accept a particular product and making sure that they contribute to and agree the Product Description can reduce the potential for conflict at later stages of a plan's implementation.

Assistance could be sought from a 'quality specialist' when defining quality, particularly when adherence to recognised standards is part of the Acceptance Criteria.

If a product is the subject of a change, its Product Description should also be checked for any necessary updates.

22.6 Producing a Product Flow Diagram

The final task in product-based planning is producing the Product Flow Diagram (PFD). The Product Flow Diagram is created from the Product Breakdown Structure and indicates the order or sequence in which the plan's products will be created. It precedes the identification of activities in *Identifying Activities and Dependencies* (PL3).

Figure 22.7 illustrates the Product Flow Diagram for the simple example later in this chapter.

22.6.1 Creating a Product Flow Diagram

A Product Flow Diagram needs very few symbols. Each product to be developed within the plan is enclosed in a rectangle. Arrows connect the rectangles, showing the sequence in which the products are to be created. Any products that already exist or are outside the planner's control should be clearly identified by using a different type of enclosure, an ellipse.

The diagram begins with those products that are available at the start of the plan (perhaps many of these are documents, such as statements of requirements or designs) and ends with the final product(s) of the plan.

Creation of a Product Flow Diagram may reveal new products that are required. These should also be added to the Product Breakdown Structure and Product Descriptions should be written for them.

Although the Project Manager or Team Manager is responsible for creation of the Product Flow Diagram, it is sensible to involve those who are to develop or contribute the products contained in the plan.

22.6.2 Key criteria

●   On what other products is each product dependent?

- Is any product dependent on a product developed outside the scope of this plan?

- Which products can be developed in parallel?

- Have any new/previously unidentified products come to light?

Hints and tips

At project level, the dependencies can be rather crude - for example, not all elements of major product 1 need to be done before any elements of major product 2 can start. To try to break those major products down so that the dependencies can be refined is likely to confuse the diagram. It is better to accept the crude dependencies and resolve them at Stage Plan level.

The easiest way to create a Product Flow Diagram is to put all the specialist products in their required sequence and then add any relevant management products to the correct point in the flow.

It is often easiest to fill in the middle of the flow by working back from the final product and asking the question: 'Which products should be available in order to create this product?' Self-adhesive notelets on a whiteboard can be an effective way of developing a Product Flow Diagram, particularly where there is likely to be a lot of modification and adjustment.

A useful way to get started with the flow of specialist products is to 'top and tail' the diagram - that is, put the final product at the bottom of a sheet of paper and any products that are prerequisites to starting the work at the top. Take each product in the list and match it to every other product to establish if there is any particular dependency between them. Work through all the products in this way. Use this information to connect all the products in their appropriate sequence from any prerequisites to the final product.

If Project Board approvals are listed as management products, their placement in the sequence will show where the stage ends should come, if this is not already known.

The derivation section of a Product Description gives useful information about dependencies. The key question to ask is: 'From where do I get this information?'

22.7 Product-based planning example

An example of product-based planning is given in Figures 22.5, 22.6 and 22.7. The example is an extremely simple one whose purpose is to illustrate the various steps and parts of the technique without any complexity in the plan's subject. A short scenario explains the background to the example.

22.7.1 Simple example – scenario

A project is required to organise and run a conference for between 75 and 90 delegates. A required date and the selected theme of the conference have been given to you. The theme is to bring members of a particular profession up to date on recent developments in professional procedures and standards. The conference will be held at a venue that will need to be identified, checked for availability, facilities and price, and then booked. Delegates will all be members of the profession, and a mailing list is available for you to use. Suitable speakers have to be identified, approached and booked. Once the speakers are booked, a detailed agenda and programme have to be identified. One hundred delegate handout packs will be needed, the cover reflecting the selected theme; these must contain a printed agenda, reflecting the agreed programme, copies of slides and notes used by the speakers and a feedback form, based on the programme, to capture attendee reviews. You need to devise booking arrangements for those members wishing to attend. These need to be in place, the programme needs to be agreed and the venue needs to be selected and booked before the mail shots are sent out. You will need to prepare a press release based on the programme when the venue is booked. You expect some bookings to come from this publicity. The attendance list will be updated with the responses once the press release has been issued and the mail shots posted. You will need to recruit staff to help you on the day, based on the finalised attendance list.

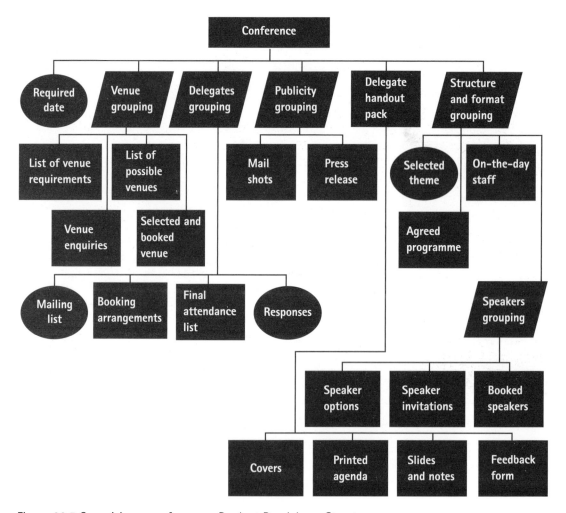

Figure 22.5 Organising a conference - Product Breakdown Structure

Title	List of Venue Requirements
Purpose	To identify all the requirements that must be met by suitable venues for the conference
Composition	The date on which availability is required Start and end times Expected numbers of attendees Accommodation requirements Facilities required Refreshment requirements Parking requirements
Derivation	Mailing list Required date Previous conference numbers Any previous conference list of requirements
Format and Presentation	Typed list with sub-headings as per Composition
Allocated to	Conference Organiser
Quality criteria	List must identify everything that will be required of a site to hold the conference List should clearly separate mandatory from desirable features List must cover all items defined under Composition Each item should be defined in a way that is measurable
Quality method	One check of the list against the headings in Composition Proof-reading by word processing software and independent reviewer Comparison against the list for any previous conferences Cheek against any offered checklist from conference sites
Quality tolerance	The list should recognise the interaction of quality and cost, with the emphasis on quality up to a 10% differential in cost Where possible, any acceptable range of tolerance for an item should be given
Quality check skills and/or people required	Proof-reader Ideally a person who has either organised a conference before or a conference director from a hotel chain

Figure 22.6 Organising a conference – Sample Product Description

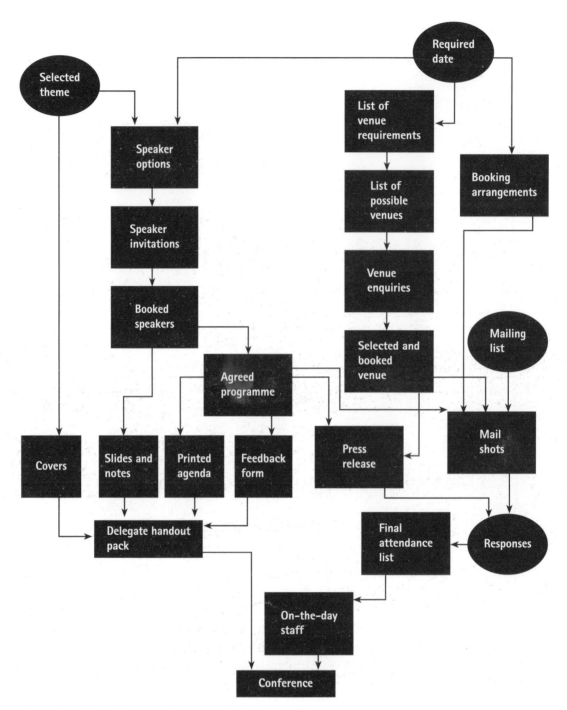

Figure 22.7 Organising a conference – Product Flow Diagram

22.8 Further examples

Two further examples of a project to procure a product are now given. The first example is at the level of a Project Plan. Figures 22.8 and 22.9 show the Project Plan Product Breakdown Structure and Product Flow Diagram, respectively. The second example is the first Stage Plan of this project. Figures 22.10 and 22.11 show the Stage Plan Product Breakdown Structure and Product Flow Diagram, respectively.

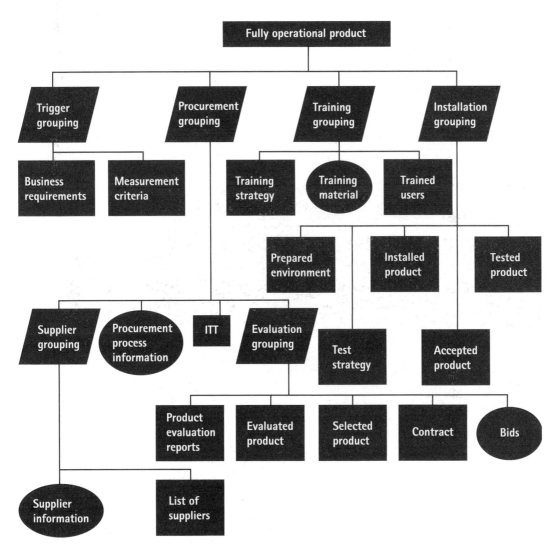

Figure 22.8 Project Plan Product Breakdown Structure

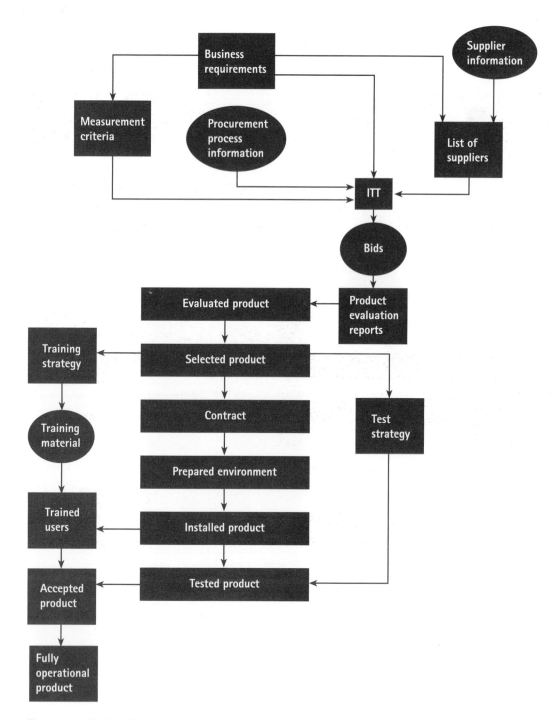

Figure 22.9 Project Plan Product Flow Diagram

17.   Check each product in the flow diagram and ensure that a dependency is shown on all products that it will require.

If the project is broken down into several stages, the products for each stage are extracted from the project Product Breakdown Structure to form the basis for that stage's Product Breakdown Structure. These may be expanded to more levels of detail and thus 'extra products' added to give the detail required of the Stage Plan. Care must be taken to use the same names in the Stage Plan diagrams as were used in the Project Plan.

The creation of Stage Plan diagrams may cause rethinking that requires further modification of the Project Plan's diagrams in order to retain consistency.

23
CHANGE CONTROL TECHNIQUE

This chapter looks at the control of changes to specialist products, not management products. Two important points need to be made:

- If a product is to be changed, its Product Description should be checked for any necessary changes

- Once a product has been approved, the Project Manager should not authorise any work that would change it without the approval of the Project Board.

A programme or organisation may have its own change control procedure and forms. This is not a problem as long as its key points are compatible with the approach detailed in this chapter.

For those without a mandatory change control procedure, the following will ensure that changes are controlled during the project.

23.1 Change control steps

All changes are treated as types of Project Issue and are handled using the same technique. *Change control*, Chapter 20 should be read in conjunction with this technique.

Changes can be:

- A request to change what the project is set to deliver, for example, the specification of requirements (Request for Change)

- A suggestion to improve one or more of the project's products (Request for Change)

- A record of some current or forecast failure to meet a requirement (Off-Specification).

Figure 23.1 shows the steps involved in capturing Project Issues and then managing those that are changes through to resolution.

23.1.1 Issue Log

Whatever its type, every issue raised is logged as a Project Issue in the Issue Log. A suggested content for this log is given in *Product Description outlines*, Appendix A. A unique number is allocated, plus the date received and the status of the issue.

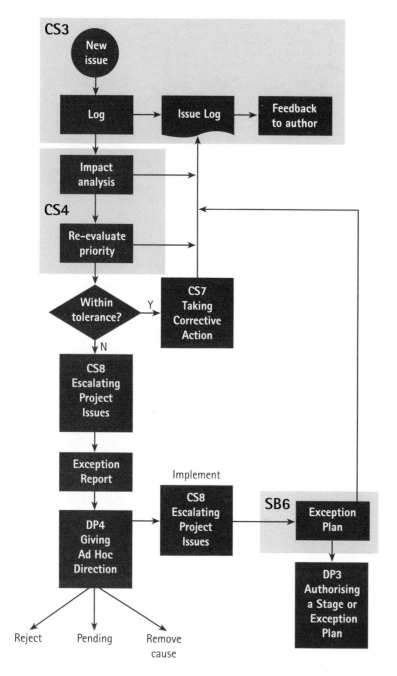

Figure 23.1 Change control steps

23.1.2 Prioritise

Each Project Issue should be assessed to indicate a priority. A suggested priority rating is:

1. A must – the final product will not work without this change

2. An important change – its absence would be very inconvenient, although a work-around is possible for a while

3. A nice-to-have but not vital

4.   A cosmetic change – of no importance

5.   This does not involve a change.

A copy of the Project Issue is returned to the author to acknowledge its receipt and entry in the project's Issue Log.

Any Project Issues that are questions or are based on misunderstandings should be answered directly. A reply is sent to the author, a copy filed and the Issue Log updated to reflect the action.

23.1.3 Impact analysis

An impact analysis is carried out on each remaining Project Issue to identify:

- What would have to change, including any changes to linked products
- What effort the change would need
- What the impact on the Team, Stage and Project Plans would be
- Whether the impact would cause deviation beyond team, stage or project tolerances
- What the impact on the Business Case would be
- What the impact on the risks would be.

The change may impact just the customer, just the supplier or both. The priority should be re-evaluated after the impact analysis. This can be done in a number of ways, depending on the project's circumstances. The Project Board may wish to do the re-evaluation. The Project Board may have decided to delegate such decisions on Project Issues to a change authority.

23.1.4 Authorisation

The use of a change authority is described in *Change control*, Chapter 20 (section 20.3).

Only the Project Board or its delegated change authority should make decisions on Requests for Change.

For Off-Specifications, the Project Manager may try to solve the problem within the stage tolerance margins. This may mean changes to the plan(s) to include extra activities. Where correction of the Off-Specification is not possible within tolerance levels, the Project Manager follows the exception procedure, *Escalating Project Issues* (CS8), to bring the matter to the attention of the Project Board in *Giving Ad Hoc Direction* (DP4). If the decision of the Project Board is to accept the Off-Specification without any corrective action; this is called a 'concession'.

After impact analysis Project Issues are passed to the Project Board/change authority. This authority can decide to reject Project Issues, put them in 'pending' status, remove the cause of the problem or ask for their implementation. The Project Issues are updated with any change in priority and the Project Board's directives.

The Project Issues are returned to the Project Manager, the Issue Log updated and an updated copy sent to the author.

Any Project Issues whose implementation would cause deviation beyond stage or project tolerances will form the basis of an Exception Report, created in *Escalating Project Issues* (CS8). According to the project environment, this may be formal or informal. The likely result will be a request for the Project Manager to produce an Exception Plan, which will include the extra work, to be submitted via *Producing an Exception Plan* (SB6).

Note: Where the Project Board has delegated decisions on the implementation of changes to some separate change authority, the name of this body should be substituted for that of the Project Board in this technique.

Hints and tips

Evaluating the impact of potential changes can be erroneously taken to mean only the impact on the customer. Impact analysis must cover the three areas of business, user and supplier. Before a change goes to the Senior User for consideration, the impact on the supplier must be known – for example, the cost and effort required and what products would have to be changed.

Where the project is partially or fully funded by the supplier, this may change the decision-making authority within the Project Board about changes. It may become more of a joint decision based on the contract terms or including contract modification. Any changes in responsibility and authority should be reflected in the job descriptions.

Where the project is part of a programme, is the project in a position to judge the impact on other projects? Does it have the authority to make decisions? There are two potential approaches:

- Screen all changes at programme level to determine where the decision should be made

- Ensure a programme representative is part of the project's change authorisation loop.

24
QUALITY REVIEW TECHNIQUE

24.1 What is a quality review?

A quality review is a structured and organised procedure designed to assess whether a product is 'fit for purpose' or conforms to requirements. The procedure begins with the identification of individuals or groups who have a vested interest in the product under review. The product is presented for review and comments from reviewers are discussed during a structured meeting. Any required changes to the product are agreed and a complete list of required actions is taken. The procedure is completed when all the required changes have been made and the product is formally 'signed off', meaning that it meets the quality criteria that were set and the product is now approved.

24.2 Quality review benefits

The following benefits can be achieved from the effective use of quality reviews:

- Early identification of defects in products and therefore a platform for product improvement, with attendant reduction in the costs of the final product during development and in operation

- An objective measurement for management progress control is provided. It is one thing being told by the developer that a product is complete, but far more useful to know that a group of peers have examined the product and accepted it. This gives the Project Manager far more certainty about the status of the product

- It provides the opportunity for all vested interests to work together to improve product quality. This helps build the team approach to development

- Once a product has gone through a quality review, user(s), who are represented on the quality review team, are more willing to commit to that product.

24.3 Context

A quality review can be invoked at any point in the project, since any product could be subject to a quality review if there are subjective elements of quality to be monitored. It has close ties with the following processes:

- *Planning* (PL) for the pre-planning and resourcing of major quality reviews at the level of Stage or Team Plan

- *Managing Product Delivery* (MP), which is the process covering the production of the project's products and hence where the application of most of the quality reviews will take place (*Executing a Work Package* (MP2))

- *Authorising Work Package* (CS1), which addresses the handover of responsibility for product production and will include any requirement for quality reviews

- *Assessing Progress* (CS2), which deals with progress monitoring and reporting, and which will receive details of completed quality reviews as updates to the Quality Log.

24.4 Overview of the quality review technique

24.4.1 Objectives

The objectives of a quality review are to:

- Assess the conformity of a product against set criteria

- Provide a platform for product improvement

- Involve all those who have an interest in the product in checking its quality

- Spread ownership of the product

- Obtain commitment from all vested interests to the product

- Provide a mechanism for management monitoring and control.

24.4.2 Responsibilities

There are four specific roles involved in the quality review procedure.

Review chairperson

This role runs the quality review. This is a different role from that of the Executive, who chairs the Project Board.

The role has the following main responsibilities:

- Check that the product is ready for review

- Ensure that the quality review is properly organised (venue, date, time, attendees, duration)

- Gather in the question lists and set the review meeting agenda

- Chair the quality review meeting

- Ensure that the quality review does not stray from its main aim

- Ensure that actions and required results are agreed

- Together with the reviewers, determine the quality review result

- Keep the Project and/or Team Manager aware of the status of all quality reviews

- Provide final review sign-off

- Institute exception procedures via the Project and/or Team Manager where problems with the product cannot be resolved within a short time frame.

Producer

This role represents the creator(s) of the product involved. Typically, the person who has produced the product, or staff from the team responsible will take this role. The role has the following responsibilities:

- Provide all reviewers with the relevant review products

- Prepare for the review meeting

- Assess question lists prior to the review meeting and use them to assist the review chairperson to set the review meeting agenda

- Answer questions about the product during the review procedure, agree errors and explain any implications of these errors

- Agree action to resolve errors

- Ensure any agreed actions are carried out

- Obtain sign-off from reviewers for changes made to the product

- Obtain final sign-off from the review chairperson when the reviewers have approved all changes.

Reviewer

The reviewer role has the following responsibilities:

- Review the product

- Assess the product against the quality criteria specified in the Product Description

- Document questions on the product against the pre-set quality criteria

- Ensure errors are fully understood by the producer and are subsequently resolved satisfactorily

- Sign off any follow-up action list items when identified as checker.

Scribe

The major responsibilities of this role are:

- Assist the chairperson in the review administrative details, such as arrangement of venue

- Take notes of agreed actions during the review meeting

- Read back the agreed actions at the end of the meeting and note who is to take corrective action and who is to check the corrections.

In addition to the specific roles involved, there are responsibilities that need to be taken by other people. These are responsibilities that form part of their standard job, but are particularly relevant to quality reviews:

Project Manager

- Plan the quality reviews in outline
- Plan to overcome any identified exception conditions raised as a result of a quality review
- Act as reviewer where appropriate.

Team Manager

- Plan quality reviews in detail
- Identify any quality review resources required from the team (additional to any reviewers chosen by Project Assurance roles)
- Monitor quality review progress against plan
- Report progress to the Project Manager.

Note that often the Project Manager will be directly managing the work that is being quality reviewed. If this is the case, the responsibilities of Project Manager and Team Manager will be combined.

Project Assurance roles

- Advise on suitable reviewers for each quality review
- Check that everyone involved with the quality review process is aware of their role and responsibilities and that adequate training in the technique has been given
- Ensure that the quality review procedure is being properly followed
- Check that reviewers are being correctly selected and that they are being correctly briefed for the work
- Check that follow-up actions are being properly monitored
- Log and report on the use of corporate standards and advise on improvements and amendments
- Act as reviewers where appropriate.

Project Support roles

If Project Support is available to the Project Manager, it can be used to assist the review chairperson and producer to organise a review venue, prepare and distribute the review documentation, act as scribe and progress-chase the follow-up action list until all errors have been corrected and signed off. People in support roles can act as reviewers where appropriate.

24.4.3 Steps in a formal quality review procedure

A quality review has a number of activities, the central element being the review meeting, where all participants gather to identify and agree on any defects in the product.

There are three basic steps in a quality review:

- Preparation, consisting of:
    - confirmation that the product is ready for review
    - confirmation of the availability of the nominated reviewers and agreement on dates for the return of comments and the review itself
    - distribution of a copy of the product and its Product Description to reviewers where this is possible, for instance if it is a printed document. Alternatively, making the product available for inspection by the reviewers
    - assessment of the product against the quality criteria
    - entry of questions or suspected errors on a question list
    - annotation of minor errors (for example, grammar and spelling) on the product
    - return of the annotated product and question list to the producer
    - a plan of the review meeting and agreement on the agenda
- Review meeting, consisting of:
    - discussion, clarification and agreement on each of the points raised by the reviewers
    - agreement of the follow-up actions appropriate to each agreed error
    - documentation of the follow-up responsibilities
    - summary of the actions at the end of the meeting
    - agreement on the quality review outcome, and sign-off of the product, if appropriate
    - update of the Quality Log
- Follow-up, consisting of:
    - notification to the Project and/or Team Manager of the quality review result
    - a plan of any remedial work required
    - sign-off of the product following successful remedial work
    - update of the Quality Log.

Tables 24.1, 24.2 and 24.3 show the detailed job contents for the quality review roles for each of the steps.

Preparation

Table 24.1 Preparation for quality review

Review chairperson	Producer	Reviewer	Project Manager/ Team Manager
Check product ready	Confirm product available for review	Read Product Description of review product	Check quality review on schedule
Confirm reviewers available and still appropriate	Distribute a copy of the product and Product Description to reviewers (or make the product available for review)	Schedule preparation and review time	Ensure quality review procedure is being followed
Confirm preparation time	Agree time and location of review meeting	Review product against Product Description	Confirm the timing
Confirm Quality Log details	Add any extra reviewer names. Update the planned date if this has changed	Complete question list and annotate product	
Receive question lists and discuss them with the producer	Assess question lists	Forward question list and annotated product to chairperson	
Agree agenda	Agree agenda with chairperson	Confirm review attendance	
Agree presentation format and timing (if any)	Confirm review details to reviewers prior to the meeting		

The scribe can do most of the administrative work for the chairperson.

Review meeting

Table 24.2 Quality review meeting

Review chairperson	Producer	Reviewer	Project Manager/ Team Manager
Open review, state objectives, duration, meeting agenda and format	Take note of comments and concerns	Expand on question list comments	Ensure all quality review documentation is filed
Invite general comments (decide if premature closure of meeting is needed)	Clarify reviewer comments	Contribute to concerns raised by other reviewers	Take appropriate action on incomplete quality reviews or errors found that are outside the scope of the normal follow-up actions

Review chairperson	Producer	Reviewer	Project Manager/ Team Manager
Walk through product as agreed in the agenda	Agree errors and follow-up actions	Agree errors and follow-up actions	
Invite reviewer comments	Collect follow-up action list and annotated product copies		
Ensure all reviewers contribute			
Ensure all agreed errors are recorded on follow-up action list			
Get agreement on responsibility for follow-up action and sign-off			
Agree quality review result			
Ensure Quality Log is updated with date of meeting and actions found			
Inform Project/Team Manager of quality review outcome			

It is recommended that a scribe record errors on the follow-up action list to allow the chairperson to concentrate on control of the meeting.

Follow-up of review meeting

Table 24.3 Follow-up of quality review

Review chairperson	Producer	Reviewer	Project Manager/ Team Manager
Raise Project Issues for any unresolved errors or errors in other products than the one being reviewed	Resolve errors	Check and sign off error corrections	Ensure plans are updated following error resolution
Notify the Project/Team Manager if the correction schedule is exceeded	Obtain follow-up action list sign-off from quality review chairperson	Assist in error resolution as appropriate	File all sign-off documentation

Review chairperson	Producer	Reviewer	Project Manager/Team Manager
On resolution of all errors, sign off the product and inform the Project/Team Manager	Notify the chairperson of any error corrections that exceed their schedule		Deal with any required exception actions
Update the Quality Log with details of actual sign-off date			

The scribe can do most of the progress-chasing of actions and sign-offs on behalf of the chairperson.

Quality review planning

It is important that quality reviews are properly planned, with input from the Project Assurance function. There is therefore an additional quality review planning step consisting of:

- Identifying the products that will be subject to quality review

- Planning the timescale for each quality review

- Identifying the reviewers and adding them to resource plans.

This is carried out as part of creating a Stage or Team Plan in the *Planning* (PL) process.

24.4.4 Quality review results

At the end of a quality review, the review chairperson should obtain a consensus agreement on the result of the review. If any of the reviewers is not prepared to sign off the product, then the product has not met its quality criteria and hence is not ready for use. If the reviewers' comments cannot be resolved for any reason – for example, contention between reviewers – a further discussion and agreement on the matter should be raised as an item on the follow-up action list. If the problem affects other products than the one reviewed, it should be raised via a Project Issue and this action recorded on the follow-up action list.

The result of a quality review will normally be one of three:

- The product is error free and can be approved immediately

- The product can be approved once the identified errors are corrected and signed off

- Correction of the errors found will radically alter the product and it should be reviewed again.

The review chairperson may also decide to postpone the review meeting if:

- Insufficient reviewers attend to cover the quality issues addressed by the product's quality criteria

- The reviewers who are attending are not qualified to comment on the issues being addressed

- It is clear that the reviewers have not studied the product during the preparation step
- It becomes obvious that the product is not fit to be reviewed.

24.4.5 Key criteria

- Have the product's quality criteria been specified?
- Has the Product Description been passed to the reviewers, together with the product?
- Have the reviewers fully checked the product prior to the review meeting?
- Have the question lists been sent to the producer or review chairperson prior to the review meeting?
- Has the review meeting concentrated on error detection, not error fixing or redesign?
- Have the follow-up actions been documented and allocated?
- Have reviewers been asked which changes they wish to sign off?
- Has agreement been reached on the result of the quality review?

Hints and tips

Quality review is there for error/opportunity identification NOT correction.

The temptation to agree solutions for the defects found in a product can be inviting. Should resolution become a feature of quality review, then the review procedure will lose much of its effectiveness because discussion of solutions takes time and effort away from the key objective of the quality review procedure, that is, the identification and agreement of defects in the product to provide the platform for product improvement. Also, there may be more than one solution to a problem and the group of people assembled to review a product may not be the best qualified to select the best solution. Any solutions suggested during the review process should be noted for later consideration.

There is a need to address the producer/reviewer psychology. The aim of the quality review is to identify defects in the product not in the producer. Reviewers and producers should approach the review in a constructive 'team' attitude to achieving quality products. If the team approach is not adopted, conflict can arise and be destructive to the quality review procedure. It helps if reviewers can refer to the product, rather than your product.

Quality review is not an ad hoc gathering of individuals. It is not a first sight of the product for the purpose of problem identification. As in all good meetings, all the participants should attend having checked the product involved and should be prepared to contribute, knowing the agenda and objectives and the role they should perform at the meeting.

Quality review participants must prepare for the review by identifying major questions or suspected errors on a question list, annotating the product where possible with minor errors and informing the chairperson of their findings. Not to do so wastes the time of the other reviewers and devalues the eventual product sign-off since it is more likely that errors will be left undiscovered.

Care must be taken that managers do not attend a quality review in a people management role. They do not attend to assess the performance of their staff. This is particularly true of the producer's manager; it would devalue the meeting and would cause extra stress on the producer. However, managers may attend in the role of reviewers.

Checklists should be in existence.

A major means of assessing a product's quality is against the Product Description, which defines the composition, format and quality criteria of a product. Should this not be available, a checklist of the standard criteria for this type of product should be available. Without one or other of these, the reviewers will be left with no guidance as to what the acceptable quality is.

Ideally, the chairperson should not act as a reviewer. It is difficult to both chair the review meeting and review the product involved. The review chairperson should be there just to run the meeting.

Non-attendance of a reviewer:

- If a reviewer cannot attend the meeting, the review chairperson can decide either to accept a question list from that reviewer and arrange for its points to be discussed at the meeting or replace the reviewer. If the number of non-attendees is such as to undermine the effectiveness of the review, either because of the lack of people to form discussions or because of the lack of key skills, it may be necessary to postpone the review meeting. Where reviewers are not prepared for the review or have not submitted question lists, it may be appropriate to postpone the review if it is felt that the review might be ineffective

- A Project Manager may decide to ask for reviewers to submit question lists, then hold the review meeting with only the chairperson and producer in attendance, the chairperson acting on behalf of the reviewers. In such cases, the chairperson should have any actions signed off directly by the reviewer(s) who submitted the question.

For inter-project products, there should be cross-project representation at quality reviews.

The producer can take the suggested scribe role, especially in an informal quality review. It should not be done by the chairperson, as the distraction of note-taking may impair the control of the meeting.

Errors in other products:

- A quality review may identify an error in a product other than the one being reviewed. This should be recorded as an action item, but closed on its transfer to an appropriate Project Issue. Quality reviews may reveal not only faults on the part of the creator(s), but also defects caused by deficiencies in the quality standards and development methods. Failure to use a standard may indicate that the standard is no longer practical or suitable. Such events should cause a review of the suspect standards area.

GLOSSARY

Acceptance Criteria

A prioritised list of criteria that the final product(s) must meet before the customer will accept them; a measurable definition of what must be done for the final product to be acceptable to the customer. They should be defined as part of the Project Brief and agreed between customer and supplier no later than the project initiation stage. They should be documented in the Project Initiation Document.

Activity network

A flow diagram showing the activities of a plan and their interdependencies. The network shows each activity's duration, earliest start and finish times, latest start and finish times and float. Also known as 'planning network'. *See also* Critical path.

Baseline

A snapshot; a position or situation that is recorded. Although the position may be updated later, the baseline remains unchanged and available as a reminder of the original state and as a comparison against the current position. Products that have passed their quality checks and are approved are baselined products. Anything 'baselined' should be under version control in configuration management and 'frozen', i.e. no changes to that version are allowed.

Benefits

The positive outcomes, quantified or unquantified, that a project is being undertaken to deliver and that justify the investment.

Benefits realisation

The practice of ensuring that the outcome of a project produces the projected benefits claimed in the Business Case.

Business Case

Information that describes the justification for setting up and continuing a PRINCE2 project. It provides the reasons (and answers the question: 'Why?') for the project. An outline Business Case should be in the Project Mandate. Its existence is checked as part of the Project Brief, and a revised, fuller version appears in the Project Initiation Document. It is updated at key points, such as end stage assessments, throughout the project.

Change authority

A group to which the Project Board may delegate responsibility for the consideration of Requests for Change. The change authority is given a budget and can approve changes within that budget.

Change budget

The money allocated to the change authority to be spent on authorised Requests for Change.

Change control

The procedure to ensure that the processing of all Project Issues is controlled, including submission, analysis and decision making.

Checkpoint

A team-level, time-driven review of progress, usually involving a meeting.

Checkpoint Report

A progress report of the information gathered at a checkpoint meeting which is given by a team to the Project Manager and provides reporting data as defined in the Work Package.

Communication Plan

Part of the Project Initiation Document describing how the project's stakeholders and interested parties will be kept informed during the project.

Concession

An Off-Specification that is accepted by the Project Board without corrective action.

Configuration audit

A comparison of the latest version number and status of all products shown in the configuration library records against the information held by the product authors.

Configuration control

Configuration control is concerned with physically controlling receipt and issue of products, keeping track of product status, protecting finished products and controlling any changes to them.

Configuration management

A discipline, normally supported by software tools, that gives management precise control over its assets (for example, the products of a project), covering planning, identification, control, status accounting and verification of the products.

Contingency budget

The amount of money required to implement a contingency plan. If the Project Board approves a contingency plan, it would normally set aside a contingency budget, which would only be called upon if the contingency plan had to be implemented when the associated risk occurs. *See also* Contingency plan.

Contingency plan

A plan that provides details of the measures to be taken if a defined risk should occur. The plan is only implemented if the risk occurs. A contingency plan is prepared where other actions (risk prevention, reduction or transfer) are not possible, too expensive or the current view is that the cost of the risk occurring does not sufficiently outweigh the cost of taking avoiding action – but the risk cannot be simply accepted. The Project Board can see that, should the risk occur, there is a plan of action to counter it. If the Project Board agrees that this is the best form of action, it would put aside a contingency budget, the cost of the contingency plan, only to be used if the risk occurs.

Critical path

This is the line connecting the start of an activity network with the final activity in that network through those activities with zero float, i.e. those activities where any delay will delay the time of the entire end date of the plan. There may be more than one such path. The sum of the activity durations on the critical path will determine the end date of the plan.

Customer

The person or group who commissioned the work and will benefit from the end results.

Customer's quality expectations

A statement from the customer about the quality expected from the final product. This should be obtained during the start-up of a project in *Preparing a Project Brief* (SU4) as an important feed into *Planning Quality* (IP1), where it is matched against the Project Approach and the standards that will need to be applied in order to achieve that quality.

Daily Log

A record of jobs to do or to check that others have done, commitments from the author or others, important events, decisions or discussions. A Daily Log should be kept by the Project Manager and any Team Managers.

Deliverable

An item that the project has to create as part of the requirements. It may be part of the final outcome or an intermediate element on which one or more subsequent deliverables are dependent. According to the type of project, another name for a deliverable is 'product'.

Earned value analysis

Earned value analysis is a method for measuring project performance. It indicates how much of the budget should have been spent in view of the amount of work done so far and the task, assignment or resources.

End Project Report

A report given by the Project Manager to the Project Board that confirms the handover of all products and provides an updated Business Case and an assessment of how well the project has done against its Project Initiation Document.

End stage assessment

The review by the Project Board and Project Manager of the End Stage Report to decide whether to approve the next Stage Plan (unless the last stage has now been completed). According to the size and criticality of the project, the review may be formal or informal. The approval to proceed should be documented as an important management product.

End Stage Report

A report given by the Project Manager to the Project Board at the end of each management stage of the project. This provides information about the project performance during the stage and the project status at stage end.

Exception

A situation where it can be forecast that there will be a deviation beyond the tolerance levels agreed between the Project Manager and the Project Board (or between the Project Board and corporate or programme management, or between a Team Manager and the Project Manager).

Exception assessment

This is a meeting of the Project Board to approve (or reject) an Exception Plan.

Exception Plan

This is a plan that often follows an Exception Report. For a Team Plan exception, it covers the period from the present to the end of the Work Package; for a Stage Plan exception, it covers the period from the present to the end of the current stage. If the exception were at a project level, the Project Plan would be replaced.

Exception Report

Description of the exception situation, its impact, options, recommendation and impact of the recommendation to the Project Board. This report is prepared by the relevant manager to inform the next higher level of management of the situation.

Executive

The single individual with overall responsibility for ensuring that a project meets its objectives and delivers the projected benefits. This individual should ensure that the project or programme maintains its business focus, that it has clear authority and that the work, including risks, is actively managed. The Executive is the chairperson of the Project Board, representing the customer, and is the owner of the Business Case.

Feasibility study

A feasibility study is an early study of a problem to assess if a solution is feasible. The study will normally scope the problem, identify and explore a number of solutions, and make a recommendation on what action to take. Part of the work in developing options is to calculate an outline Business Case for each as one aspect of comparison.

Follow-on Action Recommendations

A report that can be used as input to the process of creating a Business Case/Project Mandate for any follow-on PRINCE2 project and for recording any follow-on instructions covering incomplete products or outstanding Project Issues.

Gantt chart

This is a diagram of a plan's activities against a time background, showing start and end times and resources required.

Gate review

A generic term, rather than a PRINCE2 term, meaning a point at the end of a stage or phase where a decision is made whether to continue with the project. In PRINCE2 this would equate to an end stage assessment.

Highlight Report

Time-driven report from the Project Manager to the Project Board on stage progress.

Issue Log

Contains all Project Issues including Requests for Change raised during the project. Project Issues are each allocated a unique number and are filed in the Issue Log under the appropriate status. *See also* Project Issue.

Lessons Learned Log

An informal collection of good and bad lessons learned about the management and specialist processes and products as the project progresses. At the end of the project, it is formalised and structured into a Lessons Learned Report. *See also* Lessons Learned Report.

Lessons Learned Report

A report that describes the lessons learned in undertaking the project and includes statistics from the quality control of the project's management products. It is approved by the Project Board and then held centrally for the benefit of future projects.

Off-Specification

Something that should be provided by the project, but currently is not (or is forecast not to be) provided. This might be a missing product or a product not meeting its specifications. It is one type of Project Issue.

Operational and maintenance acceptance

Acceptance by the person/group who will support the product during its useful life that it is accepted into the operational environment. The format of the acceptance will depend on the product itself – it could be in the form of an acceptance letter signed by the appropriate authority, or a more complex report detailing the operational and maintenance arrangements that have been put in place.

Outcome

The term used to describe the totality of what the project is set up to deliver, consisting of all the specialist products. For example, this could be an installed computer system with trained staff to use it, backed up by new working practices and documentation, a refurbished and equipped building with all the staff moved in and working, or it could be a new product launched with a recruited and trained sales and support team in place.

Peer review

Specific reviews of a project or any of its products where personnel from within the organisation and/or from other organisations carry out an independent assessment of the project. Peer reviews can be done at any point within a project but are often used at stage-end points.

Phase

A part, section or segment of a project, similar in meaning to a PRINCE2 stage. The key meaning of stage in PRINCE2 terms is the use of management stages, i.e. sections of the project to which the Project Board commits one at a time. A phase might be more connected to a time slice, change of skills required or change of emphasis.

Post-implementation review

See Post-project review.

Post-project review

One or more reviews held after project closure to determine if the expected benefits have been obtained. Also known as post-implementation review.

PRINCE2

A method that supports some selected aspects of project management. The acronym stands for **PR**ojects **IN** Controlled **E**nvironments.

PRINCE2 project

A project whose product(s) can be defined at its start sufficiently precisely so as to be measurable against predefined metrics and that is managed according to the PRINCE2 method.

Process

That which must be done to bring about a particular result in terms of information to be gathered, decisions to be made and results to be achieved.

Producer

This role represents the creator(s) of a product that is the subject of a quality review. Typically, it will be filled by the person who has produced the product or who has led the team responsible.

Product

Any input to or output from a project. PRINCE2 distinguishes between management products (which are produced as part of the management or quality processes of the project) and specialist products (which are those products that make up the final deliverable). A product may itself be a collection of other products.

Product-based planning

A four-step technique leading to a comprehensive plan based on creation and delivery of required outputs. The technique considers prerequisite products, quality requirements and the dependencies between products.

Product Breakdown Structure

A hierarchy of all the products to be produced during a plan.

Product Checklist

A list of the major products of a plan, plus key dates in their delivery.

Product Description

A description of a product's purpose, composition, derivation and quality criteria. It is produced at planning time, as soon as possible after the need for the product is identified.

Product Flow Diagram

A diagram showing the sequence of production and interdependencies of the products listed in a Product Breakdown Structure.

Product life span

This term is used in this manual to define the total life of a product from the time of the initial idea for the product until it is removed from service. It is likely that there will be many projects affecting the product during its life, such as a feasibility study and development, enhancement or correction projects.

Product Status Account

A report on the status of products. The required products can be specified by identifier or the part of the project in which they were developed.

Programme

A portfolio of projects selected, planned and managed in a co-ordinated way.

Project

A temporary organisation that is created for the purpose of delivering one or more business products according to a specified Business Case.

Project Approach

A description of the way in which the work of the project is to be approached. For example: Are we building a product from scratch or buying in a product that already exists? Are the technology and products that we can use constrained by decisions taken at programme level?

Project Assurance

The Project Board's responsibilities to assure itself that the project is being conducted correctly.

Project Brief

A description of what the project is to do; a refined and extended version of the Project Mandate, which the Project Board approves and which is input to project initiation.

Project closure notification

Advice from the Project Board to inform all stakeholders and the host location that the project resources can be disbanded and support services, such as space, equipment and access, demobilised. It should indicate a closure date for costs to be charged to the project.

Project closure recommendation

A recommendation prepared by the Project Manager for the Project Board to send as a project closure notification when the board is satisfied that the project can be closed.

Project Initiation Document (PID)

A logical document that brings together the key information needed to start the project on a sound basis and to convey that information to all concerned with the project.

Project Issue

A term used to cover any concern, query, Request for Change, suggestion or Off-Specification raised during the project. They can be about anything to do with the project.

Project life cycle

This term is used in this manual to define the period from the start-up of a project to the handover of the finished product to those who will operate and maintain it.

Project management

The planning, monitoring and control of all aspects of a project and the motivation of all those involved in it to achieve the project objectives on time and to the specified cost, quality and performance.

Project management team

Covers the entire management structure of Project Board, Project Manager, plus any Team Manager, Project Assurance and Project Support roles.

Project Manager

The person given the authority and responsibility to manage the project on a day-to-day basis to deliver the required products within the constraints agreed with the Project Board.

Project Mandate

Information created externally to the project that forms the terms of reference and is used to start up the PRINCE2 project.

Project Plan

A high-level plan showing the major products of the project, when they will be delivered and at what cost. An initial Project Plan is presented as part of the Project Initiation Document. This is revised as information on actual progress appears. It is a major control document for the Project Board to measure actual progress against expectations.

Project Quality Plan

A plan defining the key quality criteria, quality control and audit processes to be applied to project management and specialist work in the PRINCE2 project. It will be part of the text in the Project Initiation Document.

Project records

A collection of all approved management and specialist products and other material, which is necessary to provide an auditable record of the project.

Note: This does not include working files.

Project start-up notification

Advice to the host location that the project is about to start and requesting any required Project Support services.

Project Support

An administrative role in the project management team. Project Support can be in the form of advice and help with project management tools, guidance, administrative services such as filing, and the collection of actual data. The provision of any Project Support on a formal basis is optional. Tasks either need to be done by the Project Manager or delegated to a separate body and this will be driven by the needs of the individual project and Project Manager. A full description of the role can be found in *Project management team roles*, Appendix B.

One support function that must be considered is that of configuration management. Depending on the project size and environment, there may be a need to formalise this and it quickly becomes a task with which the Project Manager cannot cope without support. Details of the Configuration Librarian role can be found in *Project management team roles*, Appendix B.

Project Support Office

A group set up to provide certain administrative services to the Project Manager. Often the group provides its services to many projects in parallel.

Proximity (of risk)

Reflects the timing of the risk, i.e. is the threat (or opportunity) stronger at a particular time, does it disappear some time in the future, or does the probability or impact change over time?

Quality

The totality of features and characteristics of a product or service that bear on its ability to satisfy stated needs. Also defined as 'fitness for purpose' or 'conforms to requirements'.

Quality Log

Contains all planned and completed quality activities. The Quality Log is used by the Project Manager and Project Assurance as part of reviewing progress.

Quality management system

The complete set of quality standards, procedures and responsibilities for a site or organisation.

Quality review

A quality review is a quality checking technique with a specific structure, defined roles and procedure designed to ensure a product's completeness and adherence to standards. The participants are drawn from those with an interest in the product and those with the necessary skills to review its correctness. An example of the checks made by a quality review is: 'Does the document match the quality criteria in the Product Description?'

Quality system

See Quality management system.

Request for Change

A means of proposing a modification to the current specification of a product. It is one type of Project Issue.

Requirements

A description of the user's needs. *See also* Specification.

Reviewer

A person asked to review a product that is the subject of a quality review.

Risk

Risk can be defined as uncertainty of outcome, whether positive opportunity or negative threat. Every project has risks associated with it. Project management has the task of identifying risks that apply and taking appropriate steps to take advantage of opportunities that may arise and avoid, reduce or react to threats.

Risk Log

Contains all information about the risks, their analysis, countermeasures and status. Also known as Risk Register.

Risk profile

A graphical representation of information normally found in the Risk Log.

Risk register

See Risk Log.

Risk tolerance line

The risk tolerance line is one drawn between risks that can be accepted or for which suitable actions have been planned, and risks that that are considered sufficiently serious to require referral to the next higher level of project authority.

Senior responsible owner

This is not a PRINCE2 term, but is used in many organisations. Its equivalent in PRINCE2 terms would be the 'Executive' role. *See also* Executive.

Senior Supplier

The Project Board role that provides knowledge and experience of the main discipline(s) involved in the production of the project's deliverable(s). Represents the supplier interests within the project and provides supplier resources.

Senior User

The Project Board role accountable for ensuring that user needs are specified correctly and that the solution meets those needs.

Specification

A detailed statement of what the user wants in terms of products, what these should look like, what they should do and with what they should interface.

Sponsor

Not a specific PRINCE2 role but often used to mean the major driving force of a project. May be the equivalent of Executive or corporate/programme management.

Stage

A stage is the section of the project that the Project Manager is managing on behalf of the Project Board at any one time, at the end of which the Project Board wishes to review progress to date, the state of the Project Plan, Business Case and risks, and the next Stage Plan in order to decide whether to continue with the project.

Stakeholders

Parties with an interest in the execution and outcome of a project. They would include business streams affected by or dependent on the outcome.

Supplier

The group or groups responsible for the supply of the project's specialist products.

Team Manager

A role that may be employed by the Project Manager or Senior Supplier to manage the work of project team members.

Tolerance

The permissible deviation above and below a plan's estimate of time and cost without escalating the deviation to the next level of management. Separate tolerance figures should be given for time and cost. There may also be tolerance levels for quality, scope, benefit and risk. Tolerance is applied at project, stage and team levels.

User(s)

The person or group who will use the final deliverable(s) of the project.

Work Package

The set of information relevant to the creation of one or more products. It will contain a description of the work, the Product Description(s), details of any constraints on production such as time and cost, interfaces, and confirmation of the agreement between the Project Manager and the person or Team Manager who is to implement the Work Package that the work can be done within the constraints.

APPENDIX A: PRODUCT DESCRIPTION OUTLINES

This Appendix contains Product Description outlines for the standard management products. These outlines do not include all of the standard headings and content of a Product Description, such as 'format and presentation' and 'quality method'. These may vary from project to project, so no attempt has been made to define what a specific project may need.

Those wishing to turn these outlines into full Product Descriptions will need to add the missing information. This is a good opportunity to compare the given material against the circumstances of a specific project and tailor the text to be a more precise fit. A full description of the contents of a Product Description is given in A.22.

A.1 Acceptance Criteria

This is not a stand-alone PRINCE2 management product, but its inclusion may help in understanding what the content might be.

A.1.1 Purpose

A definition in measurable terms of the characteristics required of the final product(s) for it/them to be acceptable to the customers and staff who will be affected. In many cases, the Acceptance Criteria will be the same as the quality criteria in the Product Description of the final product.

A.1.2 Composition

This will vary according to the type of final product. Suggestions are:

- Target dates
- Major functions
- Appearance
- Personnel level required to use/operate the product
- Performance levels
- Capacity
- Accuracy
- Availability
- Reliability (mean/maximum time to repair, mean time between failures)

- Development cost
- Running costs
- Security
- Ease of use
- Timings.

A.1.3 Derivation

Acceptance Criteria are derived from:

- The Senior User
- Customer's quality expectations.

The criteria are either provided by programme management or developed during *Starting up a Project* (SU).

A.1.4 Quality criteria

- All criteria are measurable
- Each criterion is individually realistic
- The criteria as a group are realistic, for example, high quality, early delivery and low cost may not go together
- Acceptance Criteria form a complete list of criteria to define what will constitute a product acceptable to the customer.

A.2   Business Case

A.2.1   Purpose

To document the justification for the undertaking of a project based on the estimated cost of development and implementation against the risks and the anticipated business benefits and savings to be gained. The total business change must be considered, which may be much wider than just the project development cost.

The Business Case is used to say why the forecast effort and time will be worth the expenditure. The Project Board will monitor the ongoing viability of the project against the Business Case.

A.2.2   Composition

- Reasons
- Options (brief description of the different options considered for the project including recommendation of the chosen option)
- Benefits expected (expressed in measurable terms against today's situation)
- Risks (summary of the key risks of the project)
- Cost (extracted from the Project Plan)
- Timescale (summary of the Project Plan)
- Investment appraisal
- Evaluation.

A.2.3   Derivation

Information for the Business Case is derived from:

- Project Mandate/Project Brief (reasons)
- Project Plan (costs and timescales)
- The customer.

The existence of a provisional Business Case is checked during *Starting up a Project* (SU). If the Project Mandate does not contain a Business Case, this would be created. The Business Case is refined in sub-process *Refining the Business Case and Risks* (IP3).

A.2.4   Quality criteria

- All the benefits must be justified
- The Project Plan and Business Case must be aligned
- The reasons for the project must be consistent with corporate or programme strategy.

A.3   Checkpoint Report

A.3.1   Purpose

To report, at a frequency defined in the Stage Plan and/or Work Package, the status of work for each member of a team.

A.3.2   Composition

- Date of checkpoint
- Period covered
- Follow-ups from previous reports
- Activities during the period
- Products completed during the period
- Quality work carried out during the period
- Work Package tolerance status
- Actual or potential problems and risk update
- Work planned for the next period
- Products to be completed during the next period.

A.3.3   Derivation

- Verbal reports from team members
- Stage or Team Plan
- Previous checkpoint (checkpoints are held as part of *Executing a Work Package* (MP2)).

A.3.4   Quality criteria

- Every item in the Stage or Team Plan for that period covered
- Every team member working to an agreed schedule
- Every team member's work covered
- An update on any unresolved problems from the previous report.

A.7   Customer's quality expectations

Customer's quality expectations is not a stand-alone PRINCE2 management product, but its inclusion here may help in understanding what the content may be.

A.7.1 Purpose

To capture the quality aspirations of the customer.

A.7.2   Composition

The customer's quality expectations should be stated within the Project Brief. The format should be flexible. Consider the following questions:

- What elements of the customer's existing QMS should be used?

- What other standards should be considered when planning the project?

- What arrangements are being made to manage the change into the business?

- What arrangements are being made to ensure that the staff/customers affected by the change are managed effectively?

- What is being done to ensure that the organisation can manage this change after the project is completed?

- What level of team satisfaction should be achieved if surveyed?

- What level of customer satisfaction should be achieved if surveyed?

A.7.3   Derivation

Customer's quality expectations are derived from:

- The Senior User

- Customer's expectations.

The criteria are either provided by programme management or developed during Starting up a Project (SU).

A.7.4   Quality criteria

- The customer's quality expectations define a list of what will make the final product acceptable to the customer

- Customer's quality expectations should be stated in such a way that Acceptance Criteria can be derived from them.

A.8   Daily Log

A.8.1   Purpose

To record required actions or significant events not caught by other PRINCE2 documents. It acts as the Project Manager's or a Team Manager's diary.

A.8.2   Composition

- Date of entry
- Action or comment
- Person responsible
- Target date
- Result.

A.8.3   Derivation

- Risk Log
- Stage Plan
- Checkpoint Reports
- Quality Log
- Conversations and observations.

A.8.4   Quality criteria

- Entries are understandable at a later date
- Anything of a permanent nature is transferred to the appropriate record, for example Project Issues should be transferred to the Issue Log
- Date, person responsible and target date are always filled in.

A.9   End Project Report

A.9.1 Purpose

This report is the Project Manager's report to the Project Board (who may pass it on to corporate or programme management) on how well the project has performed against its Project Initiation Document, including the original planned cost, schedule and tolerances, the revised Business Case and final version of the Project Plan.

A.9.2 Composition

- Achievement of the project's objectives
- Review of benefits achieved to date (if any)
- Performance against the planned target time, cost and project tolerances
- The effect on the original Project Plan and Business Case of any changes that were approved
- Final statistics on Project Issues received during the project
- The total impact of approved changes
- Statistics for all quality work carried out
- Post-Project Review Plan and date.

A.9.3 Derivation

The End Project Report is derived from:

- Updated Project Plan (including Team, Stage and Exception Plans)
- Project Initiation Document
- Risk Log
- Quality Log
- Business Case
- Lessons Learned Report(s)
- End Stage Report(s)
- Issue Log
- Post-Project Review Plan.

The End Project Report is produced during *Closing a Project* (CP).

A.9.4 Quality criteria

- The report describes the impact of the approved changes on the Project Initiation Document

- The report covers all the benefits that can be assessed at this time

- The quality work done during the project meets the quality expectations of the customer.

A.10 End Stage Report

A.10.1 Purpose

To give a summary of progress to date, the overall project situation and sufficient information to ask for a Project Board decision on what to do next with the project.

The Project Board uses the information in the End Stage Report to decide what action to take with the project: approve the next stage, ask for a revised next Stage Plan, amend the project scope or stop the project.

A.10.2 Composition

- Current Stage Plan with all the actuals
- Performance against stage tolerances
- Project Plan outlook
- Business Case review
- Risk review
- Project Issue situation
- Quality statistics
- Project Manager's report on any events that affected stage performance.

A.10.3 Derivation

Information for the report is obtained from:

- Stage Plan and actuals
- Next Stage Plan (if appropriate)
- Updated Project Plan
- Risk Log
- Lessons Learned Log
- Quality Log
- Issue Log
- Exception Report/Plan
- Completed Work Packages data.

The End Stage Report is an output from *Managing Stage Boundaries* (SB).

A.10.4 Quality criteria

- The report clearly shows stage performance against the plan

- Any abnormal situations are described, together with their impact
- Any appointed Project Assurance roles agree with the report.

A.11 Exception Plan

A.11.1 Purpose

An Exception Plan is a plan prepared for the appropriate management level to show the actions required to recover from the effect of a tolerance deviation. It is based on the recommendations made in the Exception Report.

It can replace a Project, Stage or Team Plan. If approved, it will replace the plan that is in exception and the Exception Plan will become the new baselined Project, Stage or Team Plan as appropriate.

A.11.2 Composition

- For an Exception Plan to replace the Project Plan – follow the composition of the Project Plan Product Description (A.30.2)

- For an Exception Plan to replace a Stage Plan – follow the composition of the Stage Plan Product Description (A.35.2). It is likely that a change in the Stage Plan will require the Project Plan to be updated but this change should not affect the overall tolerances for the project

- For an Exception Plan to replace a Team Plan – since this is an optional plan, follow the local planning procedures and plan content currently in force. It is likely that a change in the Team Plan will require the Stage Plan to be updated, but this change should not affect the overall tolerances for the stage.

A.11.3 Derivation

The plan is derived from:

- The plan that is in exception
- The Project Issue that contains the reason for the deviation.

A.11.4 Quality criteria

- The plan is achievable
- All quality aspects of the Project or Stage Plan Product Description outline have been considered
- The plan corrects the deviation defined in the associated Exception Report
- The plan is in line with the decisions made after presentation of the Exception Report
- New tolerances have been defined for the Exception Plan.

A.12 Exception Report

A.12.1 Purpose

An Exception Report is produced when a Team, Stage or Project Plan is forecast to exceed tolerance levels set. It is prepared by the relevant manager in order to inform the next higher level of management of the adverse situation.

A.12.2 Composition

- Description of the cause of a deviation from the relevant plan
- Consequences of the deviation
- Available options
- Effect of each option on the Business Case, risks and tolerances
- Project or Team Manager's recommendations.

A.12.3 Derivation

The information for an Exception Report may come from:

- Current plan and actuals
- Issue Log
- Risk Log
- Project Plan
- Quality Log
- Highlight Reports
- Checkpoint Reports
- Project Board advice of an external event that affects the project.

When a Stage or Project Plan is in exception, an Exception Report is output from *Escalating Project Issues* (CS8); if a Team Plan is in exception, an Exception Report is output from *Executing a Work Package* (MP2) and sent to the Project Manager as a Project Issue.

A.12.4 Quality criteria

- The current plan must accurately show the status of budget and schedule
- The reason(s) for the deviation must be stated.

A.16 Lessons Learned Log

A.16.1 Purpose

To be a repository of any lessons learned during the project that can be usefully applied to other projects. At the close of the project it is written up formally in the Lessons Learned Report. Minimally it should be updated at the end of a stage, but sensibly a note should be made in it of any good or bad point that arises in the use of the management and specialist products and tools at the time of the experience.

A.16.2 Composition

- What management and quality processes:
  - went well
  - went badly
  - were lacking
- A description of any abnormal events causing deviations
- Notes on the performance of specialist methods and tools used
- Recommendations for future enhancement or modification of the project management method
- Useful measurements on how much effort was required to create the various products
- Notes on effective and ineffective quality reviews and other tests, including the reasons for them working well or badly.

A.16.3 Derivation

Information for the records in the Lessons Learned Log is derived from:

- Observation and experience of the processes
- Quality Log
- Completed Work Packages
- Risk Log
- Highlight Report(s)
- Checkpoint Report(s)
- Stage Plans with actuals.

A.16.4 Quality criteria

- Each management control has been considered
- The reasons for all tolerance deviations and corrective actions have been recorded
- Input to the log is being done, minimally, at the end of each stage

- Project Assurance and Project Support have been asked for their input
- Statistics of the success of quality reviews and other types of test used are included.

A.17 Lessons Learned Report

A.17.1 Purpose

To pass on any lessons that can be usefully applied to other projects.

The data in the report should be used by a corporate group, such as quality assurance, who are responsible for the quality management system, in order to refine, change and improve the standards. Statistics on how much effort was needed for products can help improve future estimating.

A.17.2 Composition

- What management and quality processes:
  - went well
  - went badly
  - were lacking
- A description of any abnormal events causing deviations
- An assessment of technical methods and tools used
- An analysis of Project Issues and their results
- Recommendations for future enhancement or modification of the project management method
- Useful measurements on how much effort was required to create the various products
- Statistics on how effective quality reviews and other tests were in error trapping (for example, how many errors were found after products had passed a quality review or test).

A.17.3 Derivation

Information for the report is derived from:

- Lessons Learned Log
- End Stage Reports
- Quality Log
- Issue Log.

The Lessons Learned Report is completed in *Evaluating a Project* (CP3).

A.17.4 Quality criteria

- Every management control has been examined
- Statistics of the success of quality reviews and other types of test used are included
- Details of the effort taken for each product are given.

A.18 Off-Specification

A.18.1 Purpose

To document any situation where a product is failing, or is forecast to fail, to meet its specification.

A.18.2 Composition

- Date
- Issue Log number
- Status
- Description of the fault
- Impact of the fault
- Priority assessment
- Decision
- Allocation details, if applicable
- Date allocated
- Date completed.

A.18.3 Derivation

An Off-Specification can be raised by anyone associated with the project at any time. It would be gathered in as part of *Capturing Project Issues* (CS3). The Project Manager may also decide that a Project Issue is an Off-Specification during *Examining Project Issues* (CS4).

A.18.4 Quality criteria

- Logged in the Issue Log
- Accurate description of the problem.

A.19 Post-Project Review Plan

A.19.1 Purpose

To define for the Executive how and when a measurement of the achievement of the project benefits can be made. The plan is presented to the Executive at the end of the project.

The plan has to cover the effort to find out:

- Whether the expected benefits of the product(s) have been realised
- Whether the product(s) has caused any problems in use.

Each expected benefit has to be assessed for the level of its achievement so far or any additional time needed for the benefit to materialise. Use of the product may have brought unexpected side effects, either beneficial or adverse. Time and effort have to be allowed to document explanations of why these side effects were not foreseen. The plan must include time for recommendations on how to realise or improve benefits or counter problems.

A.19.2 Composition

- How to measure achievement of expected benefits
- When the various benefits can be measured
- What resources are needed to carry out the review work
- Other areas that may need consideration, such as user reaction.

A.19.3 Derivation

- Business Case
- Discussion with the users and product support people.

The post-project review is planned as part of *Identifying Follow-on Actions* (CP2), but the Executive is responsible for ensuring that the review happens after the project has finished.

A.19.4 Quality criteria

- Covers all benefits mentioned in the Business Case
- Describes a suitable timing for measurement of the benefits, together with reasons
- Identifies the skills or individuals who will be needed to carry out the measurements
- Is realistic in terms of effort when compared to the anticipated benefits.

A.20 Product Breakdown Structure

A.20.1 Purpose

To show all products to be developed and quality controlled. To understand the content and function of all products to be developed.

A.20.2 Composition

Top-to-bottom diagram showing breakdown of all products to be developed. External products must be included in the Product Breakdown Structure, clearly distinguished from the products developed by the project. The PRINCE2 convention is for project products to be shown as rectangles, product groupings as rhomboids and external products as ellipses.

A.20.3 Derivation

- Project Brief
- Project Quality Plan.

A.20.4 Quality criteria

- External products and project products are included
- The Product Breakdown Structure is consistent with the Product Checklist
- Genuine integration products (i.e. non-bottom level but requiring a separate Product Description) are distinguished from collective groupings (memory joggers)
- Management and specialist products are identified and distinguished
- Product Descriptions for the bottom-level products can be written without further decomposition
- Enough bottom-level products have been identified to meet management planning and control requirements
- The combination of all the products identified will fulfil the business need
- All quality products have been identified that meet the needs of customer, audit and Project Assurance as described in the Project Quality Plan.

A.21 Product Checklist

A.21.1 Purpose

To list the products to be produced within a Stage Plan, together with key status dates.

Used by the Project Board to monitor progress.

A21.2 Composition

- Plan identification
- Product names (and reference numbers if appropriate)
- Planned and actual dates for:
  - draft ready
  - quality check
  - approval.

A.21.3 Derivation

- Extracted from the Product Flow Diagram.

Produced as an output from *Defining and Analysing Products* (PL2) and finalised in *Completing a Plan* (PL7) and updated throughout *Controlling a Stage* (CS).

A.21.4 Quality criteria

- The details and dates match those in the Stage Plan.

A.22 Product Description

A.22.1 Purpose

The purpose is to:

- Understand the detailed nature, purpose and function of the product
- Identify the sources of information or supply for the product
- Describe the required appearance of the product
- Identify the level of quality required of the product
- Enable identification of activities to develop and quality control the product
- Define the people or skills required to develop and check the product.

A.22.2 Composition

- *Identifier*: unique key, probably allocated by the configuration management method
- *Title*: name by which the product is known
- *Purpose*: this defines the purpose that the product will fulfil. Is it a means to an end or an end in itself? It is helpful in understanding the product's functions, size, quality, complexity, robustness, etc.
- *Composition*: this is a list of the parts of the product. For example, if the product were a document, this would be a list of the expected chapters or sections
- *Derivation*: what are the source products from which this product is derived? Examples are:
    - a design is derived from a specification
    - a product is bought in from a supplier
    - a statement of the expected benefits are obtained from the user
    - a product is obtained from another department or team
- *Format and presentation*: any standard appearance to which the product must conform
- *Allocated to*: the person, group or skill type needed to create this product
- *Quality criteria*: to what quality specification must the product be produced and what quality measurements will be applied by those inspecting the finished product? This might be a simple reference to one or more common standards that are documented elsewhere or it might be a full explanation of some yardstick to be applied
- *Quality method*: what kind of quality checking – for example, test, inspection or review – is to be used to check the quality or functionality of the product?
- *Quality tolerance*: details of any range in the quality criteria within which the product would be acceptable. This may be accompanied by a series of time periods during which the product quality is required to improve so that it remains within tolerance

- *Quality check skills and/or people required*: either identification of the people who are to check the quality, an indication of the skills required to do so or a pointer to which area(s) should supply the checking resources. Identification of the actual people may be left until planning the stage in which the quality check is to be done.

A.22.3 Derivation

- Product Breakdown Structure
- The end users of the product
- Existing customer or supplier quality management systems.

A.22.4 Quality criteria

- The purpose is clear and consistent with other products
- The product is described to a level of detail sufficient to plan and manage its development
- The composition of the product describes the contents/elements of the product, rather than being a requirements specification
- Responsibility for the development of the product is clearly identified
- Responsibility for the development of the product is consistent with the roles and responsibilities described in the project management team organisation and the Project Quality Plan
- The quality criteria are consistent with the project quality standards, standard checklists and Acceptance Criteria
- The quality criteria can be used to determine when the product is fit for purpose
- The types of quality check required are able to verify whether or not the product meets its stated quality criteria.

A.23 Product Flow Diagram

A.23.1 Purpose

To show the required sequence of delivery of a plan's products and identify dependencies between those products, including any external products.

A.23.2 Composition

A diagram showing the product delivery sequence from top to bottom or left to right, plus the dependencies between those products. Arrows indicate dependencies between products. External products must be clearly distinguished from the products developed by the plan. The PRINCE2 convention is for project products to be shown as rectangles and external products as ellipses.

A.23.3 Derivation

- Product Descriptions
- Product Breakdown Structure.

A.23.4 Quality criteria

- The topmost product from the Product Breakdown Structure (PBS) is at the end of the Product Flow Diagram (PFD)
- All external products are identified and the dependencies understood
- All bottom-level products on the PBS are identified on the PFD
- All integration products identified on the PBS are shown on the PFD
- All products identified in the PFD are identified as products on the PBS
- There are no products without dependencies
- Dependencies have been identified at a level suitable to that of the plan of which the PFD is a part
- Dependencies are consistent with the derivation fields (from the Product Description) of all the products.

A.24 Product Status Account

A.24.1 Purpose

The Product Status Account provides information about the state of products within defined limits. The limits can vary. For example, the report could cover the entire project, a particular stage or a particular area of the project. It is particularly useful if the Project Manager wishes to confirm the version number of products.

A.24.2 Composition

The composition will vary but will normally consist of the following information:

- Project name
- Product type
- Product identifier
- Version number.

For each product identified the following additional information may be provided:

- Date Product Description baselined
- Date product baselined
- List of related products
- Date on which a copy of product was issued for change
- Planned date for next baseline
- Planned date for next release
- Any relevant notes, for example, change pending, under review.

A.24.3 Derivation

- Configuration Item Records.

A.24.4 Quality criteria

- Covers all items requested
- Accurate.

A.25 Project Approach

A.25.1 Purpose

To define the type of solution to be developed by the project and/or the method of delivering that solution. It should also identify any environment into which the solution must fit.

A.25.2 Composition

- Options considered, for example:
  - bespoke
  - contracted out
  - current product modified
  - 'design from scratch'
  - use company staff
  - hire in contract staff
  - buy a ready-made solution
- Chosen option
- Reasons for selection/rejection, for example, part of programme approach
- Operational environment (identification of any environment into which the solution must fit).

A.25.3 Derivation

- Project Brief
- Design authority or equivalent
- Marketplace – that is, what is available.

A.25.4 Quality criteria

- It must conform to the strategy that relates to the product's operational environment
- It must be achievable within all known time and cost constraints for the project
- It must be achievable with known technology.

A.26 Project Brief

A.26.1 Purpose

To provide a full and firm foundation for the initiation of the project.

The contents are extended and refined into the Project Initiation Document, which is the working document for managing and directing the project.

The Project Brief is a key document in its own right. It is the basis of the Project Initiation Document. Any significant change to the material contained in the Project Brief will thus need to be referred to corporate or programme management.

A.26.2 Composition

The following is a suggested list of contents, which should be tailored to the requirements and environment of each project:

- Background
- Project definition, explaining what the project needs to achieve. It will contain:
  - project objectives
  - project scope and exclusions
  - outline project deliverables and/or desired outcomes
  - constraints
  - interfaces
- Outline Business Case
  - description of how this project supports business strategy, plans or programmes
  - reasons why the project is needed
- Project tolerances
- Customer's quality expectations (see Appendix A.7 for a more detailed explanation)
- Acceptance Criteria (see Appendix A.1 for a more detailed explanation)
- Any known risks.

If earlier work has been done, the Project Brief may refer to the document(s) containing useful information, such as Project Plan outline, rather than include copies of them.

A.26.3 Derivation

The Project Brief is developed from the Project Mandate supplied at the start of the project, produced by *Preparing a Project Brief* (SU4), and accepted via *Authorising Initiation* (DP1).

If the project is part of a programme, the programme should provide the Project Brief. In such circumstances it will not have to be derived from a Project Mandate.

If no Project Mandate is provided, the Project Manager has to generate the Project Brief 'from scratch' in discussions with the customer and users.

A.26.4 Quality criteria

- The Project Brief accurately reflects the Project Mandate

- It forms a firm basis on which to initiate a project (*Initiating a Project* (IP))

- It indicates how the customer will assess the acceptability of the finished product(s).

A.27 Project Initiation Document

A.27.1 Purpose

To define the project, to form the basis for its management and the assessment of overall success.

The Project Initiation Document gives the direction and scope of the project and forms the 'contract' between the project management team and corporate or programme management.

The two primary uses of the document are to:

- Ensure that the project has a sound basis before asking the Project Board to make any major commitment to the project

- Act as a base document against which the Project Board and Project Manager can assess progress, Project Issues and ongoing viability questions.

A.27.2 Composition

The base elements of information needed to direct and manage a project are covered by the following fundamental questions:

- **What** a project is aiming to achieve

- **Why** it is important to achieve it

- **Where** it will be developed, in the case of a geographically distributed product

- **Who** is going to be involved in managing the project and what their responsibilities are

- **How** and **when** it is all going to happen.

The information will be held in various ways, and the following contents should be read not as a list of contents for one document but rather as the information needed in order to make the initiation decisions. The sections have been divided into 'Stable' and 'Dynamic' to indicate those sections that will need to have new versions created as the project progresses.

Stable

- Background, explaining the context of the project and how the current position has been arrived at

- Project definition, explaining what the project needs to achieve. Under this heading will be:

  - project objectives
  - project scope
  - project deliverables and/or desired outcomes
  - exclusions
  - constraints

- interfaces
- assumptions
- Project Approach
- Project tolerances
- Project controls, laying down how control is to be exercised within the project and the reporting and monitoring mechanisms that will support this; it will include the exception process.

Dynamic

- Initial Business Case, explaining why the project is being undertaken
- Initial Project Plan, explaining how and when the activities of the project will occur (for details of the Project Plan content, see the separate Product Description outline)
- Initial Risk Log, documenting the results of the risk analysis and risk management activities
- Project organisation structure, explaining who will be on the project management team
  - project management team structure
  - job descriptions
- Communication Plan (see the separate Communication Plan Product Description outline)
- Project Quality Plan (see the separate Project Quality Plan Product Description outline).

A.27.3 Derivation

- Supplier's project management standards (if known)
- Customer's specified control requirements
- Much of the information should come from the Project Mandate, enhanced in the Project Brief.

The Project Initiation Document will be completed during *Initiating a Project* (IP). Parts of it, such as the Risk Log, Project Plan and Business Case, may be updated and refined by each pass through *Managing Stage Boundaries* (SB) and will finally be archived as part of *Closing a Project* (CP).

A.27.4 Quality criteria

- The document correctly represents the project
- It shows a viable, achievable project that is in line with corporate strategy or overall programme needs
- The project organisation structure is complete, with names and titles
- All the roles have been considered

- It clearly shows a control, reporting and direction regime that can be implemented, appropriate to the scale, business risk and business importance of the project

- The project organisation structure is backed up by agreed and signed job descriptions

- The relationships and lines of authority are clear

- If necessary, the project organisation structure says to whom the Project Board reports

- The controls cover the needs of the Project Board, Project Manager and Team Managers

- The controls satisfy any delegated assurance requirements

- It is clear who will administer each control.

A.28 Project Issue

A.28.1 Purpose

A generic term for any matter that has to be brought to the attention of the project team and requires an answer. After receiving a unique reference number, Project Issues are evaluated in terms of impact on the product, effort and cost, risks, Project Plan and Business Case. The Project Manager may make a decision on what action to take or the Project Issue may be referred to the Project Board. A Project Issue may have a negative or positive impact on the project. Project issues include:

- Requests for Change
- Off-Specifications
- Questions
- Statements of concern.

A.28.2 Composition

- Author
- Date
- Project Issue number
- Description of the Project Issue
- Priority
- Impact analysis
- Decision
- Signature of decision maker(s)
- Date of decision.

A.28.3 Derivation

Anyone may submit a Project Issue. Typical sources are users and specialists working on the project. *Capturing Project Issues* (CS3) deals with collating Project Issues. They are then examined during *Examining Project Issues* (CS4).

A.28.4 Quality criteria

- The problem/requirement/opportunity is clear
- All the implications have been thought out
- The Project Issue has been correctly logged.

A.29 Project Mandate

A.29.1 Purpose

The information in the Mandate is used to trigger *Starting up a Project* (SU). It should contain sufficient information to identify at least the prospective Executive of the Project Board and indicate the subject matter of the project.

It will be used to create the Project Brief.

A.29.2 Composition

The actual composition of a Project Mandate will vary according to the type and size of project and also the environment in which the Mandate is generated. The project may be a completely new piece of work that has just arisen, it may be the outcome of an earlier investigation or it may be part of a larger programme.

The following list contains suggested contents, which should be tailored to suit the specific project:

- Responsible authority
- Background
- Project objectives
- Scope
- Constraints
- Interfaces
- Customer's quality expectations
- Outline Business Case (reasons)
- Project tolerances
- Reference to any associated documents or products
- An indication of who are to be the Executive and Project Manager
- The customer(s), user(s) and any other known interested parties.

If the Project Mandate is based on earlier work, there may be other useful information such as an estimate of the project size and duration, and a view of the risks faced by the project.

A.29.3 Derivation

A Project Mandate may come from anywhere, but it should come from a level of management that can authorise the cost and resource usage. It is input to *Starting up a Project* (SU).

A.29.4 Quality criteria

- The level of authority is commensurate with the anticipated size, risk and cost of the project

- There is sufficient detail to allow the appointment of an appropriate Executive and Project Manager

- All the known interested parties are identified

- The Project Mandate describes what is required.

A.30 Project Plan

A.30.1 Purpose

The Project Plan is a mandatory plan that provides a statement of how and when a project's objectives are to be achieved, by showing the major products, activities and resources required on the project.

It provides the Business Case with planned project costs and it identifies the management stages and other major control points.

It is used by the Project Board as a baseline against which to monitor project progress and cost stage by stage.

A.30.2 Composition

This product forms part of the Project Initiation Document and will contain the following:

- Plan description, giving a brief description of what the plan covers
- Project prerequisites, containing any fundamental aspects that must be in place at the start of the project and that must remain in place for the project to succeed
- External dependencies
- Planning assumptions
- Project Plan, covering:
  - project-level Gantt or bar chart with identified management stages
  - project-level Product Breakdown Structure
  - project-level Product Flow Diagrams
  - project-level Product Descriptions
  - project-level activity network
  - project financial budget
  - project change budget
  - project-level table of resource requirements
  - requested/assigned specific resources
  - project-level tolerances (for example, time and budget)
- Contingency plans, explaining how it is intended to deal with the consequences of any risks that materialise.

A.30.3 Derivation

- Project Brief.

Refined from the outline Project Plan in the Project Brief during *Planning a Project* (IP2). Modified during *Updating a Project Plan* (SB2).

A.30.4 Quality criteria

- The plan is achievable
- It supports the rest of the Project Initiation Document.

A.31 Project Quality Plan

A.31.1 Purpose

The Project Quality Plan is part of the Project Initiation Document.

The purpose is to define the quality techniques and standards to be applied, and the various responsibilities for achieving the required quality levels, during the project.

A.31.2 Composition

- Customer's quality expectations (from the Project Brief)
- Quality tolerances
- Acceptance Criteria
- Quality responsibilities
- Reference to any standards that need to be met
- Quality control and audit processes to be applied to project management
- Quality control and audit process requirements for specialist work
- Change management procedures
- Configuration Management Plan
- Any tools to be used to ensure quality.

A.31.3 Derivation

The Project Quality Plan is derived from:

- Customer's quality expectations
- Acceptance Criteria
- Organisational standards
- Project Approach
- Project Brief
- Supplier and customer quality management systems (QMS)
- Configuration management requirements
- Change control requirements.

It is produced as an output from *Planning Quality* (IP1).

A.31.4 Quality criteria

- The plan clearly defines ways in which the customer's quality expectations will be met
- The defined ways are sufficient to achieve the required quality

- Responsibilities for quality are defined up to a level that is independent of the project and Project Manager
- The plan conforms to the corporate quality policy.

A.32 Quality Log

A.32.1 Purpose

The purpose is to:

- Issue a unique reference for each quality check
- Act as a pointer to the quality check documentation for a product
- Act as a summary of the number and type of quality checks held.

The log summarises all the quality checks that are planned/have taken place and provides information for the End Stage Reports and End Project Report as well as the Lessons Learned Report.

A.32.2 Composition

For each entry in the log, the following should be recorded:

- Reference number
- Product
- Method of quality checking
- Staff responsible, name, role
- Planned date
- Actual date
- Result
- Number of action items
- Target sign-off date
- Actual sign-off date.

A.32.3 Derivation

Entries are made when a quality check or test is entered on a Stage Plan. The remaining information comes from the actual performance of the check. The sign-off date is when all corrective action items have been signed off.

An initial, blank Quality Log is created during *Planning Quality* (IP1).

A.32.4 Quality criteria

- A procedure is in place that will ensure that every quality check is entered on the log
- Responsibility for the log has been allocated.

A.33 Request for Change

A.33.1 Purpose

To request a modification to a product or an acceptance criterion as currently specified.

A.33.2 Composition

- Date
- Issue Log number
- Status
- Description of the proposed change
- Impact of the change
- Priority assessment
- Decision
- Allocation details
- Date allocated
- Date completed.

A.33.3 Derivation

A Request for Change can be submitted by anyone connected with the project. A Request for Change can be submitted and gathered in by *Capturing Project Issues* (CS3); alternatively, a Project Issue can be defined as a Request for Change by the Project Manager as part of *Examining Project Issues* (CS4).

A.33.4 Quality criteria

- Source clearly identified
- Logged in the Issue Log
- Accurate description of the requested change
- Benefit of making the change clearly expressed and, where possible, in measurable terms.

A.34 Risk Log

A.34.1 Purpose

The purpose of the Risk Log is to contain all information about the risks, their analysis, countermeasures and status.

A.34.2 Composition

- *Risk identifier*: unique code to allow grouping of all information on this risk
- *Author*: who submitted the risk
- *Date identified*: when was the risk first identified
- *Description*: description of the risk
- *Risk category*: for example, commercial, legal, technical
- *Impact*: effect on the project/programme/organisation if this risk were to occur
- *Probability*: estimate of the likelihood of the risk occurring
- *Proximity*: the closeness in time in which the risk is likely to occur
- *Countermeasure(s)*: the actions that have been taken or will be taken to counter this risk
- *Owner*: the person who has been appointed to keep an eye on this risk
- *Date of last update*: when the status of this risk was last checked
- *Current status*: for example, closed, reducing, increasing, no change.

A.34.3 Derivation

Some risks may have been identified in work that led up to the Project Mandate. Risks may have been identified in the Project Brief and should be considered during project initiation when the Project Plan is being created. There should be a check for any new risks every time the Risk Log is reviewed, minimally at each end stage assessment. The Project Board has the responsibility to check external events continually for external risks.

Risks to a Stage Plan should be examined as part of the production of that plan. They should be reviewed each time the Stage Plan is updated.

The Risk Log is created during *Preparing a Project Brief* (SU4).

A.34.4 Quality criteria

- The status indicates whether action has been taken or is in a contingency plan
- The risks are uniquely identified (including to which project they refer if they came from a programme)

- The risk has been allocated to an owner
- Access to the Risk Log is controlled
- The Risk Log is kept in a safe place
- Activities to review the Risk Log are in the Stage Plans.

A.35 Stage Plan

A.35.1 Purpose

- Used as the basis for project management control throughout the stage

- Identifies all the products that the stage must produce

- Provides a statement of how and when a stage's objectives are to be achieved, by showing the deliverables, activities and resources required

- Identifies the stage's control and reporting points and frequencies

- Provides a baseline against which stage progress will be measured

- Records the stage tolerances

- Specifies the quality controls for the stage and identifies the resources needed for them.

A.35.2 Composition

This product will contain the following:

- Plan description, covering:
  - a brief description of what the plan covers
  - a brief description of the planned approach

- Quality plan, covering:
  - the quality control methods to be used for each major product
  - the timing and resources for each quality test or check (not a separate document but embedded in the Stage Plan)

- Plan prerequisites:
  - containing any fundamental aspects which must be in place at the start of the stage and which must remain in place for the plan to succeed

- External dependencies

- Tolerances

- How the plan will be monitored and controlled

- Reporting

- Planning assumptions

- Graphical plan, covering:
  - diagram showing identified resources, activities, start and end dates (usually a Gantt or bar chart)
  - Product Breakdown Structure
  - Product Flow Diagram

- activity network
- financial budget
- table of resource requirements
- Risk assessment
- Product Descriptions for the major products.

An Exception Plan or any other detailed plan will have the same format as a Stage Plan.

A.35.3 Derivation

- Refined from the Project Plan during *Planning a Stage* (SB1)
- Based on resource availability.

Updated during *Assessing Progress* (CS2) and may be modified during *Reviewing Stage Status* (CS5) and *Taking Corrective Action* (CS7).

A.35.4 Quality criteria

- The plan is achievable
- All Team Managers involved in the plan's operation believe that their portion is achievable
- The Stage Plan supports the Project Plan
- It takes into account any constraints of time, resources and budget
- It has been taken down to the level of detail necessary to ensure that any deviations will be recognised in time to react appropriately – for example, within the stage tolerances and within the activity 'floats'
- The Stage Plan has been developed according to the planning standard
- The Stage Plan contains activities and resource effort to review the Issue Log.

A.36 Work Package

A.36.1 Purpose

A Work Package is a set of information about one or more required products collated by the Project Manager to pass responsibility for work or delivery formally to a Team Manager or team member.

A.36.2 Composition

This product will vary in content and in degree of formality depending on circumstances.

Where the work is being conducted by a team working directly under the Project Manager, the Work Package may be a verbal instruction, although there are good reasons for putting it in writing, such as avoidance of misunderstanding and providing a link to performance assessment. Where the work is being carried out by a supplier under a contract and the Project Manager is part of the customer organisation, there is a need for a formal written instruction in line with standards laid down in that contract.

Although the content may vary greatly according to the relationship between the Project Manager and the recipient of the Work Package, it should cover:

- *Date*: the date of the agreement between the Project Manager and the Team Manager/person authorised

- *Team or person authorised*: the name of the Team Manager or individual with whom the agreement has been made

- *Work Package description*: a description of the work to be done

- *Product Description(s)*: this would normally be an attachment of the Product Description(s) for the products identified in the Work Package

- *Techniques/processes/procedures to be used*: any techniques, tools, standards, processes or procedures to be used in the creation of the specialist products (not including PRINCE2 processes)

- *Interfaces to be satisfied by the completed product(s)*: identification of any specialist products with which the product(s) in the Work Package will have to interface during their operational life. These may be other products to be produced by the project, existing products or those to be produced by other projects (for example, if the project is part of a programme)

- *Interfaces to be maintained during the work*: those with whom interfaces must be maintained while doing the work. These may be people providing information or those who need to receive information

- *Configuration management requirements*: this will identify any arrangements that must be made by the developer for version control of the products in the Work Package, obtaining copies of other products or their Product Descriptions, submission of the product to configuration management, and any need to advise the Configuration Librarian of changes in the status of the Work Package products

- *Stage Plan extract*: this will be the relevant section of either the Stage Plan or Product Checklist or be a pointer to it

- *Joint agreement on effort, cost, start and end dates, and tolerances*: details of the amounts and dates agreed, plus the tolerances for the Work Package

- *Any constraints to be observed*: any constraints (apart from the tolerances) on the work, people to be involved, timings, charges, rules to be followed (for example, security and safety) etc.

- *Reporting arrangements*: the expected frequency and content of Checkpoint Reports

- *Problem handling and escalation*: this will normally refer to the procedure for raising Project Issues and risks

- *Sign-off requirements*: the person, role or group who will approve the finished Work Package products

- *How completion is to be advised*: this will say how the Project Manager is to be advised of completion of the Work Package.

There should be space on the Work Package to record its authorisation and acceptance of the return of the completed Work Package. This can be enhanced to include an assessment of the work and go towards performance appraisal.

A.36.3 Derivation

- Product Description(s)
- Stage Plans.

A.36.4 Quality criteria

- The required Work Package is clearly defined and understood by the assigned resource

- There is a Product Description for the required product(s), with clearly identified and acceptable quality criteria

- The Product Description matches up with the other Work Package documentation

- Standards for the work are agreed

- The defined standards are in line with those applied to similar products

- All necessary interfaces have been defined

- The reporting arrangements include the provision for exception reporting

- There is agreement between the Project Manager and the recipient on exactly what is to be done

- There is agreement on the constraints, including effort, cost and targets

- The dates and effort are in line with those shown in the Stage Plan

B.2   Executive

The Executive is ultimately responsible for the project, supported by the Senior User and Senior Supplier. The Executive's role is to ensure that the project is focused throughout its life cycle on achieving its objectives and delivering a product that will achieve the forecast benefits. The Executive has to ensure that the project gives value for money, ensuring a cost-conscious approach to the project, balancing the demands of business, user and supplier.

Throughout the project, the Executive 'owns' the Business Case.

B.2.1   Specific responsibilities

- Oversee the development of the Project Brief and Business Case
- Ensure that there is a coherent project organisation structure and logical set of plans
- Authorise customer expenditure and set stage tolerances
- Monitor and control the progress of the project at a strategic level, in particular reviewing the Business Case continually (for example, at each end stage assessment)
- Ensure that any proposed changes of scope, cost or timescale are checked against their possible effects on the Business Case
- Ensure that risks are being tracked and mitigated as effectively as possible
- Brief corporate or programme management about project progress
- Organise and chair Project Board meetings
- Recommend future action on the project to corporate or programme management if the project tolerance is exceeded
- Approve the End Project Report and Lessons Learned Report and ensure that any outstanding Project Issues are documented and passed on to the appropriate body
- Approve the sending of the project closure notification to corporate or programme management
- Ensure that the benefits have been realised by holding a post-project review and forward the results of the review to the appropriate stakeholders.

The Executive is responsible for overall business assurance of the project – that is, that it remains on target to deliver products that will achieve the expected business benefits, and that the project will be completed within its agreed tolerances for budget and schedule. Business assurance covers:

- Validation and monitoring of the Business Case against external events and against project progress
- Keeping the project in line with customer strategies
- Monitoring project finance on behalf of the customer
- Monitoring the business risks
- Monitoring any supplier and contractor payments

- Monitoring changes to the Project Plan to see whether there is any impact on the needs of the business or the project Business Case

- Assessing the impact of potential changes on the Business Case and Project Plan

- Constraining user and supplier excesses

- Informing the project team of any changes caused by a programme of which the project is part (this responsibility may be transferred if there is other programme representation on the project management team)

- Monitoring stage and project progress against the agreed tolerances.

If the project warrants it, the Executive may delegate some responsibility for the business assurance functions.

The Project Board is not a democracy controlled by votes. The Executive is the key decision maker because he/she is ultimately responsible to the business. He/she is supported by the Senior User and Senior Supplier.

B.3   Senior User

The Senior User is responsible for specifying the needs of those who will use the final product(s), for user liaison with the project team and for monitoring that the solution will meet those needs within the constraints of the Business Case in terms of quality, functionality and ease of use.

The role represents the interests of all those who will use the final product(s) of the project, those for whom the product will achieve an objective or those who will use the product to deliver benefits. The Senior User role commits user resources and monitors products against requirements. This role may require more than one person to cover all the user interests. For the sake of effectiveness the role should not be split between too many people.

B.3.1   Specific responsibilities

- Ensure the desired outcome of the project is specified
- Make sure that progress towards the outcome required by the users remains consistent from the user perspective
- Promote and maintain focus on the desired project outcome
- Ensure that any user resources required for the project are made available
- Approve Product Descriptions for those products that act as inputs or outputs (interim or final) from the supplier function or will affect them directly
- Ensure that the products are signed off once completed
- Prioritise and contribute user opinions on Project Board decisions on whether to implement recommendations on proposed changes
- Resolve user requirements and priority conflicts
- Provide the user view on Follow-on Action Recommendations
- Brief and advise user management on all matters concerning the project.

The assurance responsibilities of the Senior User are to check that:

- Specification of the user's needs is accurate, complete and unambiguous
- Development of the solution at all stages is monitored to ensure that it will meet the user's needs and is progressing towards that target
- Impact of potential changes is evaluated from the user point of view
- Risks to the users are frequently monitored
- Quality checking of the product at all stages has the appropriate user representation
- Quality control procedures are used correctly to ensure products meet user requirements
- User liaison is functioning effectively.

Where the project's size, complexity or importance warrants it, the Senior User may delegate the responsibility and authority for some of the assurance responsibilities.

B.4   Senior Supplier

The Senior Supplier represents the interests of those designing, developing, facilitating, procuring, implementing, and possibly operating and maintaining the project products. This role is accountable for the quality of products delivered by the supplier(s). The Senior Supplier role must have the authority to commit or acquire supplier resources required.

It should be noted that in some environments the customer might share design authority or have a major say in it.

If necessary, more than one person may be required to represent the suppliers.

B.4.1   Specific responsibilities

- Agree objectives for supplier activities
- Make sure that progress towards the outcome remains consistent from the supplier perspective
- Promote and maintain focus on the desired project outcome from the point of view of supplier management
- Ensure that the supplier resources required for the project are made available
- Approve Product Descriptions for supplier products
- Contribute supplier opinions on Project Board decisions on whether to implement recommendations on proposed changes
- Resolve supplier requirements and priority conflicts
- Arbitrate on, and ensure resolution of, any supplier priority or resource conflicts
- Brief non-technical management on supplier aspects of the project.

The Senior Supplier is responsible for the specialist integrity of the project. The supplier assurance role responsibilities are to:

- Advise on the selection of development strategy, design and methods
- Ensure that any supplier and operating standards defined for the project are met and used to good effect
- Monitor potential changes and their impact on the correctness, completeness and integrity of products against their Product Description from a supplier perspective
- Monitor any risks in the production aspects of the project
- Ensure quality control procedures are used correctly, so that products adhere to requirements.

If warranted, some of this assurance responsibility may be delegated to separate supplier assurance personnel. Depending on the particular customer/supplier environment of a project, the customer may also wish to appoint people to carry out assurance on supplier products.

B.5   Project Manager

The Project Manager has the authority to run the project on a day-to-day basis on behalf of the Project Board within the constraints laid down by the board.

The Project Manager's prime responsibility is to ensure that the project produces the required products to the required standard of quality and within the specified constraints of time and cost. The Project Manager is also responsible for the project producing a result capable of achieving the benefits defined in the Business Case.

B.5.1   Specific responsibilities

- Manage the production of the required products
- Direct and motivate the project team
- Plan and monitor the project
- Agree any delegation and use of Project Assurance roles required by the Project Board
- Produce the Project Initiation Document
- Prepare Project, Stage and, if necessary, Exception Plans in conjunction with Team Managers and appointed Project Assurance roles, and agree them with the Project Board
- Manage the risks, including the development of contingency plans
- Liaise with programme management if the project is part of a programme
- Liaise with programme management or related projects to ensure that work is neither overlooked nor duplicated
- Take responsibility for overall progress and use of resources and initiate corrective action where necessary
- Be responsible for change control and any required configuration management
- Prepare and report to the Project Board through Highlight Reports and End Stage Reports
- Liaise with the Project Board or its appointed Project Assurance roles to assure the overall direction and integrity of the project
- Agree technical and quality strategy with appropriate members of the Project Board
- Prepare the Lessons Learned Report
- Prepare any Follow-on Action Recommendations required
- Prepare the End Project Report
- Identify and obtain any support and advice required for the management, planning and control of the project
- Be responsible for project administration
- Liaise with any suppliers or account managers
- May also perform Team Manager and Project Support roles.

B.6   Team Manager

The Team Manager's prime responsibility is to ensure production of those products defined by the Project Manager to an appropriate quality, in a timescale and at a cost acceptable to the Project Board. The Team Manager reports to and takes direction from the Project Manager.

B.6.1   Specific responsibilities

- Prepare plans for the team's work and agree these with the Project Manager

- Receive authorisation from the Project Manager to create products (via a Work Package)

- Manage the team

- Direct, plan and monitor the team's work

- Take responsibility for the progress of the team's work and use of team resources, and initiate corrective action where necessary within the constraints laid down by the Project Manager

- Advise the Project Manager of any deviations from plan, recommend corrective action and help prepare any appropriate Exception Plans

- Pass back to the Project Manager products that have been completed and approved in line with the agreed Work Package requirements

- Ensure all Project Issues are properly reported to the person maintaining the Issue Log

- Ensure the evaluation of Project Issues that arise within the team's work and recommend action to the Project Manager

- Liaise with any Project Assurance roles

- Attend any end stage assessments as directed by the Project Manager

- Arrange and lead team checkpoint meetings and produce Checkpoint Reports as agreed with the Project Manager

- Ensure that quality controls of the team's work are planned and performed correctly

- Ensure that the appropriate entries are made in the Quality Log

- Maintain, or ensure the maintenance of, team files

- Identify and advise the Project Manager of any risks associated with a Work Package

- Ensure that all identified risks are entered in the Risk Log

- Manage specific risks as directed by the Project Manager.

B.7   Project Assurance

Assurance covers all interests of a project, including business, user and supplier.

Project Assurance has to be independent of the Project Manager, therefore the Project Board cannot delegate any of its assurance responsibilities to the Project Manager.

B.7.1   Specific responsibilities

The implementation of the assurance responsibilities needs to answer the question: 'What is to be assured?' A list of possibilities would include ensuring that:

- Thorough liaison between the supplier and the customer is maintained throughout the project
- User needs and expectations are being met or managed
- Risks are being controlled
- The Business Case is being adhered to
- The value-for-money solution is constantly reassessed
- The project fits with overall programme or company strategy
- The right people are involved in writing Product Descriptions
- The right people are planned to be involved in quality checking at the correct points in the product's development.
- Staff are properly trained in the quality checking procedures
- The right people are being involved in quality checking
- The quality review/quality checking procedures are being correctly followed
- Quality checking follow-up actions are dealt with correctly
- An acceptable solution is being developed
- The project remains viable
- The scope of the project is not 'creeping upwards' unnoticed
- Focus on the business need is maintained
- Internal and external communications are working
- Applicable standards are being used
- Any legislative constraints are being observed
- The needs of specialist interests (for example, security) are being observed
- Quality assurance standards are being adhered to.

It is not enough to believe that standards will be obeyed. It is not enough to ensure that a project is well set up and justified at the outset. All the aspects listed above need to be checked throughout the project as part of ensuring that it remains consistent with, and continues to meet, a business need and that no change to the external environment affects the validity of the project. Project Assurance must therefore monitor Stage and Team Planning, Work Package preparation and quality review preparation.

See each of the Project Board role descriptions – B.2 Executive, B.3 Senior User and B.4 Senior Supplier – for details of Project Assurance tasks.

B.8   Project Support

The provision of any Project Support on a formal basis is optional. Tasks need to be done by the Project Manager or delegated to a separate body and this will be driven by the needs of the individual project and Project Manager. Project Support could be in the form of advice on project management tools, guidance, administrative services such as filing, and the collection of actuals, to one or more related projects. Where set up as an official body, Project Support can act as a repository for lessons learned and a central source of expertise in specialist support tools.

One support function that must be considered is that of configuration management. Depending on the project size and environment, there may be a need to formalise this and it quickly becomes a task with which the Project Manager cannot cope without support. See B.9 for details of the Configuration Librarian role.

B.8.1   Specific responsibilities

The following is a suggested list of tasks:

- Administer change control
- Set up and maintain project files
- Establish document control procedures
- Compile, copy and distribute all project management products
- Collect actuals data and forecasts
- Update plans
- Administer the quality review process
- Administer Project Board meetings
- Assist with the compilation of reports
- Specialist knowledge (for example, estimating, risk management)
- Specialist tool expertise (for example, planning and control tools, risk analysis)
- Specialist techniques
- Standards.

B.9   Configuration Librarian

The Configuration Librarian is the custodian and guardian of all master copies of the project's products. The role also maintains the Issue Log.

Major tasks are to:

- Control the receipt, identification, storage and issue of all project products
- Provide information on the status of all products
- Number, record, store and distribute Project Issues.

B.9.1   Specific responsibilities

- Assist the Project Manager to prepare the Configuration Management Plan (during initiation)
- Create an identification scheme for all products
- Create libraries or other storage areas to hold products
- Assist in the identification of products
- Maintain current status information on all products
- Accept and record the receipt of new or revised products into the appropriate library
- Prevent changes to a product version once it has been declared ready for inspection
- Control the allocation of new version numbers to changed products
- Archive superseded product copies
- Ensure the security and preservation of the master copies of all project products
- When authorised to do so, issue copies of products for review or information
- When authorised to do so, issue a new version of a product for change or correction
- Maintain a record of all copies issued
- Notify holders of any changes to their copies
- Maintain the Issue Log
- Monitor all Project Issues and ensure they are resubmitted to the configuration library after any authorised change
- Collect and retain information that will assist in the assessment of what products are impacted by a change to a product
- Produce Product Status Accounts
- Assist in conducting configuration audits
- Liaise with other Configuration Librarians where products required by the project are common to other systems.

B.10 Project Support Office (PSO)

The concept of a Project Support Office is a central pool of skilled resources to provide the roles of Project Support, such as clerical support, Configuration Librarians and possibly PRINCE2 consultants to individual projects. A Project Support Office may be established to support either a specific project or a range of projects within the organisation. The overall objectives of a Project Support Office are to supply resources that have the skills defined in roles B.8 (Project Support) and B.9 (Configuration Librarian) to one or more projects. These resources can:

- Support Project Managers in administration work

- Provide support skills in such areas as expertise in planning and control tools and risk management

- Ensure correct and efficient use of PRINCE2 standards across all projects.

A Project Support Office can be useful where:

- Resource shortages, either in numbers or skills, make it difficult to supply people to perform project administration for each current project

- There are a number of small projects of a diverse nature that individually require only limited support from Project Support

- There is a large programme, requiring co-ordination of individual projects

- A large project requires several resources to handle Project Support roles.

The Project Support Office role can provide all the services defined in the roles described in B.8 and B.9, but may also include some or all of the following, when acting for a number of projects.

B.10.1 Special responsibilities

- Operate a central filing system for several projects

- Operate a complex configuration management system

- Be a centre of expertise for estimating techniques

- Provide expertise in the planning and control software used

- Advise on the preparation of plans

- Produce multi-project reports

- Keep a historical database of how long specific activities take

- Analyse productivity

- Provide PRINCE2 expertise and advice

- Advise on cost/benefit analysis

- Co-ordinate standards

- Act as quality review scribe (and even chairperson).

APPENDIX C: RISK CATEGORIES

The following categories can be used as a starting point for identifying an organisation's main areas of risk in relation to projects or programmes.

Strategic/commercial

- Under-performance to specification
- Management will under-perform against expectations
- Collapse of contractors
- Insolvency of promoter
- Failure of suppliers to meet contractual commitments; this could be in terms of quality, quantity, timescales or their own exposure to risk
- Insufficient capital revenues
- Market fluctuations
- Fraud/theft
- Partnerships failing to deliver the desired outcome
- The situation being non-insurable (or cost of insurance outweighing the benefit)
- Lack of availability of capital investment.

Economic/financial/market

- Exchange rate fluctuation
- Interest rate instability
- Inflation
- Shortage of working capital
- Failure to meet projected revenue targets
- Market developments will adversely affect plans.

Legal and regulatory

- New or changed legislation may invalidate assumptions upon which the activity is based
- Failure to obtain appropriate approval, for example, planning, consent
- Unforeseen inclusion of contingent liabilities
- Loss of intellectual property rights
- Failure to achieve satisfactory contractual arrangements
- Unexpected regulatory controls or licensing requirements
- Changes in tax or tariff structure.

Organisational/management/human factors

- Management incompetence
- Inadequate corporate policies
- Inadequate adoption of management practices
- Poor leadership
- Key personnel have inadequate authority to fulfil their roles
- Poor staff selection procedures
- Lack of clarity over roles and responsibilities
- Vested interests creating conflict and compromising the overall aims
- Individual or group interests given unwarranted priority
- Personality clashes
- Indecision or inappropriate decision making
- Lack of operational support
- Inadequate or inaccurate information
- Health and safety constraints.

Political

- Change of government policy (national or international), for example, approach to nationalisation
- Change of government
- War and disorder
- Adverse public opinion/media intervention.

- Do reviewers unable to attend quality reviews send question lists?
- Do quality reviews generate follow-up action lists?
- Do the reviewers sign off corrections?
- Are product creators (producers) always present?
- Are second reviews carried out if needed?
- Is there a review result for each review?

Change control

- Is there a documented procedure for change control?
- Is that procedure the same as stated in the Project Plan?
- Are Project Issues recorded?
- Is there an Issue Log?
- Are Project Issues assessed regularly?
- Is the impact of Project Issues on the Business Case assessed?
- Is the impact of Project Issues on the Risk Log assessed?
- Are all Project Issues actioned?
- Is the status of Project Issues monitored?
- If the impact of a Project Issue exceeds tolerance, is it escalated to the Project Board?
- Are plans updated to incorporate agreed changes?
- Is a distinction made between Off-Specifications and Requests for Change?

Configuration management

- Is there a formal configuration management method in use?
- Are products controlled once submitted to configuration management?
- Are products uniquely identified?
- Are relationships between products identified?
- Are products identified as complete?
- Do products have version identifiers?
- Are product records up to date?
- Is the accuracy of the product records checked regularly?
- Are all old versions preserved?
- Is it easy to retrieve old versions?

- Are the configuration management records in line with the support requirements?

- Is the Configuration Librarian role well defined, allocated and agreed?

- Are new records created during product-based planning?

Project filing

- Is there a recognisable filing system?

- Is its structure documented and available?

- Does it cover management and specialist products?

- Does it cater for multiple versions – for example, of plans?

- Does the filing system provide an audit trail?

- Is it easy to find things in the filing system?

- Is the filing kept up to date?

- Is filing responsibility clearly defined in a job description?

APPENDIX E: PROJECT DOCUMENT MANAGEMENT

PRINCE2 offers this suggested document management structure to be used by a project to hold the PRINCE2 management documents.

There are three types of file:

- Project file
- Stage files for each stage
- Quality file.

E.1 Project file

This has sections as shown in Table E.1.

Table E.1 Project file sections

Project Initiation Document	The original approved Project Initiation Document
Organisation	The project organisation chart and signed job descriptions
Plans	The Project Plans. These should include any versions developed, not only the one approved as part of the Project Initiation Document. The various components of each version should be kept (such as Product Breakdown Structures, Product Flow Diagrams) with clear identification of their date, version number and reasoning, such as change of assumptions, scope, stage results or resource availability. The Project Plan should be updated at least at the end of each stage
Business Case	Versions of the Business Case, updated at each stage end or when Exception Plans are created
Risk Log	Updated details of all identified risks, their status and countermeasures
Control	Copies of project initiation and closure, and documents such as the Project Mandate, Project Brief, Project Board stage approvals and Lessons Learned Log. During *Closing a Project* (CP), the Post-Project Review Plan, Lessons Learned Report, Follow-on Action Recommendations and End Project Report will be filed here
Communication Plan	Created in *Initiating a Project* (IP) and updated if necessary to include new interested parties

E.2   Stage files

One of these would exist for each stage of the project (see Table E.2).

Table E.2 Stage file sections

Organisation	Stage organisation, details of team members. These should reflect all work assignments, achievements and the Project Manager's or Team Manager's assessment of work performance
Plans	Copies of Stage Plans, Team Plans (if used) and Exception Plans, updated as available
Control	Copies of Work Package authorisations, Checkpoint Reports, Highlight Reports, Exception Reports, end stage assessments, plus any exception assessments held
Daily Log	The Project Manager's notebook of events, problems, questions, answers, informal discussions with Project Board members and actions for the stage
Correspondence	Copies of management correspondence or other papers associated with the stage

E.3   Quality file

The objective of a quality file is to permit an audit, at any time, of the quality work being done and to confirm adherence to quality standards. There is one quality file that runs through the whole project and is not divided into stages. It contains:

- Customer's quality expectations

- Acceptance Criteria

- Project Quality Plan – the original and any subsequent versions of the Project Quality Plan should be filed here

- Configuration Management Plan

- Configuration Item Records – there should be minimally a Product Description for every product in the project. As more information is created, a full Configuration Item Record for each product can be produced

- Quality inspection products – it is useful to head this section with the Quality Log, giving a number to each check, the type of quality check or test (for example, quality review), the product and the date. This is a quick reference to see or show how many checks have been held in a particular stage and a guide to where the appropriate documentation can be found

  The subdivision of the quality inspection section will depend on the type(s) of check or test being carried out. There should be a separate file for the documents relating to each entry in the Quality Log. This file should keep details of the method used, the resources used, the sign-off document where appropriate, details of the tests carried out, and expected and actual results. The filing for quality reviews should include:

  - invitations
  - action lists
  - result notifications

- Project Issues – this should have the Issue Log at the front to facilitate sequential numbering and to record the status and allocation of Project Issues. The Project Issue masters should be filed in sequence behind it. The subject of Project Issues is covered fully in *Change control technique*, Chapter 23.

FURTHER INFORMATION

Best practice guidance from OGC

OGC has developed a wide range of guidance covering strategy, programme management, service management, procurement and performance management.

Details of OGC guidance may be obtained from:

The OGC Service Desk
Rosebery Court
St Andrews Business Park
Norwich NR7 0HS

Telephone: 0845 000 4999
Email: ServiceDesk@ogc.gsi.gov.uk
Website: http://www.ogc.gov.uk

PRINCE2 accreditation and qualifications

APM Group Ltd

The APM Group Limited (APMG) is the certification body for PRINCE2 accredited by UKAS in accordance with EN45011 and EN45013.

APMG has been working as a strategic partner of OGC since 1996 on the development and promotion of professional standards associated with the use and implementation of PRINCE2.

The Group's activities extend beyond the UK and full information can be seen on its website at http://www.apmgroup.co.uk

The APM Group Limited
Sword House
Totteridge Road
High Wycombe
Buckinghamshire HP13 6DG

Telephone: 01494 452450
Fax: 01494 459559
Email: info@apmgroup.co.uk
Website: http://www.prince2.org.uk

The Best Practice User Group

The Best Practice User Group is an independent not-for-profit organisation whose aims are to support and encourage the use of OGC guidance on project, programme and risk management. The Best Practice User Group provides a forum for sharing experience for users of the guidance.

Membership is open to individuals and organisations, and brings a range of benefits, including regular newsletters, a subscription to *Project Manager Today*, the opportunity to attend regional workshops and the annual conference, and to contribute to the maintenance and development of OGC's guidance.

The Best Practice User Group
c/o WG Services
20 Tracious Close
Horsell
Woking
Surrey GU21 3AF

Telephone: 0870 901 5583
Fax: 0870 901 6581
Email: admin@usergroup.org.uk
Website: http://www.usergroup.org.uk

Comments and feedback on *PRINCE2*, *Managing Successful Programmes* and *Management of Risk: Guidance for Practitioners* can be logged on the OGC Guidance Issue Log at http://www.usergroup.org.uk/issues

INDEX

Page numbers in *italics* refer to glossary entries; page numbers in **bold** refer to Product Outline Descriptions or Roles; the suffix (Fig.) indicates a figure.

A

acceptance
  response to risk 256
  see also operational and maintenance
    acceptance; Work Packages,
    acceptance
Acceptance Criteria *329*, **341–2**
  change control 286, 287
  product definition and analysis 176
  Product Descriptions 302
  project authorisation 80
  Project Brief preparation 38
  project closure 90, 155
  project decommissioning 157, 158
  Project Quality Plan 38
  quality management 50, 51, 52, 268–9
  Work Packages 124
  see also customer's quality expectations
accreditation 4, 425
activities 54, 176–80, 178 (Fig.),
    182 (Fig.), 188
  see also Product Flow Diagram;
    scheduling
activity networks 184, 185 (Fig.), 186, *329*
  see also critical path
ad hoc direction 14, 71, 73, 85–9
  corrective action 117
  Exception Plans 152
  Exception Reports 83, 87, 88, 241, 262
  intermediate Lessons Learned Reports
    245
  Off-Specifications 317
  Project Issues 87–8, 89, 121
  Project Manager 86, 87, 88, 89, 262,
    317
  risk management 262
administration *see* Project Support
APM Group 425
appointment
  Configuration Librarian 65
  Executive 28–31, 72, 212

Project Assurance 35, 209, 211, 214–15
Project Board
  by Executive 31, 32, 33, 36, 212
  by programme management 27, 32,
    33, 36, 72, 208, 212
  confirmation and late appointments
    79
  project management team 13, 26, 27,
    28, 31, 34–7
  confirmation 72, 74, 79
  Project Manager 28–31, 72, 208, 212
  Project Support 35
  Team Managers 35
  see also membership
approval *see* authorisation
archiving 17, 155, 156, 158, 159
  see also Project Files; records
assembly, Project Initiation Document
    52, 65–8, 215
assessment *see* end stage assessment;
    exception assessment; progress
    assessment; risk assessment
asset management *see* configuration
    management
auditing *see* configuration audits; internal
    audit functions
authorisation
  change control 287–8, 317
  Exception Plans 81–5, 137, 201, 225–6,
    229, 243, 261
  initiation Stage Plans 72
  Project Brief 75, 231
  project initiation 26, 74–6, 229, 231,
    261
  Project Initiation Document 77–81, 231
  Project Plan 220
  Team Plans 220, 225, 229
  see also Acceptance Criteria; change
    authority; project authorisation;
    Stage Plans, authorisation; Work
    Packages, authorisation
authority levels 212, 287–8

B

balancing, risks 256–7, 288
baselines 199, 277, *329*
baselining 60, 78, 278
  benefit measures 201
  change control 282
  end stage assessment 242
  Product Descriptions 300
  Project Brief 75
  Project Initiation Document 77–8, 231
  Project Plan 224, 232
  quality review 272
  releases 277
  Work Package completion 124
  see also version control
benefit tolerance 235
benefits *329*
  baselining measures of 201
  Business Case statement of 9–10, 57,
    59, 78, 145, 198, 200
  defining 198, 199, 201
  delivery risks and 263, 264
  PRINCE2 2–4
  Project Issue effects on 108, 288
  quality review 319
  see also project evaluation
benefits realisation 56, 59, 60, 71, 200,
    210, *329*
Best Practice User Group 426
budgets *see* change budgets; contingency
    budgets; risk management budgets
business
  PRINCE2 relationship with 9 (Fig.)
  Project Board membership 206, 208,
    211
Business Case 18, 197–201, **343**
  benefit tolerance 235
  benefits statement 9–10, 57, 59, 78,
    145, 198, 200
  change control 10, 83
  configuration management 200, 232,
    281
  content 198–9, **343**
  corrective action 119
  costs 57, 59, 78, 199, 200
  customer/supplier environment and
    207, 208
  customers 60, 199, 208

definition 6, *329*
End Project Reports 245, 246
end stage assessment 197, 229, 242
End Stage Reports 147, 148, 149, 201,
    243
evaluation 53, 82, 83, 199
Exception Plans 82, 83, 145, 152, 243
Exception Reports 83
Executive 198, 199–200, 209, 210, *332*
Follow-on Action identification 160–1,
    201
GAP analysis 199, 200
healthcheck 415
impact analysis 143, 145, 201, 288, 317
initiation stage planning 44, 72
Issue Log 145
plans and 220
post-project review 57, 161, 200, 201,
    210
programme management 58, 83, 145,
    200
Project Approach 41, 57, 59
Project Assurance 44, 58, 145, 215, 216
project authorisation 76, 80, 81, 201,
    229, 261
Project Board
  control of deviations 10
  referral to programme management
    58, 78, 145
  review by 18, 197, 201, 229
Project Brief preparation 38, 39, 201, 261
project closure 200, 244
project direction 71, 72, 73
project evaluation 164, 165
project initiation 14, 49, 57, 200, 201
Project Initiation Document 38, 56, 58,
    67, 78, 201, 261
Project Issues
  escalating 58, 121, 122, 123
  examining 109, 110, 201
  impacts 87, 201, 288, 317
Project Manager 58, 78, 145, 200, 201,
    229, 261
Project Mandate 83, 198, 200–1
Project Plan
  input from 53, 78, 199, 201, 224
  interaction with 53, 56–9, 143, 145,
    146, 200, 261

project start-up 13, 27, 198
Project Support 58, 145
revision 9–10, 38, 56–60, 144–6, 200–1,
    261
  configuration management 232
  stage boundary management 137
  time for 220
risk analysis 58, 59
Risk Log 198, 199, 200
  updating 56, 57, 58, 59, 145, 146
risk management 56–60, 199, 200, 252,
    257, 261, 262
risk owner responsibilities 254
risk tolerance 252
Senior Supplier 210, 211
stage boundary management 15, 137
stage control 95
Stage Plans 82, 83, 84, 146
stage status review 112, 113, 262
suppliers 60, 208

C

capture, Project Issues 97, 105–7, 286,
    316 (Fig.)
Central Computer and
    Telecommunications Agency
    (CCTA) see Office of Government
    Commerce
change authority 89, 109, 287–8, 289,
    317, 318, 329
  see also Requests for Change
change budgets 54, 287–8, 289, 330
  agreement 89
  creation 51, 54
  plan design 172, 173
  Project Board 54, 89, 287
  Project Issues 109, 112
  tolerances and 236
change control 10, 18, 19, 285–9, 291,
    315–18, 330
  ad hoc direction 87
  baselining 282
  Business Case 10, 83
  configuration management and 282–3,
    289
  contracts 109, 289, 318
  healthcheck 419

Product Descriptions 266, 300, 315
programme management 56, 63, 287,
    289, 315, 318
project authorisation 77
Project Board 10, 87, 89, 287–8, 289,
    315, 317–18
Project Issues 238–9, 282, 285–9, 317,
    318
Project Manager 254, 289, 315, 317, 318
quality planning 51, 53
risk management 89, 288
Team Managers 100, 102
Work Packages 100, 102, 124
see also Project Issues; version control
change integrity 288–9
checklists
  PRINCE2 healthcheck 413–20
  quality review 328
  see also Product Checklist
Checkpoint Reports 240, 330, **344**
  Highlight Reports and 115, 116, 240
  plan completion 191
  product delivery management 16
  progress assessment 103, 104, 105
  Project Manager 16, 133, 229, 240
  risk owners 254
  Senior User 241
  Team Managers 16, 229
  Work Package execution 133, 230
checkpoints 103, 105, 239–40, 330
closing a project see project closure
collective groupings 295–6, 300, 311, 312
communication
  Executive responsibilities 209
  organisational structure and 81, 205,
    309
  project and programme 34, 50, 63, 70,
    73, 88
  project direction 70, 71
  project management team appointment
    35
  risk management 253
  see also Communication Plan; Project
    Controls; reports and reporting
Communication Plan 330, **345**
  ad hoc direction 88
  Business Case 200
  content 61, 233, **345**

creation 61, 62
Daily Log 244
End Project Reports 246
end stage reporting 148, 149
Highlight Reports 114, 115, 116, 241
programme management and Project
    Board 70, 79, 88, 89
project closure confirmation 92
Project Controls 61, 62, 232–3
project decommissioning 158, 159, 160
Project Files 64
project initiation 50
Project Initiation Document 67, 79, 80
project management team appointments
    35
Project Manager 79
Stage Plan authorisation 84
completion, plans 190–3, 216
components 12 (Fig.), 17–18, 19–20, 43,
    195–289
concessions
    definition 317, *330*
    impact analysis 112
    Project Board 91, 112, 113, 121, 122,
        123, 317
    project closure 91
    Project Issues 119, 121, 122, 123, 273
    quality tolerance 236
    stage status review 112, 113
    see also Off-Specifications
configuration audits 280, *330*
    end stage reporting 148, 149, 150
    Lessons Learned Reports 164
    Project Assurance 149, 280
    project decommissioning 158, 159, 164
configuration breakdown 282 (Fig.)
configuration control 278, 279, *330*
Configuration Item Records **346–7**
    Business Case revisions 232
    corrective action 118
    creation 174, 175, 279
    end stage reporting 148, 149
    Exception Plan production 151
    product definition and analysis 174,
        175, 279
    progress assessment 104
    project decommissioning 158
    project evaluation 165
    Project Issue escalation 121, 122

Project Plan revisions 232
    stage status review 111, 113
    Work Packages 100, 101, 124, 125
Configuration Librarian 217, 278, 281,
    406
    appointment 65
    configuration audits 280
    corrective action 118
    end stage reporting 149
    Exception Plan production 151
    Issue Log maintenance 109
    product definition and analysis 175
    product issue 279
    Product Status Accounts 279
    product submission 279
    progress assessment 104
    project decommissioning 158
    Project Issues 106, 109, 122, 281, 282
    Project Manager as 217
    Project Quality Plan 271
    stage status review 112
    Work Packages 100, 125, 135
configuration management 10, 18,
    275–83
    Business Case 200, 281
    change control and 282–3, 289
    definition 18, *330*
    healthcheck 419–20
    Product Status Accounts 103
    progress assessment 103
    project decommissioning 159
    Project Issues 276, 281, 282, 289
    quality review 272
    Risk Log 232, 281
    Work Packages 124, 125, 131, 134, 136
    see also archiving; product delivery
        management; Project Files; records
Configuration Management Plan 278,
    348
    change control 289
    creation 51
    product definition and analysis 175
    project decommissioning 158, 159
    Project Files 63, 64
confirmation
    Project Board appointment 79
    project closure 89–93, 156, 158, 162,
        163, 164, 229

project management team appointment
72, 74, 79
contingency budgets 54, 58, 172, 173,
236, 258, *330*
see also risk management budgets
contingency plans 54, 58, 78, 84, 147,
258, *330–1*
see also risk management
contingency responses to risk 256
contractors 237, 271
see also stakeholders; sub-contractors
contracts
  change control 109, 289, 318
  organisational structure and 206
  PRINCE2 and 8–9
  project authorisation 80
  project decommissioning 159
  Project Initiation Document and 9
  Project Issues 109
  quality control 271
  third-party suppliers 289
  Work Package authorisation 102
control
  healthcheck 417–18
  multiple changes 283
  see also change control; configuration
    control; copy control; plan controls;
    progress control; Project Controls;
    quality control; stage control; version
    control
control loop 228 (Fig.)
control points 186, 222, 224, 232
  see also decision points; stage boundaries
copy control 279
corporate management *see* programme
  management
corrective action 117–19
  Highlight Reports 115, 118
  replanning 240
  stage control 15, 97, 99
  stage status review 111, 112, 113
  Work Package authorisation 99, 118
cost/time tolerance graph 235 (Fig.)
costs
  balancing risks 256–7
  Business Case 57, 59, 78, 199, 200
  change control 288, 289
  closing date for charging 91

corrective action 119
  Project Issues 108
  tolerances 234, 236
  see also change budgets; contingency
    budgets; payment; risk management
    budgets
critical path 187, *331*
  see also activity networks
critical path items 114, 133
customer/supplier environment 10, 203,
207–8
  PRINCE2 manual assumptions 10, 228
  product definition and analysis 176
  Project Assurance 217
  Project Manager role 212, 213
customers 10
  Business Case 60, 199, 208
  definition 6, *331*
  impact analysis 318
  organisational structure and 206
  product definition and analysis 175
  Product Descriptions 226, 272, 301,
    302
  Project Approach 41, 42, 270
  project authorisation 80, 81
  Project Board representation 88, 206–7,
    208, 211
  project closure 17, 90, 92, 155, 156
  project decommissioning 156, 157, 158,
    159
  project funding 59
  Project Issue examination 109
  project management team 33, 34, 36
  quality assurance function 214, 271
  quality criteria 272, 301, 302
  quality management 10, 51, 174, 269,
    270
  quality policy 269–70
  risk management 59
  Senior Supplier role 208
  see also customer's quality expectations;
    stakeholders; users
customer's quality expectations *331*, **349**
  post-project review 161
  Project Approach 270
  Project Brief preparation 38
  Project Quality Plan 38, 78, 271
  project start-up 13, 27, 266

quality management 50, 52, 266, 268,
    269, 272
Senior User 38
stage planning 140
see also Acceptance Criteria

D

Daily Log 243–4, *331*, **350**
    corrective action 118
    creation 13, 38
    progress assessment 105
    Project Brief preparation 39
    project evaluation 165
    Project Manager 13, 38, 112, 243–4,
        255, 264, 274
    project start-up 13
    quality management 274
    risk management 255, 264
    stage boundary management 139
    stage status review 112, 243
    Team Managers 244, 274
    Work Packages 132, 133, 244
decision points 14, 54, 70, 71, 176, 197,
    247
    see also control points; stage boundaries
decommissioning 121, 156–60, 164, 216
definition
    products 174–6, 216, 279, 293
        see also Product Breakdown Structure
    project 66, 78
    Project Approach 28, 40–3, 57, 215, 261
delegation 206
    Project Board responsibilities 34, 206
        change authority 109, 317, 318, 387
        monitoring external sources 89
        Project Assurance 32, 36, 81, 206,
            211, 214, 237
        risk ownership 254
    Project Manager responsibilities 212
    Senior User responsibilities 34
deliverables *331*
delivery
    Work Packages 134–6
    see also product delivery management
delivery risks, benefits and 263, 264
dependencies 10–11
    constraints as 179

external products 299
identification 176–80
plan completion 190
planning 222
Product Flow Diagram 176, 179, 294,
    302–3, 312, 313
Project Approach definition 41
risk analysis 189
scheduling 184, 187
stage planning 141, 142
see also interdependencies
design
    plans 170, 171–4, 175, 216
    project management team 13, 26, 27,
        31–4, 36, 214, 215
deviations *see* change control; corrective
    action; Exception Reports; Project
    Issues; tolerances
diagram and text notation 23
directing a project 13–14, 21, 69–93, 207,
    212, 215
    see also ad hoc direction
document management 421–3

E

earned value analysis 105, *331*
end project recommendation 17, 158
End Project Report 245–6, *331*, **351–2**
    content 164, **351–2**
    evaluation of estimating method 172
    impact analysis 164, 246
    premature closure 74
    Product Status Accounts 279
    Project Board 91, 246
    project closure 17, 91, 92, 155
    project evaluation 163–4, 165, 166
    Project Manager 155, 163
end project triggers 113
end stage assessment 242–3, *331*
    Business Case 197, 229, 242
    decision points 247
    programme management 264
    Project Board 79, 229, 242
    timing 85
end stage notification 113, 141
End Stage Reports 147–50, 243, *332*,
    353–4

Business Case 147, 148, 149, 201, 243
plan completion 191
Product Status Accounts 279
Project Assurance 149, 216
Project Board 15, 147, 150, 243
Project Manager 15, 148, 149, 150, 243
Project Plan 143, 147, 148, 150, 243
risk owner responsibilities 254
scheduling 186
stage boundary management 15
Stage Plan authorisation 84
escalation, Project Issues 119–23
Business Case 58, 121, 122, 123
change control 318
Exception Reports 85, 121, 122, 123, 152, 262, 318
Off-Specifications 123, 317
Project Assurance 122, 216
Project Board 110–11, 112, 119–21, 122, 123
Project Controls 61
Project Manager 119–22, 262, 317
Project Plan 121, 122, 123
risk management 121, 123, 262
stage control 97
stage status review 111, 112, 121
estimating 172, 180–3, 217, 223
evaluation
Business Case 53, 82, 83, 199
estimation methods 172
projects 71, 162–6
risks 253, 255–6
see also earned value analysis; End Project Report; End Stage Report; impact analysis; lessons learned; post-project review; risk analysis; stage status review
event-driven controls 228
examination, Project Issues 107–10
Business Case 109, 110, 201
corrective action 117
Exception Reports 242
Project Assurance 109, 215
Project Board 109, 317
risk management 108, 262, 287
stage control 97
exception *332*

exception assessment 150, 229, 243, 287–8, *332*
Exception Plans 223, 225–6, *332*, **355**
ad hoc direction 88
authorisation 81–5, 137, 201, 225–6, 229, 243, 261
Business Case 83, 145, 152, 243
change control 318
Configuration Item Records 151
Configuration Librarian 151
End Stage Reports 148, 149
exception assessment 150, 243
Exception Reports 150
impact analysis 243
Issue Log 152
production 73, 83, 121, 137, 150–2, 318
programme management 83, 152, 225–6
Project Assurance 83, 151, 216
Project Board
authorisation 83, 225, 229, 243, 261
Business Case and 201, 243
requests for 83, 87, 150
risk management 261
Project Initiation Document 152
Project Issues 84, 119, 121, 122
project management team 152
Project Manager 83, 223, 225, 243, 318
Project Plan 83, 142, 143, 151, 152, 225–6, *332*
Quality Log 152
Risk Log 83, 152
risk management 152, 243, 261
stage boundary management 15, 137
Stage Plans 152, 225, *332*
Team Plans 223, 225, *332*
tolerances 83, 150, 151, 152
Work Package authorisation 101
Exception Reports 241–2, *332*, **356**
ad hoc direction 83, 87, 88, 241, 262
Business Case 83
change control 318
content 83, **356**
corrective action 118
end stage reporting 148
Exception Plans 150
impact analysis 83, 121

Project Board 83, 112, 121, 229, 241,
  262
project direction 73
Project Issues
  escalation 85, 121, 122, 123, 152,
    262, 318
  examination 242
Project Manager 83, 87, 121, 241, 242
Project Plan 83
risk management 83, 258, 262
stage control 16, 98
stage status review 112, 113
tolerances 234, 241–2
execution, Work Packages 102, 132–4,
  216, 230, 238, 320
Executive 208, 209–10, *332*, **397–8**
  appointment 28–31, 72, 212
  Business Case 198, 199–200, 209, 210,
    332
  customer representation 206
  customer's quality expectations 38
  Exception Reports 242
  job description 29, 30, 33, 81
  post-project review 91, 210, 246
  Project Board appointment 31, 32, 33,
    36, 212
  Project Brief preparation 38, 39
  project direction 69
  project initiation 76, 209
  project management team 32, 36
  Project Mandate 29, 30
  risk ownership 253–4
  risk tolerance line 259
  tolerances 233
external products 299, 311, 312
external risks 263

F

feasibility studies 11, 28, 200, *332*
files *see* Project Files; quality files
finance *see* costs; funding
Follow-on Action identification 160–2,
  164, 201, 216, 262–3
Follow-on Action Recommendations 245,
  332, **357**
  Follow-on Action identification 160,
    162, 262–3

programme management 91
Project Board 73, 91, 160, 245
project closure 17, 91, 92, 155, 156
project evaluation 166
Project Issues 91, 92, 161
Project Manager 155
risk management 245, 262–3
follow-up, quality reviews 323, 325, 326,
  327
funding 34, 59, 75, 76, 80, 81, 287–8

G

Gantt charts 170, 184, 186 (Fig.), 191,
  192, 271, *332*
GAP analysis 199, 200
gate review 247, *333*
  see also end stage assessment
glossary 329–40
guidance, PRINCE2 425–6

H

healthcheck, PRINCE2 413–20
Highlight Reports 114–16, 240–1, *333*,
  358–9
  ad hoc direction 88, 89
  corrective action 115, 118
  plan completion 191
  Product Checklists 115, 116, 174, 240
  product definition and analysis 174
  Project Assurance 115, 216, 241
  Project Board 83, 89, 114–16, 229,
    240–1, 259, 262
  Project Issue escalation 123
  Project Manager 16, 87, 209, 240, 241,
    254, 262
  risk management 254, 259, 262
  Senior User 241
  stage control 16, 98
  Stage Plans 83, 115, 116, 240
  stage status review 110, 113, 114, 115

I

identification
  activities and dependencies 176–80, 302
  Follow-on Actions 160–2, 164, 201,
    216, 262–3

products 277, 278–9, 280
   see also version control
impact, definition 255
impact analysis
   Business Case 143, 145, 201, 288, 317
   change requests 226
   concessions 112
   End Project Report 164, 246
   Exception Plans 243
   Exception Reports 83, 121
   Project Assurance involvement 215, 216
   Project Brief changes 37
   Project Issues 107–10, 120, 123, 201,
      288, 317, 318
   Project Plan 143, 145, 317
   see also change control; risk analysis
information dissemination *see*
      communication; publicity
information retrieval *see* archiving; Project
      Files; records
initiation 10, 14, 47–68, 231–2, 247–8
   authorisation 74–6, 229, 231, 261
   Business Case 14, 44, 49, 57, 72, 200,
      201
   change control 287
   Executive 76, 209
   healthcheck 413–14
   job descriptions 75
   planning 43–5, 48, 72, 215, 220
   programme management 50, 75, 76
   Project Approach 40, 44, 75
   Project Assurance 44, 45, 75, 76, 215
   Project Board
      authorisation 14, 44, 48–9, 71, 74–6,
         229, 231
      authority levels 287
      risk assessment 261
   Project Brief 40, 44, 49, 75, 76, 231
   Project Initiation Document 14, 48, 49,
      50, 65, 231
   Project Issues and 109, 287
   project management team structure 75
   Project Manager 48–9, 75, 76, 261
   Project Quality Plan creation 271
   project start-up 26, 40, 49, 75
   Project Support 44
   Quality Log creation 272
   quality planning 273

Risk Log 75, 261
risk management 76, 261
Senior Supplier 76
suppliers 76
third-party funding 76
see also Project Initiation Document
initiation Stage Plans 43–5
   authorisation 72
   Project Assurance 215
   Project Board 43, 44, 45, 75, 230
   Project Brief 38, 44
   Project Controls 230
   project start-up 13, 25, 27, 230
integration products 295, 296, 312
integrity of change 288–9
interdependencies 142, 255, 263, 264,
      312
intermediate products 245, 295–6
internal audit functions 33
internal risks 263
investment appraisal 57, 199, 200
ISO (International Organisation for
      Standards) 269
Issue Log *333*, **360**
   Business Case updating 145
   change control 286, 315, 317
   Configuration Librarian 109
   configuration management 281
   corrective action 118
   creation 14, 64
   end stage reporting 149
   Exception Plan production 152
   Follow-on Action identification 160, 161
   Highlight Reports 116
   progress assessment 104
   project decommissioning 159
   project evaluation 165
   Project Issues
      capture 106, 107, 286, 315, 317
      escalation 122
      examination 108, 109, 286
   Project Plan updating 143
   Risk Log updating 147
   stage control 16
   stage planning 141
   stage status review 113
   Work Package authorisation 101
issuing products 279

J

job descriptions
    change control 287, 318
    configuration management 281
    Executive 29, 30, 33, 81
    Product Descriptions and 9
    Project Assurance 9
    Project Board 32, 88
    Project Controls 61, 62
    project initiation 75
    Project Initiation Document 66, 67, 68
    project management team 33, 36, 52,
        68, 140, 205, 281
    Project Manager 29, 30, 32, 33
    project roles conversion to 9
    quality planning 52
    risk ownership and 9
    Senior Supplier 81
    stage planning 140

L

layers
    organisational structure 204, 233,
        234 (Fig.)
        see also programme management;
        Project Board; Project Manager;
        Team Managers
layout see presentation
lessons learned 15, 73, 90, 138, 210, 217
    see also evaluation
Lessons Learned Log 244, 333, **361–2**
    change control 289
    configuration management 281
    content 163, 164, 165, 244, **361–2**
    creation 14, 64, 163, 164, 244
    end stage reporting 148, 149, 150
    project closure 155, 156
    project evaluation 163, 164, 165
    Project Initiation Document 232
    stage boundary management 15
    Work Package delivery 136
Lessons Learned Report 245, 333, **363**
    configuration audits 164
    content 164, 245, **363**
    estimating 172, 183
    planning 170
    premature closure 74, 164

programme management 166
    Project Board 91, 164, 165
    project closure 17, 91, 92, 155
    project evaluation 163, 164, 165, 166
    project initiation 50
    project start-up 28
life cycle 7, 8 (Fig.), 11, 336
life span 7, 8 (Fig.), 335

M

maintenance see operational and
        maintenance acceptance
maintenance contracts 159
management see configuration
        management; organisational
        structure; product delivery
        management; programme
        management; project management;
        quality management; risk
        management; stage boundaries,
        management
management by exception 14, 70, 71, 72,
        73, 208
    definition 3–4, 18, 228
    Highlight Reports 241
    see also Exception Plans; Exception
        Reports
management layers 204, 233, 234 (Fig.)
    see also programme management; Project
        Board; Project Manager;
        Team Managers
management levels 21–2
management products 297–8, 303, 334
management stages see stages
membership
    Project Board 32–4, 206–12
        changes 8, 87, 88, 89
        programme management 30, 33, 63,
            89, 212
        suppliers 76, 88, 206, 207, 208, 211
        users 34, 75, 206, 207, 208, 211
    project management team 10, 31
    see also appointment
monitoring
    Executive's role 209
    Project Board's role 14, 60, 70, 88, 89,
        224

Project Manager's role 209, 229
Project Plan 224
risk analysis 188, 190
risk management 254, 258
scheduling time for 187
see also progress assessment; Project
    Assurance; Project Controls;
    stage control
multiple changes, controlling 283
multiple versions, in Product Breakdown
    Structure 298

N

notification
  end stage 113, 141
  project closure 91, 92, 159, 245, 336
  project start-up 75, 337

O

Off-Specifications 317, 333, **364**
  ad hoc direction 87
  change control 286–7, 289, 315, 317
  project evaluation 165
  Project Issues 106, 123, 317
  quality management 236, 273
  see also concessions
Office of Government Commerce 1, 425,
    426
operational and maintenance acceptance
    92, 93, 156, 157, 158, 159, 333
organisational structure 18, 203–18,
    414–15
  communication and 81, 205, 309
  layers 204, 233, 234 (Fig.)
  Project Initiation Document and 66, 79
  project management team design 31
  see also programme management; Project
    Board; project management team;
    Project Manager; quality organisation
    structure; roles; Team Managers
outcomes 333

P

payment, suppliers 60, 80
peer review 247, 333–4

phase 334
plan completion 190–3, 216
plan controls 191
plan design 170, 171–4, 175, 216
plan deviations see change control;
    corrective action; Exception Reports;
    Project Issues; tolerances
plan elements 222 (Fig.)
plan levels 18, 222–6
plan narratives 190–1, 192, 221
planning 17, 167–93
  configuration management 277
  initiation stage 43–5, 48, 72, 215, 220
  product delivery management 127, 130
  Product Descriptions 237
  progress assessment 105
  Project Approach and 42, 44, 54, 55,
    170, 171, 172
  Project Assurance 171, 172, 216
  project initiation 44, 48
  quality review 319, 326
  replanning and 240
  risk management 222, 258
  stage boundary management 137
  Team Plans 127, 130, 171, 326
  tolerance setting 234
  see also plans; product-based planning;
    project planning; quality planning;
    stage planning
planning networks 184, 185 (Fig.), 186,
    329
  see also critical path
planning standards 54, 172, 174
planning tools 54, 171–2, 173, 192
plans 18, 169, 219–26
  Executive responsibilities 209
  presentation 171, 190, 191, 192, 193,
    221
  Project Controls 61
  see also Exception Plans; planning;
    Project Plan; Project Quality Plan;
    Stage Plans; Team Plans
post-project review 246, 334
  Business Case 57, 161, 201, 210
  date for 73, 160–1, 162
  Executive 91, 210, 246
  Follow-on Action identification 160,
    161, 162

function 161
premature closure 74
Project Board 73, 91, 162, 246
project closure 155
project decommissioning 158
see also project evaluation
Post-Project Review Plan 246, **365**
Business Case 57, 161, 200, 201
Executive 91, 246
Follow-on Action identification 161,
164
Project Assurance 216
Project Board 91, 246
project closure 17, 91, 92
Project Manager 201
premature closure 71, 73–4, 84, 155
ad hoc direction 88
Lessons Learned Reports 164
project decommissioning 157, 158,
159
project evaluation 164
Project Issue escalation 119, 121, 122
tolerance deviations 85
see also project closure
preparation, Project Brief 38
presentation
planning for 54
plans 171, 190, 191, 192, 193, 221
Project Initiation Document 68
prevention, response to risk 256
PRINCE2 2–4, 7–20, 228, *334*, 413–20,
425–6
PRINCE2 project *334*
prioritising, Project Issues 108, 316–17
probability 255–6, 259
problem referral 209, 259
process description 22–3
processes 12–17, 19–20, 21–193, *334*
producer 321, 324–6, 327, 328, *334*
product-based planning 18–19, 168,
169–70, 250, 291, 293–313, *334*
see also Product Breakdown Structure;
Product Descriptions; Product Flow
Diagram
Product Breakdown Structure 293,
294–300, 311, *335*, **366**
conference organisation 304 (Fig.),
307 (Fig.)

product definition and analysis 174, 175
Product Descriptions and 237, 294,
298, 299, 300, 312
Product Flow Diagram and 302, 312
Project Plan 307 (Fig.), 313
Stage Plans 309 (Fig.), 313
see also product definition and analysis
Product Checklist **367**
corrective action 118
creation 17, 174
definition 17, *335*
Highlight Reports 115, 116, 174, 240
plan completion 191, 192
planning 170
product definition and analysis 174, 175
progress assessment 102, 104
Project Board 170, 240
stage status review 111, 113
Work Package authorisation 101
product control *see* configuration
management
product copies, issuing 279
product definition and analysis 174–6,
216, 282, 293–313
see also Product Breakdown Structure
product delivery management 16, 127–36
Project Issues 16, 108
Project Manager 16, 127–9, 212
quality review 320
stage control 96, 99, 127, 129
Team Managers 16, 21, 127–8, 212
Work Packages 16, 99, 128–36
see also configuration management; Work
Packages, delivery
Product Descriptions 236–7, 300–2, *335*,
368–9
activities and dependencies identification
179, 303
change control 266, 300, 315
conference organisation 305 (Fig.)
customers 226, 272, 301, 302
estimating aid 181
integration products 295
job descriptions and 9
product-based planning 293, 294,
300–2, 311, 312
Product Breakdown Structure and 237,
294, 298, 299, 300, 312

438

programme management 27, 37, 75, 230

Project Approach definition and 40, 41, 42

Project Assurance 39, 215

Project Board 37, 38, 39, 40, 75, 78

project initiation 40, 49, 75, 76, 231

Project Initiation Document 40, 44, 66, 67, 78

project management team 32, 37

Project Manager 39, 230

Project Mandate 37, 38, 39

project planning 55, 56

project start-up 13, 26, 27, 28, 230

Project Support 39

quality management 38, 51, 52, 268

Risk Log 37, 38, 39, 56

risk management 260–1

Senior User 38

stakeholders 38, 231

terms of reference 38

tolerances 233

user requirements 38

see also Acceptance Criteria

project closure 16–17, 89–93, 153–66

Business Case 200, 244

confirmation 73, 89–93, 156, 158, 162, 163, 164, 229

control of 244–6

Executive responsibilities 210

notification 91, 92, 159, 245, 336

Project Board 14, 71, 83, 166, 229, 244–6

confirmation 73, 89–93

project definition changes 78

project direction 14, 70, 73–4

Project Initiation Document 17, 92, 154, 155, 229

Project Manager 16–17, 83, 89, 92, 155, 229, 245

recommendation 159, 336

stage status review 113

see also premature closure

Project Controls 18, 60–3, 227–50

Project Assurance 215

Project Board 60, 72, 75, 79, 228, 229

Project Initiation Document 62, 67, 79, 231–2

time constraints 81

see also configuration management; quality control

project decommissioning 121, 156–60, 164, 216

project definition 66, 78

project direction 13–14, 21, 69–93, 207, 212, 215

see also ad hoc direction

project document management 421–3

project evaluation 71, 162–6

see also End Project Report; lessons learned; post-project review

Project Files 17, 63–5, 158, 215, 281, 421

see also archiving; configuration management; quality files

project filing, healthcheck 420

project initiation 14, 47–68, 231–2

authorisation 26, 74–6, 229, 231, 261

Business Case 14, 49, 57, 200, 201

change control 287

Executive 76, 209

healthcheck 413–14

job descriptions 75

planning 44, 48

programme management 50, 75, 76

Project Approach 40, 44, 75

Project Assurance 75, 76

Project Board

authorisation 14, 44, 48–9, 71, 74–6, 229, 231

authority levels 287

risk assessment 261

Project Brief 40, 49, 75, 76, 231

Project Initiation Document 14, 48, 49, 50, 65, 231

Project Issue examination 109

project management team structure 75

Project Manager 48–9, 75, 76, 261

Project Quality Plan creation 271

project start-up 26, 40, 49, 75

Quality Log creation 272

quality planning 273

Risk Log 75, 261

risk management 76, 261

Senior Supplier 76

stakeholders 50

suppliers 76

third-party funding 76
Project Initiation Document *336*, **375–7**
  ad hoc direction 87
  assembling 52, 65–8, 215
  authorisation 77–81, 231
  baselining 77–8, 231
  changes to 87
  content 78–9, **375–7**
  contracts and 9
  End Project Reports 245, 246
  Exception Plans 152
  Highlight Reports 241
  initiation stage planning 43, 44, 45
  job descriptions 66, 67, 68
  Lessons Learned Log 232
  organisation and 79
  plan design 173
  product definition and analysis 176
  Product Descriptions 68
  programme management 44, 67, 68, 76,
    79
  Project Approach 66, 67, 78
  Project Assurance 45, 67, 215
  project authorisation 65, 66, 77–81
  Project Board 14, 48–50, 75, 78, 81, 87,
    231
  Project Brief 40, 44, 66, 67, 78
  project closure 17, 92, 154, 155, 229
  project decommissioning 158, 159
  project definition 66, 78
  project direction 14, 75
  project evaluation 163, 165, 166
  project initiation 14, 48, 49, 50, 65, 231
  Project Issues 110, 122
  project management team 44, 66, 67,
    68, 78
  Project Manager 48–9, 67, 78, 79, 81,
    212, 261
  project organisation structure 66
  project start-up 28
  Project Support 67
  quality planning 52, 266
  revision 232
  risk assessments 78
  risk management 261
  stage boundary management 65, 139
  Stage Plan authorisation 84
  stage planning 141

  tolerances 67, 79
  see also Acceptance Criteria; Business
    Case; Communication Plan;
    Product Breakdown Structure;
    Project Controls; Project Plan;
    Project Quality Plan; Risk Log
Project Issues 285–9, *336*, **378**
  ad hoc direction 87–8, 89, 121
  benefits 108, 288
  Business Case 109, 110, 121, 122, 123,
    201
    impacts 201, 288, 317
    refinement 58
  capturing 97, 105–7, 286, 316 (Fig.)
  change authority 109, 287
  change budgets 109, 112
  concessions 119, 121, 122, 123, 273
  Configuration Item Records 121, 122
  Configuration Librarian 106, 109, 122,
    281, 282
  configuration management 276, 281,
    282, 289
  contracts 109
  corrective action 117, 118
  costs 108
  customer's interests 109
  End Project Reports 246
  end stage reporting 148, 149
  escalation 119–23
    Business Case 58, 121, 122, 123
    change control 318
    Exception Reports 85, 121, 122, 123,
      152, 262, 318
    Off-Specifications 123, 317
    Project Assurance 122, 216
    Project Board 110–11, 112, 119–21,
      122, 123
    Project Controls 61
    Project Manager 119–22, 262, 317
    risk management 121, 123, 262
    stage control 97
    stage status review 111, 112, 121
  examination 107–10
    Business Case 109, 110, 201
    escalation 120, 121
    Exception Reports 242
    Project Assurance 109, 215
    Project Board 109, 317

risk management 108, 262, 287
  stage control 97
Exception Plans 84, 119, 121, 122
Executive responsibilities 209
Follow-on Actions 91, 92, 160, 161, 162
Highlight Reports 123
impact analysis 107–10, 120, 123, 201, 288, 317, 318
premature closure 119, 121, 122
prioritising 108, 316–17
product delivery management 16, 108
Product Descriptions 273
programme management 58, 87, 107, 108, 162
progress assessment 108
Project Assurance 109, 122, 215, 216
project benefits and 108
Project Board
  capture 106
  change authority 287, 317
  escalation 110–11, 112, 119–21, 122, 123
  examination 109, 317
  project closure 91
  speed of reaction to 89
  see also concessions
project closure 91, 92, 155, 156
project decommissioning 121, 159
project initiation 109, 287
Project Initiation Document 110, 122
project management team appointment 36
Project Manager 254, 289
  capture 106
  escalation 87–8, 119–22, 230, 239, 262, 317
  examination 109
Project Mandate 162
Project Plan 107, 109, 112, 121, 224, 317
Project Support 106, 109
quality management 108, 272–3, 325, 326, 328
Risk Log 108, 109, 110, 122, 146, 287, 288
risk management 108, 121, 123, 254, 262, 287

stage control 16, 97, 98
Stage Plans 109, 110, 317
stage status review 108, 110, 111, 112, 113, 262
Team Managers 239, 242
Team Plans and 317
timescale 108
tolerances 119, 120, 121, 122, 123
training in raising 230
users 123
Work Packages 133
see also change control; Issue Log; Off-Specifications; Requests for Change
project life cycle 7, 8 (Fig.), 11, 336
project management 1–2, 336
  see also management levels; PRINCE2; project direction
project management structure see organisational structure
project management team 208–18, 336, 395–407
  appointment 13, 26, 27, 28, 31, 34–7
    confirmation 72, 74, 79
  changes 15, 84, 138
  communication 35
  contracting activities 8
  customers 33, 34, 36
  design 13, 26, 27, 31–4, 36, 214, 215
  Exception Plans 152
  Executive 32, 36
  internal audit functions 33
  job descriptions 33, 36, 52, 68, 140, 205, 281
  membership 10, 31
  organisational structure 204
  programme management 33, 34, 36, 72
  Project Approach 32, 34
  Project Assurance 33, 35, 206, 215
  Project Brief 32, 37
  Project Initiation Document 44, 66, 67, 68, 78
  Project Issues 36
  Project Mandate 33
  project planning 55
  project start-up 13
  Project Support 31, 32, 33, 35, 36
  purchasing activities 8
  quality management 33, 34, 52

reporting and communication lines 35
Senior Supplier 34
stage boundary management 15
Stage Plan authorisation 84
stage planning 140, 141
stakeholders 33
structure 33, 36, 152, 204–6
    project initiation 75
    Project Initiation Document 66, 67, 68
    stage planning 140, 141
suppliers 31, 33, 34, 36
users 31
see also Executive; Project Assurance;
    Project Board; Project Manager;
    Project Support; Team Managers
Project Manager 212–13, *336*, **401**
    activities and dependencies identification 179
    ad hoc direction 86, 87, 88, 89, 262, 317
    appointment 28–31, 72, 208, 212
    Business Case 58, 78, 145, 200, 201, 229, 261
    change budgets 54
    change control 254, 289, 315, 317, 318
    Checkpoint Reports 16, 133, 229, 240
    Communication Plan 79
    configuration audits 280
    Configuration Librarian role 217
    contingency plans and budgets 54, 58
    corrective action 117–19
    Daily Log 13, 38, 112, 243–4, 255, 264, 274
    end project recommendation 158
    End Project Reports 155, 163
    end stage assessment 242–3
    End Stage Reports 15, 148, 149, 150, 243
    estimating 181
    exception assessment 243
    Exception Plans 83, 223, 225, 243, 318
        production 83, 150, 151, 152
    Exception Reports 83, 87, 121, 241, 242
    Follow-on Actions 155, 161, 201
    Highlight Reports 16, 87, 209, 240, 241, 254, 262
    initiation stage planning 44, 45
    job description 29, 30, 32, 33
    Lessons Learned Report 245
    monitoring by 209, 229
    Off-Specifications 317
    organisational structure 203–4, 205, 206, 209, 212
    plan completion 191, 193
    plan design 172, 173
    plans and 220
    Post-Project Review Plan 201
    Product Breakdown Structure 295
    Product Checklists 174
    product definition and analysis 174, 175
    product delivery management 16, 127–9, 212
    Product Descriptions 237, 301
    Product Flow Diagram 302
    Product Status Accounts 279
    product submission 279
    Project Approach definition 42, 43
    Project Assurance and 32, 36, 212, 215, 216, 217
    project authorisation 78, 79, 80, 81
    Project Board and 73, 83, 87–9, 110, 208, 212, 233
    Project Brief 39, 230
    project closure 16–17, 83, 89, 92, 155, 229, 245
    Project Controls 61, 228, 229–30
    project decommissioning 121, 156, 157, 158, 159
    project direction 69, 70, 71, 72, 73
    project evaluation 163, 164
    Project Files 64
    project initiation 48–9, 75, 76, 261
    Project Initiation Document 48–9, 67, 78, 79, 81, 212, 261
    Project Issues 254, 289
        capture 106
        escalation 87–8, 119–22, 230, 239, 262, 317
        examination 109
    project management team 32, 36
    Project Mandate 29, 30, 230
    Project Plan 80, 143, 179, 181, 220
    project planning 54, 55
    Project Quality Plan 271

project start-up 13, 28, 230
Project Support 32, 36, 212, 217–18
Quality Log 229, 230, 238
quality management 16, 212, 271, 274
quality planning 52, 53
quality review 238, 320, 321, 322, 323,
    324–6, 328
replanning 240
risk analysis 188, 189, 262
Risk Log 146, 230, 255, 259, 261
risk management 58, 59, 89, 254, 261–2
risk ownership 253, 254, 264
risk profiles 259
risk tolerance 252
scheduling 187
stage boundaries 15, 73, 139
stage control 15–16, 21, 95–125, 250
stage planning 15, 73, 139
Stage Plans 82–3, 85, 179, 181, 220,
    224, 250
stage selection and definition 250
stage status review 82, 110–11, 112,
    243, 262
stages 246
Team Manager role 32, 98, 127, 129,
    132, 322
Team Managers and 212, 213, 214, 233
Team Plan approval 220, 225, 229
tolerances 229, 233–4
Work Packages
   acceptance 129–32
   authorisation 16, 229–30, 237,
     261–2
   completion 125
   content 237
   delivery 134, 135, 136
   execution 133, 134, 230
Project Mandate **379–80**
 definition 26, 27, *336*
 Executive appointment 29, 30
 feasibility studies 28, 200
 programme management 26, 162, 233
 Project Approach 28, 41
 Project Board and 208
 Project Brief preparation 37, 38, 39
 Project Issues 162
 project management team design 33
 Project Manager 29, 30, 230

Project Plan 30
 project start-up 13, 26, 27, 28, 230
 quality planning 51
 risk management 260
 tolerances 233
 see also Business Case
Project Plan 223–4, *336*, **381–2**
 activities and dependencies identification
    179, 180
 approval 220
 Business Case
   input to 53, 78, 199, 201, 224
   interaction with 53, 56–9, 143, 145,
     146, 200, 261
 Configuration Item Records 232
 configuration management 281
 contingency plans 58
 creation 43, 44, 48, 49, 53, 54, 55
 End Project Reports 246
 end stage assessment 242
 End Stage Reports 143, 147, 148, 150,
    243
 estimating 180, 181, 183
 exception assessment 243
 Exception Plans 83, 142, 143, 151, 152,
    225–6, *332*
 Exception Reports 83
 Executive and Project Manager
    appointment 30
 healthcheck 416
 impact analysis 143, 145, 317
 Issue Log 143
 plan completion 192
 plan design 173, 174
 Product Breakdown Structure
    307 (Fig.), 313
 product definition and analysis 175
 Product Flow Diagram 308 (Fig.)
 programme management 56, 79, 150,
    225–6
 Project Approach 40, 42, 143
 Project Assurance 143, 215, 216
 project authorisation 56, 80
 Project Board 56, 72, 79, 142–3, 220,
    221, 224
 Project Controls 62
 project evaluation 163, 164, 165
 Project Files 63, 64

Project Initiation Document 53, 66, 67, 79, 224
Project Issues 107, 109, 112, 121, 224, 317
Project Manager 80, 143, 179, 181, 220
Project Mandate 30
project start-up 27
resource requirements 53, 59, 62, 224
revision 151, 224, 232
Risk Log 143, 146, 147
risk management 55, 58, 224, 257, 258, 261, 262
stage boundaries 15, 73, 137, 139
stage control 97
stage planning 140, 141, 142
Stage Plans 82–3, 84, 142, 143, 224, 247
stage status review 112, 113, 262
timescale and resource requirements 53
updating 59, 121, 142–4
project planning 53–6, 215, 250
Project Quality Plan 271, *337*, **383–4**
  Acceptance Criteria 38
  creation 50, 271
  customer's quality expectations 38, 78, 271
  plan design 172
  product definition and analysis 175
  Project Approach definition 40
  Project Assurance 215
  Project Board 78, 271
  Project Controls 62
  project evaluation 165
  Project Files 64
  Project Initiation Document 67, 78, 224, 266, 271
  Project Plan updating 143
  project planning 53, 55
  quality management 265–6, 271
  quality planning 51, 52, 53, 266
  stage boundary management 139, 140, 141
  stage planning 140, 141
  suppliers 53
  see also Configuration Management Plan
project records *337*
  see also Project Files; records
project start-up 13, 25–45, 230–3

Business Case 13, 27, 198
customer's quality expectations 13, 27, 266
healthcheck 413
notification 75, *337*
Project Approach 13, 27, 28, 270
project initiation 26, 40, 49, 75
quality planning 266
Project Support 217–18, *337*, **405**
  activities and dependencies identification 179
  appointment 35
  Business Case 58, 145
  corrective action 118
  end stage reporting 149
  estimating and 181, 217
  Exception Plan production 151
  Highlight Reports 115
  initiation stage planning 44
  plan completion 191
  progress assessment 104, 229
  Project Approach definition 42
  Project Board 75
  Project Brief 39
  Project Controls 61
  project decommissioning 158
  Project Files 64
  project initiation 75
  Project Initiation Document 67
  Project Issues 106, 109
  project management team 31, 32, 33, 36
  Project Manager 32, 36, 212, 217–18
  Project Plan updating 143
  project planning 55
  quality review 272, 322
  Risk Log updating 146
  scheduling 187
  stage planning 140
  stage status review 112
  see also Configuration Librarian; configuration management
Project Support Office 36, 166, 218, 283, *337*, **407**
PROMPTII 1
proximity of risk 256, *337*
publicity 71, 209
purchasing 8–9

Q

qualifications 4, 425
quality 18, 265–74, *337*, 418
   see also evaluation
quality assurance 214, 266
   customers 33, 214, 271
   Lessons Learned Report 245
   project closure 166
   project management team design 33, 34
   Project Quality Plan 271
   quality planning 51, 52, 53
   suppliers 33, 214, 269, 271
   see also Project Assurance
quality control 237–8, 273
   configuration management 276–7
   contracts 271
   definition 266
   End Stage Reports 148
   plan completion 191
   Product Descriptions 266
   Project Approach and 270
   Project Assurance 217, 271
   quality planning 51
   Senior Supplier 210
   see also quality criteria; quality review
quality criteria
   customers 272, 301, 302
   defining 274
   product definition and analysis 175
   Product Descriptions 237, 266, 272,
      273, 301, 302, 312
   Project Assurance 216
   quality planning 52
   Stage Plans 266, 272
   Work Packages 102, 128, 130
   see also quality control; quality review
quality expectations *see* Acceptance
      Criteria; customer's quality
      expectations
quality files 124, 238, 422–3
   see also Project Files
Quality Log 238, 272, *337*, **385**
   configuration management 281
   creation 14, 51, 52, 238, 272
   end stage reporting 149
   Exception Plan production 152
   Highlight Reports 116
   product delivery management 16, 130

   progress assessment 23, 102, 103, 104,
      105, 238, 320
   Project Assurance 104, 215, 216
   project evaluation 165
   Project Manager 229, 230, 238
   quality review 238, 320, 323, 324, 325,
      326
   stage planning 140, 141, 238
   stage status review 111, 112, 113, 238
   Team Managers 229, 230, 238, 272
   Work Packages 229
      acceptance 130, 131
      authorisation 100, 101
      completion 124, 125
      delivery 135
      execution 133
quality management 265–6, 270
   Acceptance Criteria 50, 51, 52, 268–9
   activities and dependencies identification
      180
   customers 10, 51, 174, 269, 270
   Daily Log 274
   End Stage Reports 148, 149, 150
   ISO (International Organisation for
      Standards) 269
   Off-Specifications 236, 273
   Product Descriptions 237
   programme management 51, 270
   progress assessment 273, 320
   Project Approach and 42, 50, 52, 270
   Project Assurance 216, 217, 271
   project evaluation 166
   Project Issues 272–3
   project management team 33, 34, 52
   Project Manager 16, 212, 271, 274
   stage planning 140, 141, 142
   stage status review 112
   suppliers 51, 270, 273
   Team Managers 271, 274
   Team Plans 134, 271
   Work Packages 100, 101, 131, 133, 134
   see also customer's quality expectations;
      Project Quality Plan; quality
      assurance; quality control;
      quality planning
quality management system *338*
quality organisation structure 270
quality path 266–73

quality planning 50–3, 271–3
 customer's quality expectations 50, 52, 266, 272
 definition 266
 Project Approach 42, 50, 52, 270
 Project Assurance 50, 51, 52, 215, 225, 271, 272
 Stage Plans 51, 171, 225, 266, 271–2, 273
 Team Plans 51, 171, 225, 271–2
 see also Project Quality Plan
quality policy 269–70
quality products 298 (Fig.)
quality responsibilities 51, 52, 78, 271
quality review 19, 237–8, 272, 291, 319–28
 definition 319, 338
 Gantt charts 271
 healthcheck 418–19
 product definition and analysis 176
 Project Assurance 216, 225, 238, 322, 326
 Stage Plans 225, 271, 272, 326
 Team Plans 225, 238, 271, 326
 Work Packages 124, 238, 320
 see also quality control
quality review chairperson 225, 238, 271, 320–1, 324–7, 328
quality review meetings 323
quality reviewers 272, 319, 321, 322, 324–7, 328, 338
 Project Assurance 216, 271
 stage and team quality plans 225, 271
quality specialists 302
quality standards 51, 52, 53, 55, 108, 133, 216
 see also Acceptance Criteria; Project Quality Plan
quality systems see quality management
quality tolerance 236

R

receiving Work Packages see Work Packages, acceptance; Work Packages, completed
records 155, 156, 158, 337
 see also archiving; Configuration Item Records; Project Files; quality files

reduction, response to risk 256
refining, Business Case see Business Case, revision
releases 277
replanning 240
 see also stage boundaries
reports and reporting
 initiation stage planning 43, 45
 project management team appointment 35
 resource requirements 191, 221
 risk management 258
 Work Packages 134, 230
 see also Checkpoint Reports; End Project Report; End Stage Reports; Exception Reports; Highlight Reports; Lessons Learned Report; monitoring; Project Controls
requests for advice 88, 118
Requests for Change 338, 386
 ad hoc direction 87, 89
 change control 286, 287, 289, 315, 317
 Follow-on Action Recommendations from 245
 Project Board 245, 317
 Project Issues 106, 121
 see also change authority; change budgets
requirements 338
resource availability 45, 112, 131, 184, 186, 187–8
resource requirements
 Business Case refinement 56, 59
 estimating 223
 Project Controls 61, 62
 Project Plan 53, 59, 62, 224
 project planning 53, 54
 reports on 191, 221
 risk management 258
 scheduling 187
responses to risk 256
review see peer review; post-project review; quality review; stage status review
review points see decision points
reviewers see quality reviewers
risk
 definition 251, 338
 healthcheck 415–16
 proximity of 256, 337
 responses to 256

risk action selection 257 (Fig.)
risk analysis 188–90, 253, 255–7, 261
  Business Case refinement 58, 59
  Project Assurance 189, 216
  Project Board 189, 253, 262
  Project Manager 188, 189, 262
  project planning 54
  Team Managers 130, 189
  see also impact analysis; risk assessment;
    risk profiles
risk appetite see risk tolerance
risk assessment 41, 44, 54, 56, 76, 78,
    215
  see also risk analysis
risk categories 255, 409–11
risk evaluation see risk analysis
risk flow 260 (Fig.)
Risk Log 239, 338, **387–8**
  activities and dependencies identification
    176, 179
  Business Case 198, 199, 200
    updating 56, 57, 58, 59, 145, 146
  configuration management 232, 281
  corrective action 118
  creation 17, 27, 38–9, 260
  end stage reporting 149
  estimating 183
  Exception Plans 83, 152
  Follow-on Action identification 160,
    161
  Highlight Reports 116
  initiation stage planning 44
  Issue Log 147
  product delivery management 16
  programme management 59
  Project Approach definition 42
  Project Assurance 147, 215, 216
  project authorisation 261
  Project Board 261
  Project Brief preparation 37, 38, 39, 56
  Project Controls 62, 230
  project evaluation 165
  project initiation 75, 261
  Project Initiation Document 44, 67, 78
  Project Issues 108, 109, 110, 122, 146,
    287, 288
  Project Manager 147, 230, 255, 259,
    261

Project Plan 143, 146, 147
project planning 55
project start-up 13, 27, 28
Project Support 147
revision/updating 56, 57, 145, 146–7,
    232, 261
risk analysis 189, 190, 255, 261
risk evaluation 256
risk management 261, 262
risk profiles 258, 259
risk proximity 256
stage boundary management 15
stage control 16
Stage Plan authorisation 84
stage planning 141
stage status review 112, 113, 262
Work Packages 101, 131
risk management 10, 18, 251–64
  balancing of risks 256–7, 288
  Business Case 56–60, 199, 200, 252,
    257, 261, 262
  change control 89, 288
  customers 59
  End Project Report 246
  End Stage Reports 147, 148, 150, 243
  Exception Plans 152, 243, 261
  Exception Reports 83, 258, 262
  external products 299
  Follow-on Action Recommendations
    245, 262–3
  plan completion 191, 192
  planning 222, 258
  product definition and analysis 175
  programme management 56, 58, 59,
    114, 252, 253, 264
  Project Approach 42
  Project Assurance 44, 189, 215, 216,
    262
  project authorisation 80, 229, 261
  Project Board 58, 59, 72, 252, 261, 262
  project direction 71, 72
  project evaluation 163, 166
  project initiation 76, 261
  Project Issues 108, 121, 123, 254, 262,
    287
  Project Manager 58, 59, 89, 254, 261–2
  Project Plan 55, 58, 224, 257, 258, 261,
    262

stage boundary management 137
stage control 16
Stage Plans 224, 257, 258, 261–2
stage status review 112, 114, 262
Work Packages 100, 131, 133, 258, 261–2
see also contingency plans; Risk Log
risk management budgets 190, 259, 263
see also contingency budgets
risk management cycle 254–8
risk monitoring 258
risk ownership 9, 147, 253–4, 261, 264
risk profiles 59, 258–9, *338*
risk proximity 256
Risk Register *see* Risk Log
risk responses 256–7
risk responsibilities *see* risk ownership
risk tolerance 235, 252
risk tolerance line 259, *338*
roles 9, 204, 205–12, **395–407**
see also job descriptions

S

scalability 22, 247
scheduling 63, 81, 181, 183–8, 190
see also timescale
scope tolerance 235, 236
scribe 321, 324, 325, 326, 328
senior responsible owner *339*
see also Executive
Senior Supplier 8, 34, 207–8, 209,
210–11, *339*, **400**
job descriptions 81
Project Approach definition 42
Project Assurance 217
project initiation 76
project management team design 34
stage planning 142
Team Managers and 214
Senior User 34, 208, 209, 210, 211, *339*,
399
change control 318
Checkpoint and Highlight Reports 241
customer's quality expectations 38
delegation of responsibilities 34
Project Brief preparation 38
quality assurance 34
stage planning 142

sensitivity analysis 59, 199
service agreements 159
simple products 295, 296, 300, 312
skills matrix 188
specialist products 297, 298, 299, 303,
311, 315–18, *334*
see also suppliers
specialist work 8, 43, 248–9, 250, 302
see also suppliers
specification *339*
sponsor *339*
stage boundaries
Business Case 15, 137
Daily Log 139
defining 54, 73
End Stage Reports 15
Exception Plans 15, 137
Lessons Learned Log 15
management 14–15, 65, 113, 137–52,
224–5, 250
Product Flow Diagram 303
products and 249 (Fig.)
Project Approach 139
Project Board 14–15, 73, 85, 137, 138,
139
Project Controls 61
project direction 73
project evaluation 71
Project Initiation Document 65, 139
project management team 15
Project Manager 15, 73, 139
Project Plan 15, 73, 137, 139
Project Quality Plan 139
replanning at 240
Risk Log 15
risks 137
Stage Plans 15, 137, 138
stage status review 113, 137
Team Managers 225
Team Plans 15, 225
timing 250
tolerances 15, 138
see also control points; decision points;
End Stage Report; stages, selection
stage control 15–16, 21, 95–125, 127,
129, 150, 246–50
see also end stage assessment; Stage
Plans; stage status review

stage files 281, 422
stage planning 139–42, 214, 216, 238,
    273
    see also initiation Stage Plans
Stage Plans 139–42, 146, 223, 224–5,
    247, **389–90**
    activities and dependencies identification
        179
    authorisation 81–5, 208, 231, 242–3
        Business Case revision and 83, 201
        risk management 261
        stage boundary management 137
        summary versions 221
    Business Case 82, 83, 84, 146, 201
    Communication Plan 84
    corrective action 118, 119
    End Stage Reports 84, 148, 149
    estimating 180, 181, 183
    exception assessment 243
    Exception Plans 152, 225, *332*
    Gantt charts 271
    healthcheck 416–17
    Highlight Reports 83, 115, 116, 240
    impact analysis 317
    plan completion 191, 193
    plan design 173
    planning 171, 326
    presentation 221
    Product Breakdown Structure
        309 (Fig.), 313
    product definition and analysis 175
    Product Descriptions 272
    Product Flow Diagram 310 (Fig.)
    programme management 85, 142, 150
    progress assessment 102, 103, 104
    Project Assurance 83, 171, 225, 271,
        272
    Project Board 240, 248
        authorisation 81–5, 201, 208, 221,
            231, 242–3, 261
    project initiation 14, 48
    Project Initiation Document 84
    Project Issues 109, 110, 317
    project management team 84
    Project Manager 82–3, 85, 179, 181,
        220, 224, 250
    Project Plan 82–3, 84, 142, 143, 224,
        247

quality criteria 266, 272
Quality Log 272
quality planning 51, 171, 225, 266,
    271–2, 273
quality review 225, 271, 272, 326
Risk Log 84
risk management 224, 257, 258, 261–2
scheduling 186
stage boundary management 15, 137,
    138, 224
stage status review 111, 112, 113, 262
suppliers 84
tolerances 83, 85, 233
version control 281
Work Packages 101, 130, 136, 261–2
see also end stage assessment; initiation
Stage Plans; stage control
stage status information 104, 105, 113, 116
stage status review 110–14
    Business Case 112, 113, 262
    Daily Log 112, 243
    Highlight Reports 110, 113, 114, 115
    Project Assurance 112, 215, 262
    project decommissioning 156
    Project Issues 108, 110, 111, 112, 113,
        262
    Project Manager 82, 110–11, 112, 243,
        262
    Project Plan 112, 113, 262
    Quality Log 111, 112, 113, 238
    Risk Log 112, 113, 262
    risk management 112, 114, 262
    stage boundary management 113, 137
    stage control 97
    stage planning 141
    Stage Plans 111, 112, 113, 262
    see also end stage notification; progress
        assessment
stages 18, 246–50
    definition 246, *339*
    Product Breakdown Structure 313
    selection 44, 54, 73, 81, 232
        see also stage boundaries
    Work Packages 102
    see also decision points
stakeholders 10, *339*
    Business Case 200, 201
    Project Assurance 214

Project Brief 38, 231
Project Controls 61
project initiation 50
project management team design 33
see also contractors; customers; Project
    Board; suppliers; users
start-up *see* project start-up
status accounting 278
sub-contractors 10, 173, 225, 237
see also stakeholders
supplier forums 34, 211
suppliers 10
    Business Case 60, 208
    change control 287, 289, 318
    definition 6, *339*
    impact analysis 318
    payment 60, 80
    Product Descriptions 226, 301
    Project Approach definition 41, 43
    project authorisation 80, 81
    Project Board membership 76, 88, 206,
        207, 208, 211
    project decommissioning 156
    project direction 72
    project funding 59
    project initiation 76
    project management team 31, 33, 34,
        36
    Project Quality Plan 53
    quality management 51, 214, 269–70,
        271, 273
    risk management 252
    Stage Plan authorisation 84
    see also customer/supplier environment;
        Senior Supplier; stakeholders; third-
        party suppliers
support infrastructure 75, 76, 91, 156,
    158, 159–60
    see also Project Support
symbols 23

T

Team Managers 213–14, *339*, **402**
    activities and dependencies identification
        179
    appointment 35
    change control 100, 102

Checkpoint Reports 16, 229
checkpoints 239
corrective action 118
Daily Log 244, 274
estimating 181
Exception Plans 222
Exception Reports 242
organisational structure 32, 204, 205
plan completion 191
plan design 172
Product Breakdown Structure 295
product definition and analysis 175
product delivery management 16, 21,
    127–8, 212
Product Descriptions 237, 301
Product Flow Diagram 302
progress assessment 103, 104, 105
Project Issues 239, 242
project management team design 32
Project Manager and 212, 213, 214,
    233
Project Managers as 32, 98, 127, 129,
    132, 322
Quality Log 229, 230, 238, 272
quality management 271, 274
quality review 238, 320, 321, 322, 323,
    324–6
risk management 130, 189, 261, 262
scheduling 187
stage boundary management 225
stage control 98
stage planning 140
Team Plans 179, 181, 220, 225
tolerances 229, 233
Work Packages
    acceptance 129–32, 225, 262
    authorisation 99–100, 101, 102, 261
    completion 125
    content 237
    delivery 134–6
    execution 132–4, 230
work triggers 99
Team Plans 223, 225
    activities and dependencies identification
        179
    approval 220, 225, 229
    creation 16, 225
    estimating 180, 181

Exception Plans 223, 225, 332
Gantt charts 271
impact analysis 317
plan completion 191
planning 127, 130, 171, 326
product definition and analysis 175
product delivery management 16, 127,
    128, 130
progress assessment 103, 104
Project Assurance 216, 225, 271, 272
Project Issues and 317
Project Plan updating 143
Quality Log 238, 272
quality management 134, 271
quality planning 51, 171, 225, 271–2
quality review 225, 238, 271, 326
risk management 257, 262
scheduling 187
stage boundary management 15, 225
stage definition 250
Team Managers 220, 225
Work Packages
    acceptance 130, 131, 225, 238, 262
    authorisation 100, 229
    execution 133, 134
technical stages 248
techniques 18–20, 43, 291–328
    see also change control; product-based
        planning; quality review
terms of reference 27, 38, 99–100
    see also Acceptance Criteria; Project
        Brief; Project Mandate
third-party funding 76
third-party suppliers 127, 289
time, tolerance element 234, 235 (Fig.),
    236
time constraints, Project Controls and 81
time/cost/risk balance 288
time-driven controls 228
    see also checkpoints; Highlight Reports
timescale
    Business Case 199
    Project Issues 108
    project planning 53, 54
    see also scheduling
timing, stage boundary management 250
tolerances 233–6, *339*
    Business Case 199

cost/time graph 235 (Fig.)
end stage assessment 242
end stage reporting 148
estimating 181
Exception Plans 83, 150, 151, 152
Exception Reports 234, 241–2
plan completion 191, 192
plan design 173
Project Board 181, 233, 234, 235–6, 241
Project Controls 61, 62
project direction 72
project initiation 75
Project Initiation Document 67, 79
Project Issues 119, 120, 121, 122, 123
Project Manager 229, 233–4
Project Plan 224
risk management 262
setting 181, 234
stage boundary management 15, 138
stage planning 140
Stage Plans 83, 85, 233
stage status review 111, 112, 113, 262
Team Managers 229, 233
Work Packages 130, 133, 229, 233
    see also benefit tolerance; quality
        tolerance; risk tolerance; scope
        tolerance; stage status review
training
    for PRINCE2 4
    Project Board 211
    project evaluation 166
    Project Issue identification 230
    scheduling time for 187
    users 41
transference, response to risk 256
transformation 176
triggers see end project triggers; work
        triggers

U

updating
    Business Case 142, 144–6, 201, 216
        see also Business Case, revision
    Project Plan 59, 121, 142–4
    Risk Log 56, 57, 145, 146–7, 232, 261
user groups 4, 34, 211
    see also Best Practice User Group

users 10
  Business Case 199
  definition 6, *340*
  impact analysis 318
  product definition and analysis 175
  Product Descriptions 237, 301, 312
  Project Board membership 34, 75, 206,
      207, 208, 211
  Project Brief preparation 38
  project decommissioning 159
  Project Issue escalation 123
  project management team membership
      31
  quality management 237, 319
  see also customers; Senior User

V

verification
  configuration management 278
  see also quality management
version control 10, 134, 277, 278, 281,
      282–3
  see also baselining; change control;
      configuration audits; Project Files
versions, in Product Breakdown Structure
298

W

Work Packages 124–36, 237, **391–3**
  acceptance 129–32, 237
    planning 168
    Project Assurance 131, 216
    quality review 238
    risk management 262
    Team Managers 129–32, 225, 262
    Team Plans 130, 131, 225, 238, 262
    Work Package authorisation 100, 129,
        132
  authorisation 98–102
    configuration management 280
    corrective action 99, 118
    Product Descriptions 237
    Project Assurance 100, 101, 215
    Project Manager 16, 229–30, 237,
        261–2
    quality management 100, 273, 320

risk management 100, 261–2
stage control 96, 97
Stage Plans 101, 261–2
stage status review 110, 112, 113, 114
Team Managers 99–100, 101, 102, 261
Team Plans 100, 229
Work Package acceptance 100, 129,
    132
Work Package delivery 134, 135
change control 100, 102, 124
checkpoints 239
completed 96, 102, 124–5
Configuration Item Records 100, 101,
    124, 125
Configuration Librarian 100, 125, 135
content 130, 229, 230, 237, **391–3**
contracts 102
corrective action 99, 118
Daily Log 132, 133, 244
definition 99, *340*
delivery 134–6
Exception Plans 101
execution 102, 132–4, 216, 230, 238,
    320
Issue Log 101
Product Checklists 101
product delivery management 16, 99,
    128–36
Product Descriptions 99, 100, 101, 102,
    130, 237, 238
progress assessment 99, 102, 104, 105,
    128, 134
Project Assurance 100, 101, 130, 131,
    133, 215, 216
Project Controls 61, 237
Project Support 100, 125
quality 273
quality criteria 102, 128, 130
quality management 100, 101, 131,
    133, 134, 230
quality review 124, 238, 320
reports and reporting 134, 230
  see also Checkpoint Reports
Risk Log 101, 131
risk management 100, 131, 133, 258,
    261–2
stage control 16, 96, 97, 98
Stage Plans 101, 130, 136, 261–2

stage status review 110, 111, 112, 113,
    114
stages and 102
sub-contractors 237
tolerances 130, 133, 229, 233
see also Quality Log, Work Packages
work triggers 99, 100–1, 113, 118

Best Practice:
the OGC approach with ITIL® and PRINCE®

OGC Best Practice is an approach to management challenges as well as the application of techniques and actions.

Practical, flexible and adaptable, management guidance from OGC translates the very best of the world's practices into guidance of an internationally recognised standard. Both PRINCE2 and ITIL publications can help every organisation

- Run projects more efficiently
- Reduce project risk
- Purchase IT more cost effectively
- Improve organisational Service Delivery.

What is ITIL and why use it?

ITIL's starting point is that organisations do not simply use IT; they depend on it. Managing IT as effectively as possible must therefore be a high priority.

ITIL consists of a unique library of guidance on providing quality IT services. It focuses tightly on the customer, cost effectiveness and building a culture that puts the emphasis on IT performance.

Used by hundreds of the world's most successful organisations, its core titles are available in print, Online Subscription and CD-ROM formats. They are:

- Service Support
- Service Delivery
- Planning to Implement Service Management
- Application Management
- ICT Infrastructure Management
- Security Management
- The Business Perspective Volume 1 and 2
- Software Asset Management

What is PRINCE2 and why use it?

Since its introduction in 1989, PRINCE has been widely adopted by both the public and private sectors and is now recognised as a de facto standard for project management and for the management of change.

PRINCE2, the most evolved version, is driven by its expe and users to offer control, transparency, focus and ultima success for any project you need to implement.

Publications are available in various formats: print, Online Subscription and CD-ROM. Its main titles are:

- Managing Successful Projects with PRINCE2
- People Issues and PRINCE2
- PRINCE2 Pocket Book
- Tailoring PRINCE2
- Business Benefits through Project Management

Other related titles:
- Passing the PRINCE2 Examinations
- Managing Successful Programmes
- Management of Risk – Guidance for Practitioners
- Buying Software – A best practice approach

Ordering

The full range of ITIL and PRINCE2 publications can be purchased direct via **www.get-best-practice.co.uk** or through calling TSO Customer Services on **0870 600 5522**. If you are outside of the UK please contact your local agent, for details email **sales@tso.co.uk** For information on Network Licenses for CD-ROM and Online Subscription please email **network.sales@tso.co.uk**

You are also able to subscribe to content online through this website or by calling TSO Customer Services on **0870 600 5522**. For more information on how to subscribe online please refer to our help pages on the website.